PAVEL FLORENSKY

Early Religious Writings,
1903–1909

PAVEL FLORENSKY

Early Religious Writings,
1903–1909

Translated by

Boris Jakim

WILLIAM B. EERDMANS PUBLISHING COMPANY
GRAND RAPIDS, MICHIGAN

Wm. B. Eerdmans Publishing Co.
2140 Oak Industrial Drive N.E., Grand Rapids, Michigan 49505
www.eerdmans.com

© 2017 Boris Jakim
All rights reserved
Published 2017

ISBN 978-0-8028-7495-5

Library of Congress Cataloging-in-Publication Data

Names: Florensky, P. A. (Pavel Aleksandrovich), 1882–1937, author.
Title: Early religious writings, 1903–1909 / Pavel Florensky ;
    translated by Boris Jakim.
Description: Grand Rapids : Eerdmans Publishing Co., 2017. |
    Includes bibliographical references and index.
Identifiers: LCCN 2017006750 | ISBN 9780802874955 (pbk. : alk. paper)
Subjects: LCSH: Philosophy, Russian—20th century.
Classification: LCC BX597.F6 A25 2017 | DDC 230/.19—dc23
    LC record available at https://lccn.loc.gov/2017006750

Contents

Translator's Introduction — vi

Superstition and Miracle — 1

The Empyrean and the Empirical: A Dialogue — 25

The Goal and Meaning of Progress — 71

The Prize of the High Calling: An Appreciation of the Character of Archimandrite Serapion Mashkin — 80

Questions of Religious Self-Knowledge — 98

Dogmatism and Dogmatics — 119

Orthodoxy — 139

The Salt of the Earth: The Story of the Life of Abba Isidore, Starets of the Gethsemane Skete; Compiled and Told in Order by His Unworthy Spiritual Son, Pavel Florensky — 164

Index — 223

Translator's Introduction

1. Biographical Sketch[1]

Pavel Florensky was born on January 9, 1882, near Evlakh in the Elizavetpol'skaya district, where his father was an engineer employed building the Trans-Caucasian Railroad. He spent his childhood in Tiflis and largely in Batum. He attended the Second Tiflis Classical Gymnasium, graduating in 1900. He then enrolled in the physico-mathematical department of Moscow University, specializing in mathematics. He finished the course in 1904 with a concentration in pure mathematics, and was retained as a faculty member. He wrote his Kandidat thesis on the independently chosen theme "On singularities of planar curves as places where continuity is disrupted"; this thesis was intended to become part of a larger general-philosophical work titled "Discontinuity as an element of a worldview." In the university, Florensky's work was inspired by N. F. Bugaev's[2] theory of functions of a real variable. He also studied philosophy with the eminent philosophers S. N. Trubetskoy and L. M. Lopatin. In 1904 Florensky enrolled as a student at the Moscow Theological Academy and moved to Sergiev Posad.[3] At the Academy he studied the disciplines essential for developing a general

---

1. This section traces Florensky's biography until the end of the first decade of the twentieth century. I am indebted to Igumen Andronik's biographical essay in volume 1 of *Sochineniya v chetyrekh tomakh*.

2. Eminent mathematician, father of Andrey Bely. Bugaev's theory of discontinuity strongly influenced Florensky's philosophical ideas.

3. The town northeast of Moscow where both the Moscow Theological Academy and the Trinity Lavra of St. Sergius are located. See the comment on "The Salt of the Earth," p. xiii below.

Translator's Introduction

worldview: philosophy, philology, archeology, and the history of religion; and he continued, to some extent, his mathematical studies. When he was in the fourth course, he was named to the faculty of the history of philosophy in the fall of 1908 as an assistant docent; in 1911, after defending his master's dissertation, "On Spiritual Truth," he was named an extraordinary professor.[4]

As an adolescent, Florensky was immersed in studying the physical sciences and enthusiastically observed the world of nature—geological, meteorological, etc.—around him. Religion did not play any role in his life. In the summer of 1899, he underwent a spiritual crisis, which made itself known in two mystical experiences. Once, when he was sleeping, he dreamt that he was buried alive, like a convict in a deep mine. This was a "mystical experience of darkness, of nonbeing." His account continues:

> I experienced the sensations of someone buried alive, covered by miles of black impenetrable earth. This was a darkness before which the darkest night seems full of light. . . . No one could help me, no one upon whom I had relied before. . . . It was not that physics and the world of natural phenomena had been proven wrong. . . . They were no longer relevant. . . . All the things that had interested me before were not more than insignificant rags in this darkness and agony that surrounded me now. . . . I was overcome with despair, and I was conscious that it was absolutely impossible to escape from here, that I was cut off absolutely from the visible world. At that moment, a very slender ray of light, more like a sound perhaps than like visible light, brought me the name—God. This was not an illumination or rebirth, but news of possible light. But this news brought hope as well as the excruciating and sudden consciousness that I would perish or be saved by this name alone, and by no other. I did not know how salvation would come or why. I did not understand where I was, and why all earthly things were powerless here. But a new fact—just as incomprehensible and indisputable—rose before me: there is a realm of darkness and perdition, and yet one can find salvation in it. This fact was revealed suddenly, the way a perilous abyss is unexpectedly seen through a sea of fog in the mountains. For me this was a revelation, a discovery, a shock. I awoke from the suddenness of this shock, like one awakened by some external force; and without knowing why, but summing up the

---

4. *Avtoreferat* (Brief autobiography written in the third person), *Sochineniya v chetyrekh tomakh*, vol. 1, pp. 37–38.

whole experience, I shouted into the room: "No, it's impossible to live without God!"[5]

In the second experience, Pavel was awakened by a spiritual shock that was so sudden and decisive that he unexpectedly ran out at night into the courtyard of his house, which was bathed in lunar light.

> And then the event occurred for which I was summoned outside. In the air I heard a perfectly distinct and loud voice calling my name twice: "Pavel!" "Pavel"—and nothing else. It was not a threat or a request, or a display of anger, or even an expression of tenderness. It was precisely a call—in a major key, without any intermediate or minor keys. It expressed directly and precisely exactly what it wanted to express—a summons. . . . This call had all the directness and simplicity of the biblical "Yea, yea; Nay, nay."[6] I do not know, and still do not know, to whom this voice belonged, though I had no doubt that it came from heaven. Thinking about it, it seems more than likely that it came not from a man, however saintly, but from a heavenly messenger.[7]

In the university, Florensky begins to write scientific and philosophical works filled with critiques of evolutionism, positivism, and rationalism. His worldview becomes an idealistic and concretely symbolic one. He becomes a close friend of the leading symbolist poet Andrey Bely (N. F. Bugaev's son) and through him gains access into symbolist literary groups. Symbolism attracted Florensky because of its creative opposition to soulless rationalism.

In March 1904 Florensky made the acquaintance of Bishop Antonii (Florensov). He asked the bishop's blessing to enter into a life of monasticism, but the wise Antonii told him this was premature and counseled him instead to enroll in the Moscow Theological Academy to continue there his spiritual education. Florensky agreed that this was the best course for him. He graduated Moscow University with honors, but despite the invitation to remain in the university as a faculty member, he enrolled as a student at the Theological Academy. What Florensky thirsted after now was not abstract-philosophical learning but living spiritual knowledge. Pavel was called by the church.

---

5. *Detiam moim* (To My Children: Remembrances of Days Past) (Moscow, 1992), 211–12. *Detiam moim* is Florensky's memoir of his childhood and adolescence.

6. Matthew 5:37.

7. *Detiam moim*, 215.

Translator's Introduction

In Sergiev Posad, Florensky was mentored by the saintly elder Father Isidore, an uneducated monk whose chief traits were an exceptional tolerance and love for every human being and every living thing. One Florensky scholar writes that "the combined guidance of these two elders—of the learned theologian Bishop Antonii and of the simple peasant monk Father Isidore—gave Florensky's works that spiritual aroma which is characteristic of his writings. On his life path these two elders formed a unique grace-filled ground that could foster his exceptional gifts. The death of Father Isidore marked the end of Florensky's spiritual adolescence."[8]

2. The Essays in This Collection

Eight important religious works written by Florensky in the first decade of the twentieth century are translated in the present volume. These works show the diversity of his learning and interests; a unifying theme perhaps is his effort to develop and ground a general religious (i.e., Christian) worldview. Prominent is the interplay of religious and scientific themes, which fascinated Florensky his entire life. There is also much about the sacraments and about what it means to be a Christian. "The Salt of the Earth," perhaps Florensky's most spiritually moving work, is a major addition to the "lives of the Russian elders."[9] One could say that Father Isidore was the salt from which Florensky's writings received their mystical savor.

"Superstition and Miracle"

First published under the title "Superstition" in the magazine *Novyi Put'*, 1903, no. 8, pages 91–121. In this article Florensky concerns himself with the ontological status of supernatural phenomena and with the psychology of their perception. His approach is phenomenological. Miracle is considered to be the most adequate expression of the supernatural, and is opposed to the occultism fashionable at the time. Of particular note is Florensky's division of the perception of phenomena into religious, scientific, and superstitious modes.

---

8. Igumen Andronik, "Pavel Florensky, Student of the Moscow Theological Academy" (m.s.).

9. See, for example, Motovilov's journal of his meetings with Seraphim of Sarov, the lives of the Optina elders (especially that of Amvrosy), and the sections devoted to Father Zosima in Dostoevsky's *The Brothers Karamazov*.

TRANSLATOR'S INTRODUCTION

"The Empyrean and the Empirical"

First written in June 1904; revised a few years later and again in 1916. First published, posthumously, in *Bogoslovskie trudy*, no. 17, Moscow, 1986, pages 298–322. A chief aim of this dialogue is the development of an integral religious worldview, rooted in Christian faith. The main thesis is that "there can be no consistent worldview without a religious foundation; there can be no consistent life, a life according to the truth, without religious experience" (p. 25 of the present volume). Only Christianity can be the basis of an integral worldview, for only Christianity possesses the Absolute Truth. Behind the empirical shell of phenomena lies the divine world (the "Empyrean"), mystically connected with man. Florensky uses examples from his mathematical studies (irrational numbers, transcendental numbers, the theory of groups) to illustrate some of his points.

"The Goal and Meaning of Progress"

Transcript of a lecture read by Florensky around 1905 at a meeting of the philosophical circle of the Moscow Theology Academy. A rare sociopolitical essay by Florensky. Of particular note is Florensky's discussion of theocracy (a key concept also in Solovyov's writings): "[I]n order to realize theocracy, every member of society must unconditionally subordinate himself freely to the Truth. This is the basis of a new definition of hierarchy as an all-human society and, further, as a universal society. Theocracy is the unconditionally desirable order of society, but there is one circumstance that makes it unconditionally unrealizable: the perverseness or love of evil that characterizes man" (p. 75).

"The Prize of the High Calling"

First published in *Voprosy religii*, no. 1, Moscow 1906. This essay was originally planned to come out at the same time as the Mashkin-Florensky correspondence, edited by Florensky. Although Florensky never succeeded in personally meeting the philosopher-monk Serapion Mashkin, he regarded him as his philosophical soulmate. Florensky tells us that the goal of Father Serapion's "seekings was to formulate a universal worldview, encompassing all the domains of human interest. He had a constant vision of 'integral knowledge,' as did Solovyov and Origen, and his task was the creation of an all-embracing interconnected system" (p. 95).

This is what Florensky writes about him in *The Pillar and Ground of the Truth*: "the ideas of the late philosopher and my own have turned out to be so kindred and interwoven that I do not even know where his ideas end and where mine begin . . . our common points of departure and comparable kinds of knowledge have led us to similar conclusions. Until his very death, Father Serapion was profoundly interested in developing a system that would start with absolute skepticism and, embracing all of the fundamental questions of mankind, would end with a program of social activity."[10] Father Serapion declared that "Christian philosophy is the philosophy of the critical human spirit, illuminated by Christ's mystical light. . . . The true Christian is the true philosopher" (p. 85).

"Questions of Religious Self-Knowledge"

"Letter I" was published in *Khristianin*, 1907, vol. 1, no. 1, pages 105–210. A number of responses to "Letter I" were sent in, which, after supplying them with preface and commentary, Florensky published in *Khristianin*, 1907, vol. 2, no. 3, pages 635–53 and vol. 3, no. 10, pages 436–39, as "Letter II" and "Letter." These letters were later published as a separate volume under the title "Questions of Religious Self-Knowledge" (Sergiev Posad, 1907). This article, composed in the epistolary style fashionable at the time, treats in a multifaceted way one of the central themes of Florensky's theology—the theme of sacraments. By soliciting letters from ordinary believers, Florensky attempts to find out how these believers understand the power and meaning of the sacraments. In particular, he is interested in finding out if these believers think baptism produces any change in those baptized and if they think it is true that the sanctified Holy Gifts are the Body of Christ and whether they think this can be proved in any way. Also, he is curious to know whether they think the sign of the cross has real power. Florensky declares that "we are inquiring about the power of Christianity in general and are therefore asking where this power reveals itself. What people have thought, seen, and experienced—that is the material out of which, by our common exertion, we must build our spiritual renewal" (p. 102).

---

10. *The Pillar and Ground of the Truth*, trans. B. Jakim (Princeton: Princeton University Press, 1997), 438.

"Dogmatism and Dogmatics"

The first draft was dated September 26, 1905, and read at the first meeting of the philosophical circle of the Moscow Theological Academy. The article was first published, posthumously, in *Istoriko-filosofskii ezhegodnik*, Minsk, 1990. Florensky tells us that what his contemporaries need is a dogmatics (as opposed to dogmatism, the faith-teaching of the handbooks), "a system of fundamental schemata for the most valuable experiences, something like a concise guide to eternal life" (p. 126). Florensky urges his contemporaries to liberate themselves from the formulas of stifling dogmatism and to return to an authentic dogmatics: "The sons of the Church will be truly faithful when they cease being tied to the Church and at any moment are free to descend in their thought to the principles and motives of their faith and, having descended, are free to return, because that is what truth demands" (p. 134).

It is in this essay perhaps that Florensky first formulates his distinction between anthropodicy and theodicy, defining anthropodicy as a "*Sacrament*, a mystery, i.e., a real descent of God down to humanity, God's *self-humiliation* or *kenosis*" (p. 120).

"Orthodoxy"

First published in A. V. El'chaninov, ed., *History of Religion*, Moscow, 1909, pages 161–68. Florensky is chiefly concerned here not with dogmatic and theological questions but with the historical relation of Russia to the church, with faith, prayer, and ritual. Only Russian Orthodoxy is discussed. Florensky declares that a key aspect of Russian Orthodox religiosity is "the tendency to emphasize cult, especially ritual, instead of doctrine and morality.... Violation of chastity is forgiven more easily than the failure to attend church services; participation in the liturgy is more salvific than the reading of the Bible; the performance of cult is more important than charitable giving. It is not by chance that the Russian people assimilated Christianity not from the Bible, but from the lives of the saints; that they are enlightened not by sermon, but by liturgy; not by theology, but by the veneration and kissing of holy objects" (p. 149).

Translator's Introduction

"The Salt of the Earth"

First published in the magazine *Khristianin*, 1908 (nos. 10–11) and 1909 (nos. 1, 5). Published as a separate volume in 1909 by the press of the Trinity Lavra of St. Sergius. Florensky met Father Isidore in 1904. On November 8, 1904, Florensky writes to his mother: "I went to see Father Isidore—I went with doubt but I returned unburdened and joyous, full of strength. He is very simple, a former serf . . . but he understands theology much better than scholars do, so that I joyfully hear from him thoughts very dear to me—thoughts that many people don't understand. He is all white, affectionate, and joyful—all radiant." This simple starets was one of the great formative influences on Florensky's life and creativity. From him Florensky absorbed the very fragrance of Orthodoxy.

A Russian Orthodox "starets"[11] is an experienced and deeply spiritual monk who holds the souls of others in his hands, guiding them on their path to God. In Russian this spiritual stewardship is called "starchestvo." A hieromonk is a monk who has been ordained as a priest; unlike unordained monks, he can hear confession, celebrate the liturgy, etc. The Trinity Lavra of St. Sergius, situated in the town of Sergiev Posad about seventy kilometers to the northeast of Moscow, is, spiritually and historically, the most important Russian monastery, founded as it was by Russia's greatest saint, Sergius of Radonezh. The Gethsemane Skete[12] is part of the monastery complex. Sergiev Posad is also the home of the Moscow Theological Academy, Russia's greatest seminary, where Florensky was a student and then a lecturer.

* * *

I have used the standard edition of Florensky's works: *Sochineniya v chetyrekh tomakh* (Works in four volumes), ed. Igumen Andronik (Trubachev), P. V. Florensky, and M. S. Trubacheva. All the essays translated here appear in volume 1, Moscow, 1994. Except where indicated, all notes are the translator's.

Boris Jakim

---

11. The word "elder," which is sometimes used to translate "starets," lacks the historical specificity of the latter.

12. A skete is a monastic community that allows relative isolation for monks, but also allows for communal services. Skete communities usually consist of a number of small cells or caves that act as the living quarters, with a centralized church or chapel. This type of community is thought of as a bridge between a strict hermitic lifestyle and a communal lifestyle since it is a blend of the two.

Superstition and Miracle

In order to understand my essay adequately, the reader must have a clear idea of my point of view in writing it and, from the outset, either agree or disagree fundamentally with this point of view. Thus, I will spare no effort in explicating it, and first of all, I will say something about the task I have set for myself.

I think that no one, or almost no one, will object to the opinion that it is possible for people to look at objects or phenomena superstitiously only insofar as they do not consider them from a scientific or genuinely religious point of view.

In order to establish the meaning of the word "superstition," I will refer to a consciousness of things that is fairly highly developed but lacks a scientific or religious point of view, and especially a gnoseology. That is why I have no problem discussing phenomena such as vampirism: they are real for the consciousness I have in mind. It is not my concern whether this consciousness rejects or accepts such phenomena *after* it has received a scientific education. My aim is to observe these phenomena in their pure state. I, as the author of this essay, am not concerned with whether spiritistic phenomena are real; I am only interested in the indisputable psychic fact that spirits exist, that people who believe in miracles exist, that occultists and adherents of demonolatry exist. I refuse to put any valuation on these beliefs; the only thing that concerns me is that there exist data of consciousness related to them. These data serve as the basis of my discussion.

* * *

One fate usually awaits the majority of words associated with relatively abstract concepts that are employed in everyday life—they become worn, are devalued, and finally lose almost all definite content. This is quite evident in the case of a word that is highly significant for forming a view of the world—the word "superstition." People use it appropriately and inappropriately, and often with the implication of censure. My task is to grasp the meaning of this word in all its fuzziness, to delineate its scope of application.

To show how indefinite the meaning of this word is, I will look at a few definitions found here and there and try to put them into an order that discloses its true meaning. In *Meyers Konversations—Lexikon* we find that "superstition is a condition of trust and belief in supernatural events which do not correspond, or no longer correspond, to the belief of the majority, or rise above this belief."[1] Here, superstition is defined as a completely conditional thing—as the belief of the majority. But this word is used without any reference to statistical studies; and in the case of the "majority," of what group does belief in some phenomenon become a superstition? After all, a small group of persons calls some of the beliefs of the peasants superstitious, but where do we find a majority here? In his correspondence with Hugo Boxel, Spinoza, amid a hailstorm of ridicule that he launches at those who believe in spirits, takes apart Boxel's arguments in favor of the existence of spirits, remarking: "However, setting all this (i.e., the arguments) aside, I must say in conclusion that such arguments, as well as those similar to them, can convince no one of the existence of spirits and apparitions except those who shut their ears to the arguments of reason and give themselves over to all manner of superstition, which is so inimical to common sense that, in order to denigrate the authority of philosophers, it is ready to believe all the fairy tales of old women."[2] Spinoza, *one* man, stands alone here in opposition to *all* the common people and to the legion of authorities, calling superstitious (even if only in the sense that it is absurd) not even the belief of the majority but the belief of all people in general. The following letter to Boxel (LIX) makes particularly clear how alone he was in his opinion: ". . . not the defenders but the opponents of the existence of spirits display mistrust in philosophers, because all philosophers, both ancient and modern, share this conviction in the existence of spirits. Plutarch attests to this in his works on the views of the philosophers and on the genius of Socrates. The Stoics, Pythagoreans,

---

1. *Meyers Konversations—Lexikon. Eine Enzyklopädie des allgemeinen Wissens*, 4th ed. (Leipzig, 1885–92), vol. 1, pp. 33–45. The text quoted is translated from the Russian translation used by Florensky.

2. See *Spinoza's Correspondence*, translated into Russian by Gurevich. Petersburg, 1891, Letters 15–60, pp. 333–59. (Florensky's note.) This excerpt is translated from the Russian translation (p. 346).

Platonists, and Peripatetics attest to the same thing, as do Empedocles, Maximus Tyrius, Apuleius, and others. Of the moderns too, there is no one who denies the existence of apparitions."[3] Whether this word is used correctly or incorrectly by Spinoza is a matter of indifference. The important thing is that we clearly see how indefinite the meaning of this word is and how small the role of the majority is in clarifying the concept of superstition.

Likewise, in the definition of superstition that we are analyzing, reference to the supernatural character of an event does not explain anything, for to assert an event as supernatural depends on the point of view of the person expressing the opinion that someone is superstitious. It is clearly felt, however, that when we see superstition in someone, we regard our judgment not as relative but as objectively valid, just as we regard our judgment about behavior as objectively valid. We may admit in both cases the possibility of error, but only hypothetically. On condition that all circumstances are known and have been rigorously scrutinized, we regard our judgment as independent of arbitrary opinions, just as a judge regards the verdicts he renders to be objective.

Meanwhile, Littré's dictionary (*Dictionaire de la langue française*) defines superstition as "a sense of religious veneration based on fear or ignorance, which results in the invention for oneself of false obligations, in belief in chimeras and hope in impotent things." Here, too, the concept of superstition is made indefinite by referring it to a number of conditional (conditioned by point of view) attributes, i.e., false obligations, chimeras, impotent things. All this turns out to depend on the personal (incidental for the phenomenon itself) views of the person making statements about the superstitiousness of a given individual; and it is understandable that there can exist diametrically opposite opinions concerning the same case, and that, according to Littré's definition, the opposite opinions can both be correct. Nevertheless, Littré's definition does contain an important new element: superstition is defined as a certain sense, namely a religious one. Littré does not clarify the nature of this sense, but he does attempt to define superstition according to the *content* of the sense, according to the object of superstitious facts of the psyche, not according to their *form*, which, as we shall see later, is the unifying attribute of these facts. The important thing here is not what occasions this sense (since the object of the sense is incidental) or how it is manifested outwardly (invocations, etc.). The important thing is how the subject of the superstition, the superstitious person, relates to his representation. Thus,

---

3. *Spinoza's Correspondence*, 353.

Littré's definition fails because it seeks the essential attribute of superstitious facts in their content and does not acknowledge the special intrinsic element in the superstitious state of the spirit.

Leman brings this method to its logical conclusion.[4] Limiting himself to the material side of the fact, he gives the following definition: "Superstition is any opinion that is not acknowledged in any religion or that stands in contradiction to the scientific view of nature in a given era."[5] As we shall see, this definition is correct; or rather it is not incorrect, since in essence it does not define anything and reduces the concept of superstition to an empty place bereft of content. Leman considers only that which is not superstition; compressing his definition, we arrive at the clearly contentless formula: "superstition is neither religion nor science"—a formula that is indisputable, of course, if we take into account that superstition and religion or superstition and science are not synonyms.

The systematic use of the word "superstition" with an almost arbitrary meaning has introduced so many different attributes into the concept associated with this word and expanded the scope of this concept so indeterminately, that we are not able to cleanse or shape it. We do not have the right to exclude any attributes from the existing concept; and on the other hand these attributes resemble the heads of a hydra that keep growing back in infinite numbers after they are cut off: if we exclude an attribute that is not essential to the concept, we do not in any way prevent the sudden appearance of a dozen other attributes when the word is taken from another angle. The only recourse we have is to reject totally the existing concept and preserve just the word (the sound) "superstition."

It is incumbent upon us to construct a new concept in place of the old, to work out its attributes, and then to define it with a constructive definition. To this concept worked out by us we will conditionally give the name "superstition," symbolizing it with the former word. We have no need to fear any ambiguity; we do not have two meanings of the word, since we nullified and excluded the former one, at least until the conclusion of our investigation. When we finish creating the new concept, we can psychologically motivate the condition we have set—the condition of calling the new concept "superstition," and not something else. This motivation will consist in proving that the new concept is, so to speak, the center of the fuzzy old concept: the new concept is the type of the entire cluster of concepts previously unified

---

4. Allusion to Alfred Leman's *Illustrated History of Superstitions and Witchcraft* (1893).
5. *Illustrated History of Superstitions and Witchcraft*, Russian translation (1901), 12–16.

under the word "superstition," and at the same time it is the historical *prius* of the meaning of this word.

We took as our point of departure definitions based on the content of the outward manifestation of superstition, on the content of results of the superstitious sense (i.e., certain convictions, actions, etc.), and we arrived at the thought that those outward forms of spiritual activity in which alone the essential attribute of superstition can be sought are, in and of themselves, not yet characteristic of superstition, do not define it.

Every time such a phenomenon occurs, every time some concept, though it seems clear, cannot be defined by analysis of a certain part of its content, but melts away and vanishes as we continue to investigate it, we are induced to seek the essence of the matter in the remaining part of the attributes. In such cases it often turns out that that is where the main attribute lies, an attribute that is indivisible and irreducible to other attributes—a kind of proto-phenomenon in the spirit. Thus, for example, when we try to define the concept of morality by investigating its outward manifestations, we lose the very concept of morality as such; but when we turn to its inner side, we find the specific, irreducible side of the activity of consciousness that characterizes the phenomena of morality.

Thus, since we did not find the attribute characteristic of superstition in its outward manifestations, we turn to the inner side of this phenomenon, for it has two sides—outward (superstitious actions such as witchcraft and magic) and inner (serving as the cause of the outward manifestations).

One of the fundamental facts of consciousness, if one looks at each of its manifestations, consists in the opposition between that which is appropriate and that which is inappropriate[6] in what is apprehended by the consciousness. We evaluate a phenomenon, a conduct, an action, etc.; this valuation can be ethical, esthetic, or one touching on the truthfulness or reasonableness of a phenomenon or thing. But every valuation already includes the idea of evaluating phenomena with a certain measure, i.e., with the idea of appropriateness, and consequently it presupposes the existence of such an idea.

If a certain act is not good, that means that it does not satisfy the idea of an appropriate act, i.e., that it should be other than it is. Receiving a thought and possessing one's own thought, one's judgment, we are conscious of them as something true or untrue in a certain relation; we measure every thought by the idea of appropriate thought. A false thought is one that does not

---

6. In Russian: *dolzhnoe* and *nedolzhnoe* (literally, that which should be and that which should not be).

correspond to the idea of appropriateness and does not have the right to exist. Appropriateness and inappropriateness are compatible and are even conjoined in every phenomenon or thing, but nevertheless they are qualitatively different. They do not represent different degrees of the same thing; rather, they are determinants of a thing, forces that pull it in opposite directions. No exertion of ours can identify them; that of which we are conscious as false can be expressed, but no exertions or sophisms of ours can make us conscious of it as true. One can do evil, while being perfectly conscious that it is evil; but there is no way one can force oneself to do it as if it were good—it is impossible to nullify conscience.

Why is it we regard some objects of consciousness as appropriate and others as inappropriate? We believe that there are objective foundations for this, that the things apprehended by our consciousness possess properties that compel us to see appropriateness in some elements of consciousness and inappropriateness in other elements.

For the sake of conciseness, we will call appropriateness the Divine element in objects of consciousness, whereas we will call inappropriateness the diabolical element.

But there is also another way of looking at that which is apprehended by consciousness. We can view it as nothing more than givenness, indifferent givenness.

The human mind is limited by the world of phenomena. Sense perception is the sole source of our knowledge.

But experience alone, i.e., the totality of past experienced states, is not yet knowledge; it is not a path that can take us to reliable generalizations. The fact that certain data of experience had existed in the past does not guarantee that that was how things had been before, or that that is how things will be in the future, or that that is how things must invariably be.

Empirical knowledge rises to the level of reliable knowledge only if the data of experience are synthesized with a priori ideas or principles. As conditions, as laws of human consciousness, a priori principles have a universal and necessary significance for experience; that is, experience actualizes these principles always and everywhere. All that the human mind is conscious of cannot enter its consciousness except in these a priori forms; for example, all that the human mind is conscious of must be subordinate to the law of causal connection, or the human mind must be conscious of all external objects only in three-dimensional space, and so on.

This processing of the testimony of experience into knowledge, this acquisition of reliable empirical knowledge without complicating it by valuations from the point of view of any norms—is what it means to regard as indifferent givenness that which is apprehended by consciousness.

Indifferent givenness stands, so to speak, on the boundary between appropriateness and inappropriateness. Its position is a position of equilibrium, but this is an unstable equilibrium. I would compare this conjoined appropriateness and inappropriateness to a plane and givenness to a line: On one side of this line is unbounded appropriateness, on the other side is unbounded inappropriateness; the line is the place of transition from appropriateness to inappropriateness, and vice versa. At the same time one can say about this line that it is part of the plane of appropriateness and also part of the plane of inappropriateness.

If we consider the process of transition from appropriateness to inappropriateness as it is reflected in the consciousness of the subject, we can say that this instability of the position of indifference is clearly visible to everyone, especially in the domain of ethics. If, in and of itself, no action is either good or evil but only becomes one or the other insofar as it is produced by a subject of the action who has a definite relation to the action—then, only a single line separates the action as good from the action as evil. In particular, this question is clarified by Vladimir Solovyov:[7]

> How can I more clearly describe and define the path, a narrow path but the only reliable one (cf. Pushkin's "*Narrow* path and *strait* gate of salvation"),[8] that humanity must follow between two abysses, between the abyss of the deadly and deadening "non-resistance to evil" on the one hand and the abyss of evil and equally deadening violence on the other? Where is the line that separates compulsion as moral duty and self-renunciation for others from violence as insult, injustice, and evil-doing? This line exists, but before giving it logical definitions, let us ask human conscience whether anyone—irrespective of all religious convictions—can find it in his conscience to condemn a Christian saint when he blesses and encourages leaders and warriors who are going off to liberate "the fatherland from slavery to infidels and foreigners"? Etc.

We have established three aspects in relation to what is perceived in consciousness. But by no means does it follow that all three are given equally

---

7. In his article "Nemesis." (Florensky's note.) The quotation has been somewhat inaccurately reproduced by Florensky.
8. The parenthesis is Florensky's.

in *every* perception, taken separately. At any given moment we direct our full attention at only one of these aspects, while the other two are left in shadow, though they are indisputably present, however dimly, in our consciousness.

If, as a result of an investigation we undertake of one thing or another, our consciousness affirms the objectivity of the perception of one of these aspects and the subjectivity of the other two, then, clearly, it (our consciousness) tends to efface what it considers illusory and irrelevant for its goal. This compels every subject to perceive a thing or phenomenon from this subject's own special point of view, which is different from the points of view of other subjects. Meanwhile, the constant predominance of one of these aspects in the perception of a given person compels this person always to see his surroundings in the same light.

In accordance with the predominance of one of these three aspects in relation to what is perceived, three different types of relations are established, which lie at the basis of three different fundamental worldviews: *religious*, *scientific*, and a third one, which we have chosen to call the *superstitious* worldview, or *occultism*. We shall now examine the characteristics of these three modes of relation and three worldviews.

If a phenomenon is perceived in such a way that our consciousness sees in it exclusively, or almost exclusively, the Power of God, the power of appropriateness, directly producing this phenomenon; if a thing, as something independent, becomes transparent, allowing us to see through its transparent shell the power of the Good acting in it—then this perception of the existent as the unalloyed result of Divine activity can be called a *perception of miracle*, a miraculous perception; and the phenomenon itself, insofar and only insofar it is perceived in this way, can be called a miracle. In this phenomenon we see the direct activity of the positive power.

If always or almost always we begin to view the world in this way, if we begin to see in it an eternal miracle of God, such perceptions will produce in us a worldview that must be called religious, since such a mode of perception belongs preeminently to religion (though far from exclusively). In this sense, miracle is a result of faith, if the latter is understood to mean the direct apprehension of the actions of the Good Power. Every phenomenon, as it appears in experience, is constructed by us; it is constructed not only out of forms of contemplation and rational understanding, which give only the possibility of existence, but also out of those forms of spiritual activity that condition the perception of a phenomenon or thing as genuinely real and actual in some sense and thus link the existence of a thing with the causes that produce it. By rejecting the possibility of perceiving a miracle, we thereby reject a particular mode of perceiving the world: "faith has faded in the heart that did not recognize its dearest children—miracles."[9] In view of this, if someone is "exposed" for producing "fake miracles," if an "explanation for the miracle" is found, it would be a great error to think that there was no miracle. Such an opinion often results in the denial of miracles in general.

Miracle does not consist in fact. How do you, a nonbeliever, know that it wasn't God's desire to manifest his will precisely in this manner—through a trick? "Who then is Paul, and who is Apollos, but ministers by whom ye believed. . . . I have planted, Apollos watered; but God gave the increase. . . . For we are labourers together with God: ye are God's husbandry, ye are God's building" (1 Cor. 3:5–9). Miracle consists in a relation to fact. All things can and must be explained scientifically and be assigned their cause in the world of phenomena; in this sense, all things are natural, occur according to certain laws. But insofar as Divinity is perceivable and conceivable not only as transcendent in relation to the world but also as immanent in relation to it, that is, insofar as pure deism is impossible—every phenomenon, besides being understood scientifically, can also be perceived by someone as a miracle. In this sense, all things are miraculous; all things can be perceived as a direct creation of God's beneficence.

For example, in the lives of many scientists there were moments when they had exactly these types of perceptions. One need only think of the emotion-filled statements of Kepler, of Swammerdam,[10] and of others. Eckermann describes a stroll with Goethe during which they conversed about nature. "The hills and mountains were covered with snow," Eckermann wrote,

> and I remarked how delicate their yellow color was and that a few miles away—because of the intervening mist—the darkness tended to be bluer than the whiteness tended to be yellow. (NB: this is important for Goethe's theory of colors.) Goethe agreed with me, and we then spoke of the high significance of the proto-phenomenon behind which one seems to see Divinity directly. "I do not ask," Goethe said, "whether this Supreme Being possesses understanding and reason, but I feel that It is understanding itself, reason itself. All creatures are permeated by It and man is illuminated by It to such an extent that he can understand the Highest."[11]

---

9. Goethe, *Faust* 1, "Night."
10. Jan Swammerdam (1637–1680), Dutch biologist.
11. From Eckermann's conversation with Goethe on February 23, 1831.

There is no end to the events, sometimes seemingly very trivial ones, that Goethe attributed to the Good Power, referring to this Power as "Demonic." But even for ordinary people the perception of one's surroundings as a miracle occurs much more frequently than is usually thought. All of us, of course, have had the experience that the following words are not a mere metaphor:

> When the yellowing field is billowing . . .
> My soul's worries are soothed,
> My brow's wrinkles are smoothed,
> And I can grasp happiness on earth
> And see God in the heavens.[12]

What I have said about miracles becomes clearer when we consider the worldview of the Jews. Here is what Prince S. N. Trubetskoy writes:

> If our contemporary scientific worldview does not admit miracle since it regards it as an arbitrary violation of the laws of nature due to a supernatural intrusion, the Jew, on the contrary, did not know any law of nature other than the "commandments" of Jehovah and His continuously acting energy. The later scholastic concept of miracle is based on the acknowledgment of a more or less extensive domain of phenomena extracted from the medium of the constant living action of Providence, which intrudes only from time to time into this domain in an external fashion, violating the natural course of events. In essence, this concept of miracle is itself based on a particular premise of the mechanical worldview, and therefore in the final analysis it is powerless against the latter. The Jew does not know miracles in this sense, because for him the whole of nature with the visible lawlike regularity of its phenomena is a great unceasing Divine miracle. Among these phenomena he recognizes certain special "signs," but these Divine signs are an inseparable part of the laws of nature, as he understands the latter.[13]

Prince S. N. Trubetskoy's words so clearly illuminate the essence of the religious worldview that only one thing needs to be added: Since, in and of themselves, the facts of nature differ from the facts of spiritual life neither

---

12. From an 1837 poem by Lermontov.
13. *The Doctrine of the Logos*, vol. 1, p. 241. (Florensky's note.)

from a consistent religious point of view nor from a consistent scientific point of view, the difference between them must lie in the mode of relation to these facts. This is already indicated by the very existence of the word "miracle" (or "sign," as Trubetskoy says).

But in addition to this religious mode of looking at things, another mode is possible, one that is dominated by the isolatedness of a thing from the forces acting in it. To develop consistently this mode of perception, i.e., to crystallize in a pure form the perception of a thing as a result of forces (insofar as the thing itself differs from the forces producing it)—that is the task of science.

In order to gain all-sided knowledge of a thing, we must preliminarily examine it one-sidedly from every point of view taken separately. Synthesis is not desirable until every separate mode of perception is carried through to the end. Otherwise, instead of unification of heterogeneous views into an integral view, we would get the mixing of not fully formed elements; instead of harmony, we would get noise. Thus, the scientific worldview can and must carry through its point of view to the end; it can and must examine the world as a whole that lives its own independent life, closed to outside influences; it can and must affirm that the world is connected in its elements qua phenomena and that only these connections can be taken into account in scientific studies. But to affirm this is by no means to reject everything else; if science can and must develop in the maximally possible purity of its proper methods, this does not mean that scientists cannot have divergent views of things. The value of a worldview lies not in gray uniformity, but in the living unity of multi-diverse elements.

The aforesaid already suggests the attribute on which I will base my definition of superstition. I define the superstitious relation to that which is perceived (superstition) as the perception of a thing primarily from the inappropriate side if one directly (mystically) or indirectly (through rational understanding) observes in it the presence of the evil power. The common people characterize it very accurately when they call it the unclean power—unclean, disorderly, un-good, foul, unwashed, the king or prince of darkness,[14] since it is precisely the negation of what is clean, orderly, and good.

If superstition, the superstitious perception of one's surroundings, becomes the dominant mode of perception, a new—third and final—fundamental type of worldview is then formed: occultism, or the superstitious worldview. It can also be called a negative religious worldview, because it is

---

14. See S. Maksimov, *The Unclean Power*, 10–11. (Florensky's note.)

based on what is ignored by the religious worldview (in the sense discussed above) and, in its own turn, fails to see what lies at the basis of the religious worldview.

True miracle is accomplished in the believer's soul when he sees in the apparently random and phenomenally causal the will of him by whom all things were made, as well as the phenomenon. Pascal says that people do not believe in true miracles because of a deficiency of love. "But ye believe not, because ye are not of my sheep."[15] They also believe in false miracles because of a deficiency of love.[16] "The coming of the lawless one," says the Apostle, "is by the activity of Satan with all power and false signs and wonders, and with all wicked deception for those who are perishing, because they refused to love the truth and so be saved" (2 Thess. 2:9–10). The miracles are false precisely because they are perceived as being produced by the man of sin, the son of perdition, who "opposes and exalts himself against every so-called god or object of worship, so that he takes his seat in the temple of God, proclaiming himself to be God" (2 Thess. 2:4). The falseness of these "miracles" consists in the fact that the actions of the "son of sin" will begin to be perceived as his own actions and understood as the actions of God, whom he proclaims himself to be—in the fact that they will be perceived as miracles. These will be what we have called negative miracles; the error here will be related to the interpretation of one's perceptions and it will be caused by a deficiency of love.

Every fact can and must be explained, but every fact, as a reflection of the Eternal, can also inspire a sense of veneration toward itself. In truth, a genuine miracle must consist precisely in such a (in the broad sense) rationally explainable (though not hastily explained) phenomenon. Even the highest miracle—the resurrection of Christ—is a natural phenomenon, though so far it is the only example, so to speak, of the higher law. This is a natural phenomenon if only because all will be subject to the law of resurrection: all of us will be resurrected. And, on the other hand, resurrection is a rational necessity (Solovyov). Of course, we cannot define the life-process (in the broad sense) in terms of scientific rationalism. After all, we are even unable to explain the mechanism of the electrical charging of a conductor, or even many other, seemingly very simple, physical mechanisms. But this does not prevent us from regarding such phenomena as natural and separately explainable in terms of the scientific worldview. It would be absurd

---

15. John 10:26.
16. See the *Pensées*, ch. 22, p. 6.

to demand at the present time an explanation for all the phenomena of life, especially for those which involve spiritual causes and moral engines. We are able to see only the "divine necessity" (Leonardo da Vinci's term) or "rational necessity" (Goethe's term) of the fact of the resurrection, but at the present time it is, of course, impossible to explain its mechanism. But even if we suppose that we will never be able to explain such phenomena, that does not by any means make them impossible.

Superstition is a mode of relation to a thing or event in the case of which we see them as originating from an evil and unclean power; this thing or event is internally judged to be unclean, meaningless, evil. We regard this thing or event to be an inappropriate, sinister, and dark product of forces that strive to make everything unclean. We feel a strange horror and, curious and attracted, we are unable to tear ourselves away from the contemplation of such a thing: something alien and dark enters us and possesses us. After our curiosity is satisfied, we feel a disgust toward everything, as if we had overheard or seen something we shouldn't have. This is clarified by the following extract from Hoffmann's *Life and Opinions of Tomcat Murr*:[17]

> "People find a greater satisfaction in horror than in a natural explanation of what seems uncanny to them. Our ordinary world is not sufficient for them—they also wish to have something from another world which does not require a body for its manifestation."
>
> "I do not understand, Meister, your strange taste for such tricks," Kreisler said. "Like a chef, you concoct the miraculous out of various spicy ingredients, and you think that with these things you can excite people whose imaginations are as flat as the stomachs of slugs. After such tricks which strike our hearts with terror, there is nothing more unpleasant than suddenly to find out that they occurred in the most natural way."
>
> "Natural!" exclaimed Meister Abraham. "As someone with a first-rate mind, you have to acknowledge that nothing in the world occurs naturally. Nothing! Or do you think, honored Kapellmeister, that if with certain means we succeed in producing a certain effect, we would be able to understand its causes, which originate in the mysteries of nature? At one time your attitude toward my tricks was one of great respect, even though you had never seen the best of them, the pearl of my tricks. More than any of the others, that trick could have proved to you that the simplest things, easily susceptible to mechanical manipulation, often involve

---

17. Translated into English from the Russian translation used by Florensky.

the most mysterious miracles of nature and can produce something that is unexplained in the simplest sense of the word." (This trick is then described: a girl in an ecstatic and somnambulistic state makes predictions, and the sounds of her words are transmitted through tubes to a glass sphere suspended in an empty room.)

Let me also describe a related circumstance. Dr. Leman, who *per fas et nefas* made every effort to expose spiritism, devised a plan to prove that trickery was used in the performance of séances.[18] His plan was to learn the tricks himself and to perform séances; in Leman's opinion and judging by his accounts, the participants in the séances were indeed deceived. But after explaining his tricks, a few pages later he makes a remarkable declaration: "Even in my mediumistic experiments (earlier, he had called them 'tricks') certain indications of extremely significant psychic phenomena were revealed *which conditioned in part my successes*; and I am convinced that the existence of these kinds of phenomena is what distinguishes the medium from an outright trickster." What does this mean? Did he falsify his accounts by not mentioning phenomena whose existence he wished to deny? Was he filled with the desire to achieve the fame of a medium? Was he deceived by his own tricks?

Just as in order to perceive a miracle, one needs faith, the capacity to apprehend deeply the Divine aspect of a thing or event; so, in order to perceive a negative miracle, in order for superstition to be present, one needs the capacity to apprehend deeply the diabolical aspect of a thing. Here, by *negative miracle* we mean the object of superstition as parallel to negative religion (occultism), which constitutes systematized superstition. Just as miracle is a consequence of faith, so negative miracle is a consequence of superstition. Concerning this, let us quote the following common-folk observation: "In recent times the unclean power has appeared rarely, because almost no one believes in it."[19]

* * *

I think it will be useful to illustrate the foregoing discussion with some concrete examples; I will limit myself to a few.

---

18. See *Illustrated History of Superstitions and Witchcraft*, Russian translation, 404–13.
19. From Hans Christian Andersen, *Norwegian Fairy-Tales*. Quoted from memory. (Florensky's note.)

What could be more natural than a shadow, a reflection in water, or a reflection in a mirror? At first glance, it even seems strange to speak of such common phenomena as capable of being interpreted superstitiously. But among many primitive peoples we find shadows to be objects of superstitious terror, either as products of evil powers or as independent living beings. This may involve the notion of a dark and alien power that causes our disintegration and takes something essential out of us. What comes to mind is Balzac's theory of the daguerreotype, according to which every photograph taken of us carries off part of our soul, peels off a layer of the soul, so to speak.

The superstitious fear of shadows is most easily observable in children. One two-and-a-half-year-old boy, personally known to me, could never fall asleep with a candle burning in his room: the shadows made by it would fill him with horror. He'd often wake up at night and scream "Shadow!" This went on for about a month and it would happen every time a candle would be brought into the room. Once when he saw his shadow in the daytime, he became extremely agitated and started to jump and spin around in order to free himself of it.

Adults, too, can experience a sense of horror when they see shadows. Who has not experienced a momentary horror when suddenly seeing his shadow on the wall or when seeing shadows rise suddenly as a candle is extinguished? Will you ever remain completely indifferent to shadows if you have read Hans Christian Andersen's "Man without a Shadow" or completely indifferent to reflections in a mirror if you have read E. T. A. Hoffmann's story about a man who gave his reflection as a gift? And what about General Suvorov, who was so afraid of mirrors that he commanded that any he might encounter be covered? Finally, will anyone who has read Fyodor Sologub's story "Shadows" remain indifferent to them?

I have considered these phenomena in some detail in order to show how it is possible to interpret superstitiously things that usually seem ordinary and habitual. This phenomenon (shadows) is closely connected with the phenomenon of doubles, which inspire an even greater superstitious terror. Not having time to discuss this in detail, I will refer the reader to the strange case of the double appearances of schoolteacher Emilie Sagée, as reported by Robert Dale Owen.[20] Like shadows, these phenomena can be studied, and are being studied, by scientific methods (which does not by any means pre-decide the question of their existence: for example, we can scientifically study the accounts of these phenomena).

20. See also A. Aksakow, *Animism and Spiritism*, 2nd ed., 530–39. (Florensky's note.)

Everything connected with the phenomenon of death is of special interest; all three of the aspects highlighted above stand out very clearly here, and in the domain of the phenomena of death we find the best examples showing that one and the same phenomenon can be perceived in wholly different ways. For example, the body of the deceased can be an object of superstition, an object of scientific study, or an object of veneration, depending on what we perceive acting in it: dark powers, physico-chemical processes, or (as in relics) a Divine Power, maintaining incorruptibility. It is clear, however, that in the latter case the important thing is not the fact of incorruptibility in and of itself: in a dry climate, for example, corpses often dry up before they decompose, but nobody regards them as relics.

On the other hand, though relics are greatly venerated by Old Believers, they do not always produce the same feeling in Orthodox believers, who sometimes see in them an object of superstitious adoration. Even apart from this, a corpse can be an object of superstitious actions: "*Affin de faire perir les hommes de male mort, les sorciers ont coustume d'exhumer des cadavres & notamment de ceulx qui ont esté suppliciez & pendus au gibet. De ces cadavres ilz tirent la substance & matière de leurs sortileges, come aussi des instruments du bourrel, des pieux, des fers, etc, lesquelz sont douez d'une certain force & puissance magicque pour incantations.*"[21] As regards witches and sorcerers, this was a superstitious action: they blasphemously cut corpses for their witcheries, believing they possessed magical power. But that which we say about Bald Mountain,[22] can we apply that to the anatomical theater? The acts performed there are the same, but there the corpse is perceived not as a plaything of evil powers and a means for evil, but as a scientific object, connected by certain relations with other scientific objects. Everyone feels that the word "superstitious" is not applicable here. Also, when relics of saints are cut open for inclusion in the antimins,[23] we see an example of a similar action, but one that can be called neither witchcraft nor scientific dissection.

---

21. *Le Sabbat des Sorciers* by Bourneville and Teinturier, 31. (Florensky's note.) "In order to destroy men by an evil death, sorcerers used to exhume cadavers, especially of people who had been tortured and hanged. Out of these cadavers they made the substance and matter of their sorceries, as well as instruments of torture, stakes, irons, etc., which were endowed with a certain force and magical power for incantations."

22. In Russian folklore, the place where witches gather for their sabbaths.

23. The antimins, placed on the altar in many Eastern Christian liturgical traditions, is a rectangular piece of cloth of either linen or silk, typically decorated with representations of Christ's descent from the cross, the Four Evangelists, and inscriptions related to the Passion. A small relic of a saint is sewn into it.

Superstition and Miracle

The cutting open of a relic for the purpose of its veneration cannot seem blasphemous to those who regard relics as miracles. On the contrary, they regard this action as part of religious cult.

Closely connected with these questions is the idea of the possibility of a corpse coming back (or almost coming back) to life. This phenomenon, too, can be apprehended by the consciousness from three fundamental points of view. Abbot Calmet writes that "all lives of the saints are full of resurrections of the dead; one could compile several thick volumes of such events."[24] However, belief in such resurrections cannot be considered superstitious, even if the facts themselves are considered to be completely nonhistorical. In order to show this more clearly via an example, I will present a legend concerning St. Stanislaus, Bishop of Cracow, as recorded in Calmet's book.

> Bishop Stanislaus bought land on the Vistula near Lublin for his Cracow church from a nobleman named Peter, paying the seller in the presence of witnesses and with all the formalities common in that country, but without a written contract, for at that time in Poland such sales were rarely recorded in writing; witnesses were considered sufficient. Stanislaus took possession of this land by the authority of the king, and his church used it peacefully over a period of about three years. During that period, Peter, the seller of the land, died. Meanwhile, the Polish King Bolesław, who was nurturing an implacable hatred against the saintly Bishop for his excesses and seeking any excuse to make trouble for him, incited Peter's heirs, his three sons, to demand the land back on the pretext that the Bishop had never paid for it. The King promised to support their demand and to force the Bishop to return the land. So, those three noblemen summoned the Bishop to judgment before the King, who at that time had set up a judicial court in Solec, where he judged according to the ancient custom of the country in a general assembly of the nation. At this court the Bishop affirmed that he had bought and paid for the land in question. The witnesses did not dare to testify truthfully, and the place where the assembly was held was very close to the disputed land. Evening was approaching, and the Bishop was at great risk of being condemned by the King and his counselors. Suddenly, as if inspired by the divine Spirit, the Bishop promised to the King that in three days he would bring him Peter, the seller of the land; this was accepted with amazement, since it would be impossible

---

24. *Dissertation sur les Apparitions des esprits et sur les Vampires ou les Revenans de Hongrie, de Moravie etc.* by C. R. P. Dom Augustin Calmet, Abbé des Senonce, ch. 3, t. 1.

to fulfill. The saintly bishop returned to the disputed land and spent three days there in prayer with his retinue. On the third day, accompanied by clergy and a crowd of people, he went in pontifical vestment to Peter's grave. He ordered that it be dug up, and a desiccated and decayed corpse was revealed. The saint ordered him to come out and to testify to the truth before the King's court. The dead man rose. A mantle was put on him; the Bishop took his hand and led him, alive, to the feet of the King. No one had the boldness to question Peter, but without prompting he declared that he had properly sold the land to the prelate and that he had received money for it. Then he sternly reproached his sons for duplicitously accusing the Bishop. Stanislaus asked him if he wished to remain alive, in order to repent, but Peter thanked him and replied that he did not want to subject himself to any new perils of sin. Stanislaus conducted him back to the grave, and Peter once again found repose in the Lord.

In this legend both the corpse and the resurrection are dear and necessary to the believer; they are produced by the Good Power. But the same phenomenon of resurrection also serves as the basis for the most repulsive of figures—vampires, wurdalaks,[25] etc., figures that in one form or another exist among all peoples.[26] That which had been dear to us becomes an arena where alien and hostile forces act; dark hatred possesses the body of the dear person and transforms his corpse, which rises automatically from the grave, into an instrument for killing others, especially relatives of the deceased. The rapid withering of those who are visited by vampires, the panic of entire villages, epidemics of vampirism spread by vampire bites—are the most repulsive things imaginable if one reads the descriptions of concrete instances.

Below I will present a typical scientific view of this matter, namely the opinion presented in the magazine *Glaneur* for 1732. To be sure, it seems highly naïve to us, but because of its naïve decisiveness, it is fully rational. First, I will recount only the incident that led the magazine to express its opinion.[27]

> In that part of Hungary which bears the Latin name Oppida Heidonum, there lives a people called the Haiduks. They believe in the existence of dead people called vampires who suck the blood of living people and

---

25. A particular form of vampire.
26. The following section on vampires has been abbreviated and slightly paraphrased.
27. The following excerpt has been abbreviated.

Superstition and Miracle

get so fat with their blood that it seeps out of them. Over a short period of time this opinion has been confirmed by so many facts whose truthfulness, apparently, cannot be denied if one takes into account the character of the persons reporting them.... About five years before this, the Haiduk Arnod Paol from a Serbian village who when alive had been, they say, greatly tormented by a vampire, died (of a broken neck) and twenty or thirty days later killed four men who had witnessed his unfortunate death. Forty days after his burial, his corpse was dug up and acknowledged to be a vampire, since decomposition had not affected his body and fresh blood was flowing from his mouth and nose, drenching his clothes and forming a layer of blood on his body. As was the custom, a stake was driven through his heart; he emitted a very distinct moan and blood flowed copiously from the opening made by the stake; the corpse was then burned. Signs of vampirism were also found in the corpses of the four men killed by him.... Arnod Paol attacked not only people but also cattle, and the people who ate their meat became vampires, leading to the death of seventeen people over three months. One of the dead was Stanoska, the daughter of the Haiduk Iotuitso. She was completely well when she went to bed one night, but in the middle of night she woke up screaming that a Haiduk's son called Millo, who had died four weeks before this, was choking her, after which she felt an acute pain in her breast and died eight days later.... She was buried, and then her corpse was dug up. Millo had turned her into a vampire. On her neck beneath the right ear (where Millo had choked her), a bloody blue spot a finger in length was found. When she was dug up, blood spurted from her nose....

The girl's sorrow and fear in the days preceding her death, her profound suffering, indicated how strongly her imagination was disturbed.... The inhabitants of towns affected by plague know from their experience that fear kills many people. As soon as a person feels the most insignificant pain, he thinks that the epidemic has struck him; this affects him so powerfully that he can become seriously ill.[28]

Calmet writes the following:

The Dutch magazine *Glaneur* states that nations among which vampires appear are ignorant and gullible, for such appearances are nothing more

---

28. I have taken this account from the atrocious Russian translation of Calmet's book, since I don't have the original in my possession at this time. See vol. 3, pp. 25, 28. (Florensky's note.)

than a product of distorted imagination caused chiefly by poor nutrition. For the most part the people in such nations eat only bread made of oats, roots, and bark, a food which thickens and ruins the blood and produces somber fantasies in the imagination. It compares this sickness with infection from a rabid dog, which transmits its poison by biting people. In the same way, those infected with vampirism are said to transmit this dangerous poison to those who visit them. This explains the agitated nights, the disturbed dreams, and the so-called appearances of vampires. If a vampire screams when his heart is pierced with a stake, there is nothing unnatural about this. The air trapped in the heart, when it is rapidly expelled, necessarily produces this sound when it passes through the throat.[29]

In the chapter on "systems for explaining the phenomena of vampires," Dr. Calmet theorizes, for the most part, that the affected persons have fallen into lethargic sleep. The foregoing examples give some idea of the old scientific view of this phenomenon. Although they seem naïve to us, it cannot be denied that they possess the main feature of a scientific explanation, that is, the explanation remains within the bounds of the world of phenomena. As we can see from these examples, the majority of the facts of life are not denied; they are just explained differently.

My last example will come from Tasso's *Jerusalem Delivered*. All of you will undoubtedly remember the thirteenth canto, the description of the enchanted forest. In order to limit the size of this essay, I ask the reader to reread this canto, which presents a very vivid description of a superstitious perception, and then to compare it to the scientific attitude toward the same phenomenon as expressed in a letter of Maréchal Valiac.[30] Here is the letter:

> The experience with poplars, bored to different depths, reminded me of something that had happened to me in Algeria in September and October 1838. I had ordered that a large oak be cut down in order to build a fence, and I was astonished to hear faint moans coming from the tree so reminiscent of human moans that they caused our military hearts to tremble. A reddish liquid spurted out of the tree together with gas bubbles, and it streamed out powerfully until the moaning stopped. This incident of my

---

29. This extract has been abbreviated.
30. I quote it as it appears in the notes to Min's Russian translation of *Jerusalem Delivered* (vol. 2, p. 223). (Florensky's note.)

African life reminded me of what I had once read in *Jerusalem Delivered*. Crusaders were preparing to chop down an enchanted forest in which nymphs and fairies had found a refuge. They retreated in terror when they heard sorrowful laments coming from the trees when they were touched by the axe. What seems like a fairy tale when it is described in the verses of a poet is actually an undeniable fact; and if, instead of Algeria in the 19th century, we had found ourselves in those eastern lands in the 13th century and if in accordance with the superstition of that time we had been told that those moans were coming from nymphs confined in the trees and that the reddish liquid was their blood, our fences would, of course, have remained unfinished.

The same thing can be said about the "voices of nature." Recalling the tales of travelers and the words of Hoffmann and Maupassant, it seems difficult to keep from interpreting them superstitiously; nevertheless, they can be explained scientifically.

A question arises: Does my definition of superstition coincide with the existing and established understanding of this word? I had said earlier that superstition is a mode of the perception of a thing or event in the case of which they are perceived as originating from an unclean and evil power and inwardly condemned as inappropriate and unclean. So, does my definition coincide with the usual understanding? Yes, it does, as my analysis of the foregoing examples has clearly shown. True, sometimes the word "superstition" is used as a synonym for an absurd conclusion, a hasty generalization, or an antiquated opinion, just as the word "mysticism" is sometimes used as a synonym for obscure or fantastic conclusions. But that is an incorrect usage, of course. If we think about it, we would never call "superstitious" an erroneous or hasty induction, an absurd conclusion; rather, we would call it absurd, nonsensical, etc. We all understand or at least feel that a certain sense must be associated with superstition; and therefore, if this sense is present, though it may not be justifiable by the rational views of a given person, the perception will nevertheless be superstitious.

> Those fairy tales, which in our childhood we always listened to joyfully, never fearfully—those fairy tales would never have left such a deep trace in us if our souls did not contain independent chords resounding in harmony with them. It is impossible to deny the existence of a strange, incomprehensible world of phenomena, sometimes astonishing our ears, sometimes our eyes; and, believe me, the fear and horror felt by our earthly

organism are only outward expressions of the sufferings experienced by the spirit living within it under the yoke of these phenomena.[31]

Hoffmann's words clarify the special, specific feelings experienced during the perception of negative miracles, of dark powers possessing the consciousness. He writes that "much of what we usually consider to be insignificant and call reveries and empty fantasies points out to us perhaps, by means of symbolic revelations, the mysterious threads that pass through our life and tie up all of its manifestations into a unified whole."[32] He expressed this idea with particular vividness in "The Sandman," to which I send the reader.

The triple relation to spiritism represents a good example of the possibility of the triple perception of one and the same phenomenon. For some (e.g., Robert Dale Owen), spiritism is a gift of the Good Power, something like a new religion, a means of encounter with beloved persons; whereas for those who analyze it scientifically (e.g., Crookes, Aksakow, Zöllner, and others), it is nothing more than a fact that they study, a manifestation of forces that are not yet understood, something that in itself is neither good nor bad, though it might be useful and very interesting. Finally, for a third group, for persons of the priesthood, for Dostoevsky (see his "theory of demons" in his *Diary of a Writer*),[33] and others, spiritism is an unclean business, superstition in the full sense of the word. Persons of the first and third categories acknowledge the existence of spiritism, but view it differently; persons of the second category all view it in the same way, but some of them recognize its existence, while others deny it unconditionally. This can clarify the meaning of the word "superstition."

Someone might believe in a particular superstition: for example, that greeting a person across the threshold to a house will result in a quarrel. The superstition here does not consist in the fact that someone considers that a certain condition will result in a quarrel; we often assign the wrong causes to things that happen, and so this may be an error or a hasty conclusion, but it is not a superstition. Our belief will be a superstition if and only if we think that some *power* causes the quarrels, a power that goes beyond "physical" reality—i.e., only if we regard the cause as existing beyond the world of phenomena, but not coming from the Good Power. Perhaps the important thing

---

31. From E. T. A. Hoffmann's *The Serapion Brethren*.
32. From *The Devil's Elixirs*.
33. In the January 1876 issue of the *Diary*.

here is that we regard some force as having power over our souls and, not being able to accept it as a "physical" force, we suppose that it comes from the Devil, since the Good Power cannot produce what ethically seems absurd.

In small villages in France we find the following ritual: a key from a church dedicated to St. Peter is heated until it is red-hot, and then it is applied to the heads of bulls, dogs, and other animals, to cure them of mad-cow disease, rabies, etc. No one could, in all conscience, call this ritual a superstition, though it might be regarded as absurd. In fact, it is recommended that village priests try to eradicate such rituals only if they receive the bishop's approval and only if their efforts do not offend the popular belief. In other words, the church does not see in this anything positively bad (a quality that always characterizes superstition).

The superstitious perception of things and the resulting occultistic worldview and practice (magic) are very important because they concern themselves with aspects of things that are inappropriate par excellence and thus widen our horizon. In this sense, systematized superstition has been, and will continue to be, a necessary complement to both religion, which concerns itself with what is appropriate, and to science, which studies objects in their indifferent givenness. Nevertheless, the situation of occultism is more difficult than that of science, just as the situation of science is more perilous than that of religion (in the sense indicated above). Occultism apprehends and studies what is inappropriate, and it will itself remain an appropriate and good endeavor only insofar as it regards evil as inappropriate. If it begins to view evil as appropriate, occultism will turn into an unclean endeavor. Those who constantly deal with what is untrue, unreal, and inappropriate can be easily seduced and fall into evil. The unclean and inappropriate seduce us into believing they are true and appropriate. But an investigator will quickly begin to realize that he has been seduced. The inappropriate can take on the appearance (as if the shell) of the appropriate. Evil reveals itself as soon as the investigator pierces this shell of what seems good, this illusion of appropriateness. The seduced investigator feels guilty: "How could I have been so deceived? How could I have been so morally (and otherwise) blind as to be seduced by evil?" It is this sense of nausea, of revulsion toward any further study of superstition that characterizes the investigator's spiritual state after he has been seduced. I speak of the sense of nausea. This is more than a metaphor, for though it is a physiological sensation, nausea is essentially akin to this kind of state: in the majority of cases we experience nausea after eating excessively, that is, when for a period of time we treat food as the goal, not as a means; when we make food into an idol.

In the same way, when we read with fascination books of occultism, when we converse too much about vampires, and so on, there remains in our souls a residue of uncleanness, a kind of foulness.

Let me quote Solovyov on the topic of evil taking on the appearance of good:

"This is what I don't understand: your Antichrist is essentially good, not evil, but he hates God."

"The key thing is that he is not *essentially* good. That's the whole meaning of the thing. And I take back my earlier words that 'you can't explain the Antichrist with nothing but old sayings.' He can in fact be explained by one extremely simple saying: 'all that glitters is not gold.' This fake gold has tons of glitter, but as for essential power—it has none."[34]

The seductive tinsel appearance of evil masquerading as good cannot be described more clearly. In ordinary life, to be fascinated with the tinsel means to serve the "god of this age." In the domain of occultism, fascination with the tinsel is replaced by fascination with the object of study, which, by its resemblance to good, seduces the investigator into worshiping it, even if when he began the study, he was conscious of its inappropriateness.

---

34. From *Three Conversations*. (Florensky's note.)

The Empyrean and the Empirical: A Dialogue

Dedicated to A. V. Elchaninov[1]

A.—All of our conversations, regardless of how they've begun, have come down on your part to the eternal refrain: "There can be no consistent worldview without a religious foundation; there can be no consistent life, a life according to the truth, without religious experience." But on my part I was dubious: I did not deny, as you recall, that an absolute worldview of the kind that you want is impossible—that is, a worldview capable of embracing *everything* with a single dialectically forged chain of judgments. Likewise, I did not deny the impossibility of a fully consistent life according to the truth—that is, of a life justified in all of its details from the point of view of an absolute worldview. I consider these things impossible, however, not because we are weak and wavering, but, first of all, because to such truth it is even totally impossible to impart the full truth and meaning of life; because I cannot, as I said, recognize the absolute worldview's right to exist, and only such a worldview can (or, rather, could possibly) reveal the meaning of life and thereby justify, even if only post factum, one's conduct.

What you desire is that reality and our relation to the latter not just be *given* to the consciousness, but that they be given in their *truth*; you demand the disclosure of the rational meaning and right to exist of that which is given to us as something that is in the process of being immediately revealed. In other words, it is not enough for you know that something *is*; you also want to know *what* it is and then to examine to what extent this *what* corresponds to certain eternal norms, to what extent this *what* is that which *should be* and to what extent it can be this thing that should be. And so you proclaimed that it is impossible to

---

1. Alexander Elchaninov (1881–1934), priest and religious writer, was one of Florensky's closest friends.

construct such a worldview except on a religious foundation and on the basis of religious experience. I repeat: I would not have the slightest objection to your assertion of impossibility if you had not added the words: "except on a religious foundation and on the basis of religious experience."

B.—But that's the most important thing.

A.—And so the worldview you desire is possible if you have a religious foundation and experience?

B.—Absolutely.

A.—Do you believe that this worldview is possible for knowledge in general as its ultimate goal and never-attainable ideal? Or is it possible somewhere and sometime, if not for you, then for somebody else, in millions of years? Or, finally, do you think this worldview is possible in the concrete conditions given to us—for example, now and for you?

B.—Yes, it is possible *now and for me*. But it is also possible for anyone who wants it: "Ask, and it shall be given you."

A.—If it's not a secret, tell me: Do you already have it? Has it already been given to you?

B.—No, there's no secret. Much of it still needs to be developed; the logical formulations are not completely clear. There is still a lot I haven't worked out. But even if I don't have the finished worldview, I have its principles and foundations.

A.—Your worldview—evolving, unfinished (whatever words you might use to describe it)—can it fit into any existing category?

B.—Yes, it can.

A.—What category?

B.—Christianity.

A.—Not churchly Christianity, I hope.

B.—You hope in vain: not only churchly, but even catholic.²

A.—You know, I deliberately led the conversation up to that. I wanted you to say exactly what you just said.

B.—That catholic Christianity is the absolute worldview?

A.—Exactly. Let me explain myself. Naturally, I have no intention of discussing the absoluteness of such a worldview; I have no time to waste on this absurd and imaginary absoluteness. What I want to understand is to what extent I can grasp your views of reality . . .

B.—(*Inquisitively silent.*)

A.—You look at me, bewildered? You're silent? *Cum faces clamas*?³ Well, keep screaming silently. I am unable to pose questions concerning the absolute worldview; I am physiologically unable to, if you like. Absolutenesses get stuck in my throat and sour my spiritual disposition; all these "Truths" do nothing but enrage me. No, deliver me from absolutenesses . . .

B.—*Quid est veritas*?⁴ Is that it?

A.—Exactly. And why do you need truth? Dostoevsky's devil aptly points out the following: "If you've decided to cheat people, why do you need the sanction of truth? But such is our contemporary Russian: he loves truth so much that he can't even cheat without it being sanctioned."⁵

B.—Does that refer to me?

A.—It's just something that came into my mind. But let's get away from this sensitive subject. I say that I want to understand you. Since I myself do not recognize the possibility of absolute worldviews, naturally I will not ask you for absolute proofs of such a worldview. It would be sufficient for me to understand you if you demonstrated to me that your worldview has legit-

---

2. In the sense of universal, not in the sense of Roman Catholicism. Traditionally, the church is called *One*, *Holy*, *Catholic*, and *Apostolic*.
    3. "You scream silently?"
    4. "What is truth?" The question posed by Pilate.
    5. From *The Brothers Karamazov*.

imacy among other worldviews. For me it's now the pariah of worldviews; the others aren't that great either, but at least you can swallow them without choking. From the theoretical point of view, your worldview is a childish fantasy; while from the practical point of view, it is a social poison: *latet anguis in herba*.[6] But that's not the important thing. I can regard such a state of affairs as having come to an end only when you demonstrate to me, first of all, the *possibility* of all that you are asserting (i.e., the possibility of miracles, sacraments, and so on) not separately, but in the form of a coherent system; and, secondly, when you demonstrate that all of your assertions—even if they turn out to be possible and conceivable—have some advantage in the sense of *probability* amongst all the innumerable other assertions; that is, that they are not only conceivable but have a non-negligible probability. Thus, I will understand you when you are able to demonstrate that all your dogmas, sacraments, and so on are conceivable as such (i.e., that they do not contain absurdities) and that your decisions and your views of the mysteries and so on do not have an infinitely low probability.

B.—You're not asking for much, are you? What you demand from me now is actually the task of all of rational philosophy together with the sciences—the task, namely, of *negative* philosophy, if you allow me to use Schelling's terminology. Negative philosophy is the kind of philosophy that concerns itself with separating the possible from the impossible, the conceivable from the inconceivable, and constructing a system of the possible. Moreover, you want me to determine probabilities. But that is the task of a philosophy of the probable, if I can phrase it that way; of a philosophy that evaluates the probabilities of various possibilities and establishes gradations in the possible. There's also the question of whether I have the ability to solve such a task, which actually is a twofold one; I am probably insufficiently prepared to solve it and state my solution orally. Furthermore, what you ask for can't be expressed orally, for the simple reason that there wouldn't be enough time. What you ask for, even if one tries to express it in the most condensed way possible, would require a special course of lectures or a special treatise.

A.—Too bad. So, in that case, for the time being (but *only* for the time being, in anticipation of your *de omni re scibili atque quibusdam aliis*)[7] I will renounce my second desire, and of my first desire I will leave only the fol-

---

6. "A snake hiding in the grass."
7. "About all things knowable and about something else as well."

lowing: I will ask you a number of questions, and as I do so, I will help you however I can, taking your side, as it were. Agreed?

B.—Agreed.

A.—(*After a pause.*) The general scheme of your worldview, to the extent I understand it, can be expressed as follows: A psychophysical action of man which you call the Fall into sin brought him to a state of sickness—sickness in the broadest sense. That is, whereas previously he had been the master of himself and of the surrounding reality (i.e., of plants, animals, and so on) as well as the master of the states of his body and his spirit and of nature, with the Fall he lost his psychophysical equilibrium and his stable relation to his environment. This loss of equilibrium with the environment led to all kinds of suffering: to sicknesses in the narrower sense and, finally, to death. This sickness of the entire psychophysical organism—that is, the disruption of the former normal and existing (in your opinion) functioning of this organism, of the stream of psychic and corporeal states—was inherited by the whole race. And since you can never accuse the laws of reality of fairness, every individual is destined to be afflicted with the same ailment, even though, personally, he played no role in the Fall. Every individual suffers from this affliction the moment he appears in the world, in the same way that the descendants of alcoholics suffer from the hereditary consequences of alcoholism. That is why nobody can be a perfect master of his body and spirit, but everyone is possessed (to use your terminology) by lusts and passions, is attacked by all kinds of sicknesses, suffers and is tormented, and the result of all this is *exitus letalis*.[8] And so, since all human beings are descended from the same primordial parents, they are all sick.

That is the first, so to speak, picture of your worldview. For the time being I will not touch on all the difficulties I find in it (we will discuss them another time); I will only say that there is no proof that human beings were characterized by a particularly elevated state in ancient times. Just the opposite. In particular, there is no proof that moral will existed in ancient times; there is no proof that death did not exist for such human beings; there is no proof that they were the masters of nature—just the opposite. We do not know what sort of psychophysical effect this is that can disrupt the whole organism; we have no grounds to assert the unity of the human race and to make such a broad (even all-encompassing) application of the principle

---

8. "A lethal exit."

of the *heredity of acquired characteristics*, especially since, in general, this principle is unproven. But let's assume that all these difficulties have been overcome. Let's assume everything is as you say.

There's still the second picture: a number of persons, those you have called prophets, have indicated a means that would stop this collective sickness, this sickness of the race. If only one person healed himself, he could serve as an example for others. The prophets did not have detailed knowledge of what exactly the battle against the sickness should consist in; nor did they have sufficient power or decisiveness to use the knowledge they did have. I allow, however, that there might have been certain conditions unknown to them (conditions floating in the air, so to speak) that could have made the healing possible, such as some special composition of the atmosphere, certain hygienic conditions, assenization,[9] and so on; and the absence of these conditions might have hampered the self-healing of the prophets. They were convinced, however, that, sooner or later, the healing would occur, that *all* the necessary means would be discovered for the healing of one of the persons of the race, though this discovery would not necessarily be a conscious one, but could occur instinctively, through inspiration. They called this self-healing man the Messiah. Certain premises (I don't know what they were but I will assume for the time being that they were well founded) allowed the prophets to indicate a number of things characterizing the appearance of this Messiah; for example, for some reason the prophets thought that the blood of the line of David was particularly favorable for imparting to this man the extraordinary power that could overcome the sickness; they said that this man would be born of a virgin; they regarded the climatic conditions of Bethlehem as the most favorable for his birth and linked his birth with certain astronomical phenomena. And so on. Some of the prophets indicated some of these features, others indicated other features, so that an overall picture emerged.

B.—(*Silence.*)

A.—Without going into detail, all this seems extremely improbable to me, almost inconceivable; I say "almost" because it is impossible to assert that it is absolutely inconceivable and logically or internally contradictory. Such a doctrine contradicts our present-day information and convictions, our present-day experience. However, though our present-day experience is top

---

9. Waste removal.

flight, we still know so little and there remains so much that is unclear and unresolved, that I do not feel I have the right to say categorically that what you assert is impossible. Maybe you're right . . . even though that seems improbable and fantastic to me. Arago said: "*Celui qui en dehors des mathématiques pures, prononce ce mot impossible, manque de prudence.*"[10] I seem to remember that Pascal says somewhere that "nothing can stop the mobility of our mind. There is no rule without an exception, no truth so universal that it is not incomplete in one of its aspects. If that is true, we always have the right to categorize a miraculous case as an exception (and that is exactly what we are talking about), and then miracles become possible.[11]

Remaining scientifically conscientious, I cannot say that Pascal was completely wrong in defending your assertions in this manner.

You say that a certain phenomenon occurred that usually does not occur. So what? Perhaps it is possible to find such a combination of psychic and physico-chemical conditions, to select precedent and coexistent phenomena in such a way that they produce the effect desired by you—a strange, unusual effect, but one that is not impossible in principle. Perhaps.

Nothing prevents you, of course, from trying to go around scientific propositions in this Pascalian manner and thereby justifying many of your assertions. In your own way you are right, but . . . but the result at which you arrive is highly improbable; and though you are right formally, you are not right as to the essence of the matter—your thesis is absurd.

B.—(*Softly.*) You are justifying someone, but I don't see how it concerns me.

---

10. "Anyone who uses the word 'impossible' outside the domain of mathematics—acts imprudently." See A. Erdan, *La France mystique: Tableau des excentricités religieuses de ce temps* . . . , 2nd ed. rev. par l'aut. et augm. d'une nouv. pref. par Charles Potvin (Amsterdam: Miejek, 1858), 2:42. (Florensky's note.)

11. Mr. A. quotes Pascal from memory, somewhat changing Pascal's words and thus drastically distorting them. This is what Pascal actually said (in the *Pensées*, ch. 23): "'Miracle,' some say, 'would strengthen my certainty.' But those who say this do not see miracle. If the grounds are very remote from us this clearly limits our vision; but as soon as we move closer toward them, we begin to see further. Nothing can stop the mobility of our mind. There is no rule, they say, without an exception; no truth so universal that it is not incomplete in one of its aspects. It is sufficient for it to be not absolutely universal, and we already have a reason to classify as an exception precisely the present case and say: 'This is not always true, and so there are cases when it is not true.' After this it remains only to show that the given case is precisely such; and only someone not very skilled or not very resourceful will fail to find the means to draw this conclusion." Let us remark that the tone of the dialogue makes it indisputable that the meaning of the quotation was altered because of Mr. A.'s somewhat faulty memory, not because of any deceit on his part. (Florensky's note.)

A.—(*Didn't hear.*) For the time being I will speak as if I have accepted all of your propositions. At present, I am only conveying how I understand them, since I have to find out if I have omitted anything. Otherwise, it would be difficult to carry on a discussion. Thus, at last, when there existed in the world . . .

B.—Which one?

A.—In the world of experience, of course. The world of colors, sounds, pressures, and various psychic states. When there existed among these bunches of phenomena all the conditions necessary for this Messiah, he was born—as a natural link in the chain of existence, as a bundle or cluster of phenomena among others, as the result of very complex combinations of various circumstances. As a result, this Jesus possessed, from his very birth, all the properties necessary to fulfill what had been foretold by the prophets, or (expressing it more precisely) to fulfill all of their prescriptions, to fulfill them not by consciously acting according to some recipe, but perhaps by instinctively doing everything that was needed to heal in himself the consequences of the hereditary sickness. The chief of these psychophysical acts was the decision to submit to execution. Whether instinctively or consciously, Jesus, in your view, arrived at the conviction that with this decision and the torments of execution he would produce in himself a state so special that, after his death, the "proper" functioning of the whole organism would be renewed in his psychophysical apparatus—that he would rise from the dead with a "transfigured body," thereby serving as an example for others . . .

B.—Wait. You even have the facts wrong. He wouldn't be an example; rather, he would change everything by his death and his resurrection, so that nature and man would receive the possibility of restoring the lost order of things,

A.—We'll hear you out on this subject another time, my dear friend . . . (*He pauses to ponder.*) However, let it be so. For the time being I will accept even this formulation: Jesus's psychophysical states during his execution produced (this again is your view) certain changes in the world and in humankind because the executed man possessed certain properties and performed a number of acts that we discussed earlier. In other words, by his death he introduced into the world real conditions for the possibility of transformation; these conditions consisted in certain effects—whether by psychic waves, radiations, or certain emissions, whatever you like—on the environment in which Jesus lived. These changes (which perhaps went unnoticed at that time and, in fact, could not have been noticed *at that time* because there were no instruments to observe them), these changes were introduced by Jesus into the world for the purpose of its further transformation, its "purification." This transformation, in your view, could not have occurred immediately, since it *still* requires certain other conditions for its actualization. These conditions are being produced little by little by the activity of humankind, and when everything that is needed is fulfilled at last, that is, when all the necessary conditions are introduced into the phenomena of the world, the world catastrophe will then take place suddenly, something like a cataclysm or world fire with nature transformed. Jesus will appear again and all people will be resurrected. What could produce such a fire? The earth, for example, could fall into the sun . . . I think that's everything. Oh, yes. I forgot to add that, because of what he achieved for humankind and the world, you regard it as possible to elevate this Jesus into a god; and in gratitude for his life and activity, you give him the title "son of god and god-man.". . . Have I expressed the essence of your worldview?

B.—Though you are not Faust, I can still answer you with Margarete's reply:

> Das ist alles recht schön und gut;
> Ungefähr sagt das der Pfarrer auch,
> Nur mit ein bißchen andern Worten.[12]

A.—Why "mit andern Worten"?

B.—Because "Wenn man's so hört, möcht's leidlich scheinen, steht aber doch immer schief darum; denn du hast kein Christentum . . ."[13]

A.—But why?

B.—The question is a cunning one, but Jesus Christ himself already answered it. "Ye seek me, not because ye saw the miracles, but because ye did eat of the loaves, and were filled. Labour not for the meat which perisheth,

---

12. "This is all most excellent: The pastor says almost the same thing, but in slightly different words" (from Goethe's *Faust*, ch. 19).

13. "When one hears such speeches, they seem true; nevertheless they're false, for there is no Christianity in you" (*Faust*, ch. 19).

but for that meat which endureth unto everlasting life, which the Son of man shall give unto you: for him hath God the Father sealed ... the bread of God is he which cometh down from heaven, and giveth life unto the world. I am that bread of life.... I am the living bread which came down from heaven: if any man eat of this bread, he shall live forever: and the bread that I will give is my flesh, which I will give for the life of the world" (John 6:26–27, 33, 35, 48, 51).

A.—I don't understand how this relates to our discussion.

B.—Then, let's start from another side. What you've done is made a reproduction of the worldview such that its external form bears a great resemblance to the original, whereas the inner essences of the two are diametrically opposite to each other.

A.—What do you mean? I included all the important things in my exposition, omitting only minor details. For example, I didn't talk about sacraments.

B.—Sacraments are not minor details, but that's not the point. Even in the things you mentioned, you omitted what was most important, retaining only its *form*. The result is not Christianity (not even a distorted Christianity), but a very artful counterfeit of Christianity, an imitation so skillful that it can easily deceive anyone who does not attentively examine your "mimicry."

A.—Didn't I mention everything that's discussed in the catechism?

B.—Not quite. It's strange that when you expounded the Christian doctrine, you managed to avoid using the word "God."

A.—What do you mean? I said that you made Jesus into a god.

B.—That's the crux. You don't recognize God as such. For you, one becomes God by receiving an "achievement award." For you, the word "God" is a title of respect, something like the highest rank in the government civil service. It is not the definition of a Being.

A.—In that case, how about the following formulation: Jesus rose from the dead and by his resurrection, by his victory over death, he *became a god* in the same way that heroes became gods by their feats.

The Empyrean and the Empirical

B.—Absolutely not. Jesus Christ did not *become* a god; he *was* and *is* God. You make his Divinity out to be the result of something not primary but added-on and secondary, whereas it is a principle, an essence. You said that "Jesus became a god because he rose from the dead."

A.—I promised I would help you, and so I tried to express your doctrine in the form most advantageous for it.

B.—Yes, but Jesus Christ is God not because he rose from the dead; he rose from the dead because he is God. The Divine is primary, not the empirical. Divinity is not derived from the empirical. Just the opposite: the empirical is a manifestation of the Divine.

A.—So you sincerely believe that I didn't expound your worldview correctly?

B.—The worldview you expounded is pure positivism, while mine, in its essence, is theistic. In the worldview you expounded, man violates certain natural laws, that is, the laws of empirical existence; he therefore endures the natural consequences of this violation and then, also naturally, he finds a way out of his predicament by his own powers and becomes a godlike being. In other words, all the events here have their causation in the sensuous world; the causes and their effects do not transcend the boundaries of empirical reality. Only psychophysical humanity exists for such a worldview, that which Scripture calls "natural,"[14] as opposed to "spiritual." And so this natural humanity creates Jesus Christ out of itself—it saves and deifies itself. A man of your worldview is in reality a follower of the one who said *"eritis sicut Deus."*[15] Do I understand you correctly?

A.—Absolutely. But how could it be otherwise? What sort of humanity would this be if it didn't act from itself? And so forth.

B.—You keep talking about "bundles" and "clusters." Just as you helped me, let me help you by referring to William James.[16] Their representative, in one domain, is a "bunch" of radishes and a "bundle" of round rolls; while

---

14. See 1 Corinthians 2:14.
15. "Ye shall be as gods," the serpent's line from Genesis 3:5.
16. Here, Mr. B. satirizes James's conception of reality as a group of sensuous elements unified on the basis of subjective utility and psychological faith.

in another domain, it is a "bundle of specifically determinate reactions" called an "English gentleman" and "a useful bunch of associations" which from childhood, by the "law of propinquity," merged with the "repressive emotions" of standing in a corner and thereby "expelled" from the "field of consciousness" a bundle of "impulsive strivings and autonomous reactions" called "strolling on the street" and manifesting in the "wave of consciousness" a "core," from sensations of boredom with a "halo" or "ring" of "thoughts" about deliverance and "desires" to be on the street, as well as "remembrances" of former happy times, a "certain rim" or "half-shadow" of emotions of fear and sensations of yawning—that is the bundle that "for its possessor has a certain practical unity" which we call "Euclidean elements." Forgive me if I have caricatured them, but my aim was to express your ideas in an emphatic way.

A.—That's me. What about you?

B.—We believe that, by his Fall, man violated not natural laws, not the laws of empirical existence, but the mystical order of being. We believe that sicknesses, death, and moral corruption appeared not directly because of a violation of the laws of the sensuous world and of the laws of that psychic world which empirical psychology studies, but rather were only an external manifestation of an upheaval in the mystical domain, of a change in the inner relation to God, this relation of the spirit to God being more primary than any "state of consciousness" and lying outside the "bundle of psychic phenomena." We believe, further, that humanity could not have created means of healing out of itself, because all the things that humanity creates out of itself are only human—psychophysical, empirical, psychic. But in the case of the Fall it was necessary to act in the mystical domain, to restore a mystical order. All empirical means would have been merely palliative, and of no use; they would have been tantamount to the building of a tower of Babel; man does not have, and is incapable of having, his own mystical powers.

But, on the other hand, God as such could not change the damaged state of humanity, for humanity, being a member of the damaged mystical relation and an independent entity, could not be purified from outside by any means; nor could it purify itself from within. The only possible remedy was the incarnation of God. Since it was necessary that the action not be directed from outside and without the participation of man, God became man, making it possible to act from within. On the other hand, man did not have the power to act from within, and therefore God began to act in his place. The restoration could only be accomplished by a Being who, having in himself two natures, Divine and human, could act both as God and as man; by a Being who had two wills, giving one moral decision. The God-man resolved the dilemma the horns of which were unresolvable separately; and, having reconciled the separated horns of the dilemma, having replaced the separating "either/or" by the *uniting* "both-and," he restored humanity. But the power came from the fact that Jesus Christ did not *become* a god, but *was* the True God, while also remaining man. His mission was mystical, not a social or similar one.

A.—I don't understand. You proclaim all this as if it were indisputable, and yet . . . For an experienced investigator, Jesus was the same as any other man. There were some variations, of course, but there were no substantial differences. After all, the Apostle says: "That which was from the beginning, which we have *heard*, which we have *seen* with our eyes, which we have *looked upon*, and our hands have *handled* . . ." (1 John 1:1). Do you agree that, for all experience, Jesus turned out to be roughly the same as any other man, within the limits of individual differences, of course?

B.—I agree.

A.—Further, do you agree that the world . . .

B.—Which one?

A.—That very same empirical world, the world of "bundles" with "rims" that you made fun of. Do you agree that this world did not exhibit any substantial differences after the death of Jesus compared to the way it had been before his death, so that for any observer the change that occurred would have been the same as any other historical change—that even if it encompassed a field of action much wider than that of some great man, it was, in its general character, the same sort of historical change?

B.—I agree.

A.—In that case, the individual difference or variation that is observed in Jesus compared to all other men is the *only* reason why you consider him a god. This variation produced what you call redemption, and redemption consisted merely in the historical "plus" produced by Jesus's activity. Is that not so? All these considerations are so elementary that I am almost ashamed to refer to them. I am prepared to believe—for the sake of our conversation—in whatever characteristics of Jesus you might assign to him; but, after all, the Apostle himself said that, with respect to his personal experience, he was like any of us—and so if there was a difference, it consisted in the manner in which one man differs from another. Is that not clear?

B.—As day. But incorrect.

A.—How?

B.—By no means do I deny the individual variation in Jesus Christ about which you speak, or the historical change that was brought about by his activity and empirical existence, but I affirm that they were not the point here. Jesus Christ was a preacher of morality—yes. He was a philanthropist—yes. He was a spiritual teacher—yes. He was a social activist—yes. Nevertheless, theoretically, we can conceive all this as becoming less and less significant, so that, in the end, it can no longer be detected by any empirical observation. We can imagine all these decreasing activities as tending to a limit and vanishing, and yet Christ will remain Christ and redemption will remain redemption. Let me clarify this with a rough example. However important Jesus Christ's activity which I have indicated might have been, nevertheless it does not have fundamental significance and therefore is no more important than the color of the toga he wore or what his voice sounded like, and so on. That, too, is very important, but it does not directly relate to the Savior's mission.

A.—Consequently, you're saying (let's assume this for the sake of the argument) that if Jesus had never existed, but there had existed a certain John whose appearance and life were exactly (down to the smallest details) the same as Jesus's, that if this John had been the exact double of Jesus, that if he had died and been resurrected, you're saying that he would not have been Christ and the Son of God?

B.—The fact is, I cannot accept that your imaginary John would have been resurrected. I think this cannot be accomplished by empirical means. But if, for the sake of the argument, this John had existed (which is impossible and inconceivable), I would say that he would not have been Christ and the Son of God—that he could not have redeemed the world.

A.—So, if we could do history twice—once with the world after "redemption" and once where everything would be exactly the same in the observable picture of empirical existence except that Jesus would be replaced by someone else with exactly the same empirically observable characteristics as Jesus—are you telling me that these two states of the world would be different?

B.—Yes, because in the second case the world would not be redeemed. It would remain the former world lying in sin. Please note, however, that I am allowing your fiction only for the sake of argument; I do not really accept that anyone could imitate Christ.

A.—Now I'm beginning to understand what you really want, but I'm completely opposed to such views. If you allow me, I will pose the question on a more common ground. Two objects are given, α and β. There exists between them an empirically observable difference; but it is such that it can be made as small as you like, so that to differentiate α from β, the empirical observations would have to become increasingly finer, until finally at the extreme limit the objects α and β could not be differentiated by any empirical observation, however sensitive it might be. The empirical difference between α and β would be equal to 0; no empirical means would be able to differentiate α from β. Can α be different from β? That is, can there nevertheless be a fundamental difference between α and β? Being convinced that the whole essence and existence of an object are exhausted by what can be found out about it from the set of all conceivable experiments performed on it, I think that objects cannot be different if they cannot be differentiated by any empirical observations, however sensitive they might be. For you, on the other hand, it appears that a fundamental difference can exist even in the case of the complete empirical non-differentiability of objects.

B.—Yes, that is my opinion. Here is a concrete example to illustrate my view of the matter. There are two identical vessels; each of them contains a piece of solid matter; the pieces are of the same weight and volume. The pieces are porous, permeated with a red liquid, have the odor of wine, and have the same taste. So, elementary empirical observation—with the sensory organs—does not detect any difference between the two pieces. If, further, we were to make more sensitive measurements—of specific weight, hardness, specific heat, electroconductivity, microscopic structure, etc.—even then we would not detect the slightest difference. Finally, even a highly precise chemical analysis would show the compositions of the two pieces to be identical.

You would say that, after these measurements, these two pieces could not be different; whereas I would say that they *could* be different—fundamentally different: one of the pieces could be just a piece of bread soaked in wine, whereas the other piece could be the Body and Blood of Christ.

A.—Symbolically?

B.—No, the wine and bread were really *transubstantiated*; that is, they changed their substance and became the true Body and the true Blood of Jesus Christ.

A.—That is a decisive example, of course. One could also refer to the question of chrismation here.

B.—Yes. Baptism is another good example. One could—on the theatrical stage, for example—reproduce baptism with maximal precision, yet that would be nothing more than a series of purely empirical actions. But, in another venue, the same series of actions could represent a sacrament, which differs fundamentally from that which was presented on the stage and which in the baptized person produces a mystical change—a rebirth. For sensory experience a person *before* baptism is identical with a person *after* baptism, but nevertheless they are internally different: something substantially new has been introduced into the baptized person that cannot be detected with the eyes or hands or observed by any experimental measurement.

A.—Yes, that's certainly your opinion, but can one accept it? To me this seems nothing more than a *reductio ad absurdum*, a crazy and strange casuistry.

B.—It seems crazy and strange to you only because you are overly accustomed to sensory experience and do not have a sufficiently critical attitude toward it.

A.—But to what else could I be accustomed? I do not know any other experience. I can observe the difference between objects only by one method, not by twenty.

B.—That's not true; I will show that you have other methods for observing the difference. Let us pose the question even more broadly: assume the methods are arranged on a ladder; the higher a method stands on the ladder, the more profound the differences it will discover between the objects. But in order to clarify in advance the nature of the differences between the objects that a given method cannot detect, I will present a simple comparison. Imagine that you have a piece of glass and a piece of ice polished in an identical manner. To your eye these pieces—if the ice is pure—are almost indistinguishable, and it might appear to you that the piece of ice is in no way more interesting or beautiful than the piece of glass. But in terms of molecular structure the ice is superior to the glass the way a philharmonic orchestra is superior to random street noise. The ice is music; the glass is noise. The ice is harmony and order; the glass is chaos and disorder. The ice is organization; the glass is anarchy. Every particle of the glass stands alone and, at best, can do nothing more than bump against neighboring particles; there is no *whole*. The ice is just the opposite: every particle occupies its definite, proper place in the regular fabric of the whole, in the organization of a marvelous structure.

But this difference in internal structure, which can be taken to symbolize the difference between natural man and spiritual man, is imperceptible to the eye.

A.—You wanted to use this example as way to begin a general discussion of methods?

B.—Yes. Every science limits the domain of its investigations, creating schemata of its objects and using a specific set of characteristics that define the object of this science as such. If two objects differ with respect to one or several of the characteristics according to which the object of the given science is constructed, then we can use the methods and means proper to this science to differentiate between the objects. If it turns out that the objects differ with respect to characteristics that are not elements of the schema of the object (the schema constructed for the given science), the methods and means of this science will not be able to differentiate between the objects. We allow that, owing to the conditions in which we find ourselves, we cannot use any methods and means of investigation except those proper to the given science; that is, we allow that, because of certain conditions, we can study the given objects only from the point of view of our science. The objects, which we know beforehand to be different, would then turn out to be absolutely indistinguishable for our investigation. Thus, for example, the piece of ice and the piece of glass are absolutely indistinguishable for geometrical investigation, since it would be unable to analyze the internal structure of these bodies. If, further, we employ only methods of mechanics and limit ourselves to studying the mechanical characteristics defining a certain object, we would then be able to determine the shape of the body, its mass, its moment of inertia, etc., but there is absolutely no way we would be able to determine its temperature, its electrical state, any associated psychic phenomena, etc. We know very well that two bodies with identical mechanical characteristics but with different temperatures are different, but this difference cannot be detected by methods of mechanics. If, on the other hand, we use the methods and means of physics, the difference in temperature will readily be detected.

But, in the same way, the methods of physics cannot differentiate living from nonliving matter. Even if we were to acknowledge that living matter is characterized by certain special (compared to nonliving matter) physicochemical processes, even then we would not be able to differentiate living from nonliving matter, since it would always be possible to conceive of a system of mechanisms, to postulate a kind of adaptation of the living body, such that, from the point of view of physics, it would be possible to regard it in this respect as nonliving. Only *new* methods—nonphysical ones—can make it possible to discover the difference between living and nonliving matter. Let me give some examples of cases where two objects that cannot be differentiated by empirical observation in one level can be differentiated by empirical observation in another level. These are cases of the first type. Cases of the second type are those where two objects are absolutely indistinguishable by empirical observation, of whatever kind it might be, but are different for internal experience. Let us take an example from the moral domain: I perform an act twice under the same conditions; on both occasions, external observation can detect no difference between them. My two actions approach each other as close as you like in terms of their external expression and external conditions; in the extreme limit they can be conceived as absolutely indistinguishable for the outside observer. No external observation—whatever methods it might use (those of physics, biology, etc.) and however meticulous and precise it might be—would be able to detect any difference between the two actions. From its own point of view, such empirical observation would have to acknowledge that the two actions are identical. In their essence, however, these two actions are different. One is moral; the other is immoral. The Apostle says: "Therefore judge nothing before the time, until the Lord come, who both will bring to light the hidden things of darkness, and will make manifest the counsels of the hearts" (1 Cor. 4:5). "Every man's work shall be made manifest: for the day shall declare it, because it shall be revealed by fire; and the fire shall try every man's work of what sort it is" (1 Cor. 3:13).

"For what man knoweth the things within a man, save the spirit of man living within him?" (1 Cor. 2:11).[17]

A.—This last thing is not completely clear to me. Can you elucidate?

B.—From childhood almost every man obeys moral and governmental laws; at least he does not deviate from them very significantly. Everyone wants to be reputed to be honest and seeks to be known as just. Indeed, who would wish to appear in society *in naturalis*, with all his garments removed, if this were to lead to unpleasantness? In fact, almost all men seem honest and just, as if they were such in the depths of their hearts. Whether evil or good, "natural" or spiritual, every man—if he does not wish to be thought to be crazy or a criminal, lives, for the most part, like everyone else. The difference lies chiefly not in modes of action, but in the intimate springs of the actions—in motives. Natural man does not deviate from the norm because he is afraid of being punished or having his reputation tarnished. He may be deprived of certain honors, so he becomes a hypocrite. If natural men were not afraid of laws and punishments; if they were not afraid of losing their reputations, honors, or incomes; in other words, if external constraints stopped forcing them to perform God's work, then these men—lacking the inner consciousness of being citizens of the world, the consciousness of their vocation in the historical process and of their connection with the one organism of the church; not knowing love for God and for becoming the body of Christ; not wishing to transfer the center of their being into the Absolute; and asserting that the axis of the world exists in them and in their caprices—would rip off the chains restraining them and deceive, rob, injure, and murder others, for men who have lost their minds by willfully denying the Absolute find such crimes not only profitable, but even pleasant and agreeable. Try, then, to humanize such men and to impart to them the image of God. As long as the wheat and the tares grow together and are linked by empirical reality, these men cannot reveal their true natures and, for empirical observation, act in more or less the same way. Only the spiritual man, by internally affirming God and opening himself up to his actions, can make himself into a conscious conductor of Divine forces, a living organ of the body of Christ, and joyfully fulfill his proper function. Such a man lives not for himself and dies

---

17. The KJV has been modified to conform with the Russian Bible.

not for himself. He lives and dies for the Lord (see Rom. 14:7–8). That is why he can say: "we have the mind of Christ" (1 Cor. 2:16). That is why he has the right to declare: "yet not I, but Christ liveth in me" (Gal. 2:20).

The general foundations of the laws of morality and social life are expressed in the Ten Commandments. It is not difficult to confirm that the so-called respectable man, that is, the natural man who does not deviate too much from the average, lives his external life more or less in conformity with these prescriptions, just like the spiritual man. He accords God the usual signs of respect: he goes to church, says his prayers, listens to sermons, makes the sign of the cross over himself, wears a solemnly pious expression on his face when necessary, fulfills the fasts, and so on, just like the spiritual man. Furthermore, he does not commit crimes; that is, he does not steal, does not bear false witness, does not kill, does not take the possessions of others by force or by cunning, and so on. He does all this, however, from motives that have nothing in common with love for God; he does it from external motives, in order to seem righteous among people, in order to wield influence, in order to have power. He does not kill, but if his desire to annihilate those who oppose his wishes could kill, a thousand men would have died already. If he were not restrained by his fear of the law or of public opinion, if he did not foresee that he would fail, any enemy opposing him would have died long ago by the knife, by the axe, by the gun, or by poison. Oh, if it were possible to burn someone up by hatred, with what deliberate pleasure he would have roasted his enemies on the flame of his spiteful cruelty! With what rapture he would have poisoned them with his venomous words and iced their blood with the refined malice of his cold sarcasms! This man has killed no one, but he is an inveterate murderer.

He does not fornicate, but his "purity" annoys him. If only he could do it without people finding out! He does not steal and has never stolen. But he grows green and shakes with envy when he sees the wealth of others, and he curses twenty times a day the laws that prevent him from stealing with impunity. He does not steal, but in his heart he commits theft after theft, and he is therefore an inveterate thief.

A.—There is a poem about a "moral man." Do you remember it: "Living in accordance with strict morality, I never did anyone any harm." Among many examples, here's an example of how he "never did anyone any harm":

> "I had a daughter who loved a poor teacher
> And fervently yearned to elope with him.
> I threatened to curse her: she obeyed

And married a rich gray-beard.
Their house was brilliant and full like a goblet,
But Masha began to grow pale and wither
And a year later consumption took her.
The whole house was shrouded in grief . . .
Living in accordance with strict morality,
I never did anyone any harm."[18]

B.—This man had not yet come to the clear realization that even such "virtue" was a constraint on him. But do you know how agonizing external fetters are for men who do come to such a realization? Their "righteousness" becomes a heavy burden and a cruel yoke. Do you remember Victor Hugo's Sieur Clubin?[19] Do you remember how this "most honest man on all the seas," artistically hypocritical, calculating his game down to the minutest detail in order to create for himself the reputation of being the most honest of men—do you remember how impatiently he awaits the moment when he can insolently mock those who believed in him, when he can throw off his mask and exult in the crime for the sake of which he had been "honest" for so long? "For thirty years he had worn the mask of hypocrisy. He hated virtue. He was a monster in the image of a man. He was a prisoner of honesty: like a mummy in its tomb, he had been confined within a shell of innocence; public esteem stifled him. To appear to be an honest man is a terrible thing. He often hid the gnashing of his teeth behind a smile. Virtue choked him; and his entire life, he had desired to bite the hand that clamped down on his mouth, but he had been forced to kiss it. . . . He was liked by everyone and he therefore hated everyone. Finally, his hour had come. He took revenge. On whom? On everyone and for everything. . . . He took revenge on everyone before whom he had to wear a mask. Everyone who thought well of him was his enemy."[20]

If one reflects upon what this means, virtue without love for God, without the constant presence in one's being of the Absolute, one readily understands that the words of the Apostle, quoted so many times, are not a cruel and excessive demand, but an expression of a fundamental fact of the ethical life—they are not a condition that is imposed on man from outside, but one that flows from his very nature. Here is this condition of all life in the truth:

18. From Nekrasov's poem "A Moral Man."
19. A character in Hugo's novel *Toilers of the Sea*.
20. From *Toilers of the Sea*, part 1, book 1, ch. 6.

"Though I speak with the tongues of men and of angels, and have not love, I am become as sounding brass, or a tinkling cymbal. And though I have the gift of prophecy, and understand all mysteries, and all knowledge; and though I have all faith, so that I could remove mountains, and have not love, I am nothing. And though I bestow all my goods to feed the poor, and though I give my body to be burned, and have not love, it profiteth me nothing" (1 Cor. 13:1–3).[21]

But no external signs can reveal with certainty whether I have love or not; no empirical observation can reveal the reason why I act the way I do, the reason why I work on myself in all manner of ways, devote myself to helping others and to public service, why I appear to do all good things, and end my life in the fire of torment. No empirical observation can reveal whether I am sounding brass and a tinkling cymbal or a consciously functioning organ of the body of Christ. But this empirical *indistinguishability* conceals an essential distinction that can be revealed through self-observation or in some other way, but not empirically (this word taken in its usual sense).

A.—Amen. You've gone on for a little too long, however; no doubt carried away by the tone of your sermon. You look like a mess—when was the last time you bathed?

B.—We can now examine the third type of case—the case when two objects given in contemplation do not exhibit any difference and seem identical for the latter, whereas speculation enables us to find the fundamental difference between these objects.

Since contemplation is something we encounter primarily in geometry, we will find many examples there clarifying what we mean. We will limit ourselves to the simplest of these, though all such mathematical investigations have a decisive significance and an indisputably probative role in the consideration of our questions. To begin, I will point to the existence of incommensurable quantities, i.e., quantities of a certain kind that do not have a common measure. When a common measure exists and the relation of the quantities is commensurable, this relation can be expressed by a certain number. If it is incommensurable, no number exists that expresses this relation. Thus, the first pair of quantities has a fundamental distinction from the second pair, but this distinction cannot be detected in any empirical way.

In order to make this clearer, let us consider geometrical quantities. Let

---

21. To conform to the Russian version, "charity" (in the KJV) is replaced by "love."

us assume, for example, that through some construction we are given two linear segments. In comparing them, we find that their lengths are different: one segment turns out to be longer than the other. But we will not detect any fundamental difference by this method, by a direct comparison of the segments, however precise the comparison might be. But by examining the *manner* in which the segments were obtained, we can speculatively arrive at the conclusion that they are fundamentally—essentially—different. The length of one segment, as it is possible to determine, is expressed by a certain number, while the length of the other is not expressed by any number. In order to express the length of the second segment arithmetically, i.e., in order to characterize its length in abstract terms, it is necessary to create a completely new arithmetical symbol, a new arithmetical schema—the so-called irrational number. Thus, for example, a side of a square and its diagonal, being incommensurable, have some *internal difference* that is absolutely undetectable by the simple contemplation of these segments. This property of the lines was already known to the Pythagoreans, and its discovery is attributed to the founder of the "Union." It is easy to guess what an astonishing impression the discovery of this theorem must have made on its inventors. One of the fundamental convictions of the school was that number plays a universal role, and they understood number to mean whole number. But now it turns out that there are objects, specifically objects in the domain of contemplation, that cannot be expressed or governed by any number, as if they were deprived of essence, since, for the Pythagoreans, the essence of an object is the number that expresses it. It was as if human beings had illegitimately peered down into a bottomless mystical abyss, had seen or overheard what human beings should not know, had stolen a secret of the gods from the abyss, and stand now like accomplices to a terrible crime, not daring to look one another in the eyes, trembling from every loud word, and afraid of blurting out what they know and thus bringing down upon themselves the gods' all-destroying wrath.

The winds wailed mysteriously; the trees rocked in terror, waving their arms. Black leaves whirled and soared.

> The blizzard's bursts are sharp and severe.
> A terrible secret stirs in the soul.
> Pull down, my brother, the curtains:
> Eternity seems be looking at us through the window.[22]

22. This poem is probably by Florensky himself.

The Pythagoreans were by no means so closed and uncommunicative in their philosophical views as is usually thought. But those discoveries of theirs, *those* discoveries—they had to remain a secret, they had to remain shrouded in silence.

To disclose what has been seen by chance, to reveal what has been found through experience, is blasphemous, for it is a ripping down of the veils from what the gods have hidden; it is a shameless baring of the divine mystery. Woe to the impious man who dares to carry outside what is hidden. By his very existence he then subjects the Pythagorean Union and himself to destruction. The only way to be saved is to expel the blasphemer, to renounce him, to declare before the gods that he is an enemy. Let the eternal gods direct all their wrath at the culprit, at him alone!

And that is what happened. The founder of the Union, the seer Pythagoras, was still alive, living out his last years, when the storm suddenly struck and the Union—which had spent its time listening to melodious zithers and engaged in pious exercises and contemplations drawing one into a world of order and celestial harmony—became deeply troubled. The infidel Hippasus, impious wolf, betraying the trust of the sacred Union, disdained the wrath of the gods and, breaking the silence appropriate in the presence of divine truths, blasphemously revealed the secret to the profanes: he disclosed the sacred theorem of incommensurable quantities to the uninitiated and unpurified. Hippasus was judged and expelled dishonorably from the order; let the immortals judge him! The blessed gods living in the high aether did not wait long to announce their judgment. As soon as the insane blasphemer had sailed away into the open sea and the coast of Great Greece had sunk into blue mist, at that moment Poseidon stirred the blackening abyss with his trident, agitating the sterile sea and lashing the flimsy boat with giant waves (those monsters of the sea), and impudent Hippasus suffered the punishment for his audacity before the gods. He sank, and the dispassionate desert of water closed forever his careless lips . . .

A.—(*Laughing.*) You call those facts?

B.—I had no desire to expound facts. My task was to show how the facts could have been reflected in the consciousness of the Union. But now I will just indicate some other examples. For lack of time, I will do no more than mention the existence of so-called transcendental numbers and the quantities measured by them. It turns out that also among the irrational numbers it is possible to establish fundamental differences by dividing them into essentially heterogeneous classes. Numbers whose degrees are commensurable are one example; transcendental numbers are another. It is interesting that, though a transcendental number is essentially different from a nontranscendental or algebraic number, it is very difficult to determine about a *given* number what kind it is. For example, the famous problem of squaring the circle, exhausting the powers of mathematicians for almost four thousand years, contained a misunderstanding in the way it was originally posed, a misunderstanding based on the failure to recognize the essential distinction between the number π and algebraic numbers. In order not to linger too long on examples from this branch of mathematics, I will indicate a few examples from the so-called theory of groups. A *group* of points is taken to mean a collection of points given in a determinate manner; as a result of the uniformity of its givenness, it is regarded as something whole, unitary.

As a simple example, let us consider certain groups of points situated on a straight line; these points are threaded on the line, so to speak. In order to determine the position of a point on the line in relation to a certain invariable point, the origin, it is necessary to give a number that expresses the distance of this point from an immobile length in certain definite units, e.g., in millimeters. If the measure of the length is given and the number is given, this fully determines the point characterized by the number. By choosing collections of numbers according to one general rule or another, we begin to sequentially obtain groups of points situated according to one law or another. For example, we can demand that all the points be taken the corresponding numbers of which (the coordinates) are all the rational numbers not less than 0 and not greater than 1. This will be the group of "rational points" in the segment 0–1.

Everywhere in the theory of groups we encounter cases where two essentially different groups that must in all possible discussions be treated as very different objects *cannot* be differentiated in contemplation. Let us take, for example, the group of points defined by all possible numbers between 0 and 1 inclusive; this will be a so-called *closed* group. Let us then take the group of points defined by all possible numbers between 0 and 1 including 0, but not including 1; this group is called *nonclosed*. Both groups are absolutely indistinguishable in contemplation, "to the eye"; one looks like the other; one appears to be identical to the other. But, in fact, there is a very significant difference between them, a difference that radically distinguishes the properties of the groups. The first group, the closed one, has ends, so to speak; the points 0 and 1 are its extreme points, so that there is no point of the group that lies to the right of point 1 and no point that lies to the left of point 0. The same thing can be said about the left end of the second group, the nonclosed one; but that is not true for its right end, for strictly speaking there is no end here, no final or extreme point. However distant a point we take, there will always be a more distant one; there is no final point. We can come as close as you like to point 1 (which we do not find in the nonclosed group), yet we will never reach point 1, for if we reach point 1, we would be outside this group; however, if we find ourselves just to the left of it, we would always have the possibility of coming closer to it. It's as if the end of the closed group has melted away, obliterating the final point and producing the nonclosed group. Nevertheless, this change, though invisible and impalpable, has produced a substantial change in the properties and structure of the group; and anyone who has studied the theory of groups knows how serious such changes of structure are and how carefully the closed group must be distinguished from the nonclosed one. The latter lacks a tiny element that would make it a closed group, but the absence of this tiny element is perhaps more significant for the essence of the group than the tiny element which, in the domain of esthetics, often distinguishes a work of art from what is not art.[23]

I could present a multitude of other examples from the theory of groups, but because of a lack of time, I hasten to proceed further.

A.—Further? Where else is there to go?

B.—We must now consider the Final, or Fourth, type of objects—those that can be distinguished only by means of mystical perception. Here I do not wish to prove anything to you—after all, we began our conversation with the intention of *dicitur ad narrandum, non ad probandum*.[24] And so we can expound our convictions in an entirely dogmatic way. We think that sacraments are objects that cannot be differentiated by empirical observation (however sensitive it may be) from mere ceremonies and rituals, but that nonetheless are profoundly and substantially different from ceremonies and rituals. We know of this difference from church doctrine, just as we know of the difference between the side of a square and its diagonal from geometry. It is another question to what extent sacraments really have their proper essence, something essentially new, like a new creation; but the possibility of this cannot be denied.

---

23. At this point Mr. B. presents another page-long example from the theory of groups. This example is omitted in the present translation.

24. "Speaking for the sake of discussion, not for the sake of proof."

A.—But can you really be satisfied with this naked assertion without any factual proofs?

B.—No one compels you to be satisfied with it alone. Wholly peculiar and primary perceptions allow almost everyone (though perhaps not always) to discern the mystical element in sacraments about which the church speaks. Not only professional (so to speak) mystics but even ordinary believers commonly have such perceptions, and these specific experiences indicate the presence of a specific element in sacraments. To be sure, from the purely theoretical point of view it is necessary to subject these experiences to a theoretical-cognitive examination and to justify their objective significance and value, just as this is necessary with all kinds of experiences. Such an examination is not part of our plan, but I must remark that this task is simpler than appears at first glance. It can be affirmed a priori, irrespective of the theoretical-cognitive convictions of the investigator, that the object of these specific experiences cannot lie in the domain of objects of ordinary experiences; even if it is only a hallucination (whatever we mean by that), the cause of the hallucination must lie in the mystical domain, in a domain that is new compared to the empirical domain. After all, the empirical here, whatever it might consist in, must itself contain a mystical seed if it is to produce out of itself mystical experiences that differ fundamentally from it.

It is possible to present many examples of such experiences. Here, for example, is an excerpt from a private letter written by a young female teacher who had been brought up in the atheistic traditions of the 1860s, but who then found her way into the church: "Christ is risen, my dear . . . I am a member of Christ's church; my sins are forgiven me; and I partook of the Holy Gifts. I am astonished and overwhelmed by God's all-forgiveness. He has forgiven me, forgiven everything, because the suffering in my soul has gone away; and now, like everyone else, I am made joyful by the sun and the sky, by spring and nature. The love of my near and dear ones, and of children (my pupils), has returned to me, although it might seem that it had never been taken away. Why do I deserve this mercy of God? And formerly I had even not dared to forgive the sins of others, even though I was worse than anyone else, and yet God has forgiven me. . . . When I partook of the Holy Gifts, peace entered my soul . . . *I felt that I was in communion with my God, Jesus Christ*. I believe now that He took upon Himself the sins of the world, that He came into the world and was crucified for all people and for me, and that He redeemed all the past and future sins of people . . ."

"'Yet not I, but Christ liveth in me' (Gal. 2:20)—that is, Christ began to live in him. These words do not merely have a moral meaning in the sense that all life, all activity, all thoughts, all feelings are for Christ and for His sake. They mean much more, namely that Christ makes His home in our heart and dwells in it, that *He appears in it really*, according to His promise."

"The salvific character [of the baptismal words]," says Bishop Feofan, "cannot be denied, for *these experiences are before everyone's eyes*: they hear the baptismal words, believe, receive the baptism, and become *a new creation. They feel themselves as new and others see them as new.* . . . Those who *truly* receive [the baptismal words] *become assured of this power and wisdom* when in baptism they are buried with the crucified Lord and *taste* the salvific character of the cross. . . . These blessings are prepared for those who love God, that is, for those who abandon everything, attach their hearts to God, and *enter into living heartfelt communion and union with Him by the path indicated and prescribed by Him*."[25] I will refrain from presenting other examples.

A.—*Concedo atque distinguo*.[26] All you have said has made me change my opinion somewhat. I now concede that you view the gospel events differently than I had supposed, and moreover the formal legitimacy of your point of view in certain respects has become clear to me.

B.—What about your questions?

A.—Some of them you have answered; as for the others, I will bring them up at another time: their nature has changed. The good thing is that I now know how I should understand our further conversation. For greater clarity, however, you should briefly characterize again the two worldviews in question: yours and the one I expounded. But do it briefly.

B.—That's simple: My view is the "empyrean" one; yours is the "empirical" one.

A.—Too brief. We have a quarter of an hour left. Can you expound your idea *in extenso*?

---

25. These extracts and the letter are taken by me from M. A. Novoselov's *Forgotten Path of Experiential God-Knowledge*, 2nd ed. (Vyshnii Volochek, 1902), 42, 43, 44, 45. (Florensky's note.)
26. "I approve without reservations."

B.—Certainly. According to your worldview the world-drama is wholly played out in the empirical domain—in the domain of colors, sounds, smells, pressures, and all the other elements of the sensuously perceived world that directly or indirectly can be detected by methods of physics, chemistry, biology, and related sciences; as well as in the domain of desires, sensations, etc., observed by empirical psychology. All of the threads of action extend within the empirical domain; all of the springs that motivate events are within the limits of *this* world. Because they are too fine, or because our perception apparatus is insufficient, many of the threads are still unknown to us, perhaps; it is even possible that they will never become known to us. But between the known threads and those that are still unknown there is no fundamental difference; we regard them in the same way as we regard phenomena in physics. The difference between them is analogous to that between light and sound.

Because of these features the *conception* expounded by you can be called *naturalistic*, analogously to how this term is used to designate a certain literary school in virtue of the fact that it is satisfied with *one* plane of reality, with the protocols of this world, and wishes to reduce all other schools to this one school. Our worldview is fundamentally different. We are not satisfied with this "planarity" of reality; we demand that perspective be recognized; we see the "cold heights, the receding distances."[27] This depth of perspective means that we do not level the whole diversity of reality into one plane—the plane of sensuous perception. It means that we do not squeeze and dry reality like a flower between the pages of the thick account book of positivism. Beyond the given front plane of the empirical, there are other planes, other layers. They are not reducible to one another, but are connected by *correspondences*, which are not conditional elements imposed on reality; these correspondences are established by the same act that produces "reality" in the form in which it is represented.

Potentially, or in possibility, the same primary data or elements are given to both of us. But you—if you actually perceive the surrounding reality the way you say you do, and do not merely consider it necessary to perceive it in that way—construct out of these elements a planar world, while I construct out of them a world of depth. Allow me to continue my previous comparison of the formation of a world-representation with the formation of spatial representations.

That which exists primordially in the sensuous domain is not something

---

27. Quotation from unidentified poem.

spatial. Psychological analysis has shown sufficiently that these nonspatial elements are somehow (in the given case, it does not matter *how* precisely) constructed by our minds into an organized spatial unity, into an image of the sensuous world. But at first this image is only a planar one. Primordially, the whole of reality has the form of a picture, as it were, drawn according to all the laws of perspective on a certain surface; this picture is applied to the eye, as it were. This picture has bright and saturated colors, all possible shades and combinations of colors, brilliant, dull, luminous, dark, the play of light and shadow, and contours; but it lacks all relief; it does not have any hint of perspective or depth.

The elements remain the same, but to their arrangement are added new activities of the mind, utterly new modes of the mind's operation (whatever the nature of these modes might be), and only then is the meaning of the picture in its perspective depth suddenly revealed to us, enabling us to understand why it is drawn according to the rules of perspective. That which had seemed a twisted distortion due to the artist's ineptness turns out to be an intentional and purposive means for depicting depth. It is then and only then that the picture becomes for its creator that which it is in its intention, in its plan. Before then, it was only a collection of distorted and twisted contours and shadowy spots with only certain hints at intentionality, because, for one who does not understand perspective, that which is purposively drawn in two dimensions is a plane, not a perspective image; it is an outline, a contour, not the essence. The intentionality of a picture of reality is understood only if perspective is understood; in the opposite case, the planar one, the intentionality is different, and if the understanding of perspective is lost, then one would naturally agree with Alfonso V of Castile,[28] who said famously: "If the Creator had asked my opinion, I would have advised Him to do a better job when He was creating the world—chiefly He should have made it simpler!"

If we now go back to the subject that was our starting point, that is, the difference between the empirical and the empyrean, we can say that to those initial data which both of us equally possess, you are applying only one kind of reality-constructing act, as a result of which you obtain a uni-form reality, i.e., empirical reality; whereas we are applying to them a series of acts and obtaining an articulated multi-form reality. Out of a certain material you have constructed an object α; you have nothing beyond this; it turns out, however, that the materials of this object admit and demand further processing by new

---

28. Florensky probably means Alfonso VI.

methods of construction. In this manner, the objects β, γ, ... etc. are constructed. These objects are not separated from one another, however; though they are independent in their essence, they are linked for the consciousness by the unity of the material out of which they are constructed, and they are real by the fact that this material is given by our relation to one thing; and these objects α, β, γ, ... are particular aspects of the one thing, different sides of its idea-essence. The objects α, β, γ, ... are, so to speak, parts or sides of the thing for the consciousness. They are not identical, however. The object β, as a further processing of the same material that goes into α, contains α in a certain sense but is itself something more full of content than α, because, besides being α, it is also β—that is, it has the same relation to α as a page of Goethe examined by a person who understands the poem written on it has to the same page examined by a person who cannot read. For the first person, it comprises an esthetic experience plus "black on white" visual images, whereas for the second person it is nothing more than "black on white."

Thus, because different activities of the mind are applied to the construction of reality, our objects, though they contain all that yours do, also have much that is other; and this "other" is the chief and essential thing, constituting the *meaning* of what you have seen and not read. Objects of the religious worldview are therefore more full-bodied and richer than positivistic ones. The former can be compared to chords, and the latter to separate notes.

But after the mind has performed all this, it is then that the frontmost plane, too, the sensuous world that is constructed by the "positivistic" activity of the mind, acquires for us a special importance, a special significance. This world is given to other, higher worlds, so to speak; it becomes their representative and, in a certain sense, their bearer. Having renounced its self-assertion, its own existence as such, it becomes a being for *another world*. Having "lost its soul" and become the bearer of another world, its body, it embodies in itself this other world or is spiritualized and transformed into a *symbol*, that is, into an organically living unity of that which represents and that which is represented, of that which symbolizes and that which is symbolized. The empirical world becomes transparent, allowing us to see the flaming radiance of other worlds. "For the invisible things of Him from the creation of the world are clearly seen, being understood by the things that are made ..." (Rom. 1:20). As a result of this loss of its self-hood, of its independent color, *this* world, glowing with the flame of another world, itself becomes a flaming world, is mingled with fire. "And I saw as it were a sea of glass mingled with fire: and they that had gotten the victory over the beast, and over his image, and over his mark, and over the number of his name, stand on the sea of glass, having the harps of God" (Rev. 15:2). Those standing on the sea are those for whom this world has become fully transparent; and here, remaining in *this* world, they directly touch the element of fire which is mingled with the sea, and they see this and sing praises, saying: "Great and marvellous are thy works, Lord God Almighty; just and true are thy ways, thou King of saints" (15:3).

Thus, if I called your planar worldview "naturalistic" after a certain literary school, then mine, in all fairness, should be called "symbolic,"[29] since it believes that knowledge of the world can be attained by "touching other worlds."[30]

In reality, what is symbolic poetry if not the organic union of *this* world—the world that is represented in realistic poetry, the empirical world—with new, celestial layers of esthetic activity? Each of these layers is significant in itself, and leads to another layer, even more significant.

That, in its general contours, is what constitutes the difference between the empirical and the empyrean, if one takes the worldview as a whole. Here it would be appropriate to consider the relation of such a general worldview to the question of sacraments.

Appendix:
A Comment on Perceptions
during the Reception of Sacraments

I.

It is indisputable that the reception of the power of grace contained in sacraments is accompanied by certain special perceptions. But in addition to such perceptions noted among "ordinary" people, the literature contains examples of an extraordinary "hiero-gnosis" or (in Imbert-Gourbeyre's terminology) *flair eucharistique*,[31] a "eucharistic sense," sometimes exhibited by sensitives, visionaries, and clairvoyants—people with a special organization. Such clairvoyants have a special sense for perceiving different types of holy objects—relics, sanctified objects, and especially the Holy Gifts of the Eucharist.

---

29. Florensky is alluding to the Symbolist movement in Russian literature (especially poetry), which flowered in the first decade of the twentieth century.

30. Allusion to Father Zosima's teaching about "the touching of other worlds" in *The Brothers Karamazov*.

31. See Antoine Imbert-Gourbeyre: *La Stigmatisation*, 1894.

Many cases of the "eucharistic sense" have been recorded among Catholics in particular, perhaps because Catholic writers have the tendency to regard this sort of thing as a form of revelation, as so-called *revelationes privatae*, and, understandably, to attach great significance to it. For us the data do not provide any basis for understanding the matter in this way, but rather seem to contradict such an understanding. If the "eucharistic sense" is not a form of revelation, it is also not a type of sensuous experience. Most likely it belongs to that group of phenomena that Myers designated as "subliminal consciousness."[32]

Imbert-Gourbeyre compiled a number of examples of the *flair eucharistique*.[33] Here are some of them. Whenever he entered a church, St. Francis Borgia always knew where the Holy Gifts (the consecrated hosts) were stored. Jeanne Jugan, Marie de la Croix, would sense the fragrance emanating from priests who had received communion in the morning. Catherine of Siena once refused to partake of the host offered to her because she sensed that the priest, owing to his laziness, had not consecrated it. Lucia of Parnia identified the consecrated host among thirteen hosts. Unbelieving doctors performed experiments on Luisa Lato and became convinced that she could identify sanctified objects with absolute accuracy. By sensing their fragrance, St. Charles Borromeo discovered the relics of St. Jerome Emiliani in a church where no one had suspected they would be.

In the nineteenth century it was confirmed experimentally that Marie-Julie Jahenny possessed the eucharistic sense. But the most interesting subject was a Westphalian peasant girl, Anne Catherine Emmerich, whose years were 1774 to 1824. A stigmatic and clairvoyant, Emmerich also possessed a highly developed eucharistic sense. It should not be forgotten that the description of her experiences was subjected to a double censorship and a double series of corrections—first by her secretary, the Romantic poet Clemens Brentano, and then by her "extraordinary" confessor, the highly orthodox Catholic Oldenburg. Brentano's "scientific verification" of her visions and her own "encouragements" given the lacunae in her confessor's reports of the visions make the accounts of her visions seem "respectable," but they should also make us cautious when using them. However, any possible distortions crop up in the dogmatic and historical elements of her experiences, and there is no reason to suspect the veracity of the facts we will present below.

---

32. See F. W. H. Myers, *The Subliminal Consciousness*, 1892.

33. See *La Stigmatisation*, vol. 1. (I take this information from I. Levitsky's article "Ephesus or Jerusalem?" in *Khristianskoe Chtenie*, vol. 210, part 2 [1900], pp. 580–619—Florensky's note.)

Emmerich's "eucharistic sense" was so acute that she would know whether a priest who was visiting her had performed the Eucharist that day. With extraordinary force she'd grasp his thumb and index finger (which Catholic priests use to touch the Holy Gifts) and release his hand only when she had heard the magic (for her) word "Listen." A light invisible to others and certain special shades of this light enabled her to identify among a series of externally identical objects which of them had been sanctified by the church: not only the Holy Gifts but other sanctified objects as well, especially the relics of saints. The frequency of such perceptions, to which many investigators bore witness, led one of her friends to call her a "master of the sacred."

II.

We presented the above examples without analyzing them critically. Our aim was only to note the nature of the existing facts. By the way, one can find many other such examples in the literature on demon possession, and on clairvoyants.

Let us assume, however, that we choose to refrain from using such descriptions—if only because we do not have the opportunity to weigh critically the documents.

The question of sacraments could then be boiled down to the necessity of recognizing the existence of two facts: first, the fact of the existence of certain mysterious acts in which some people fail to see the special element of grace; and, second, the theory of sacraments, that part of dogmatics which describes the specific nature of sacraments, their "substantial" characteristics.

Thus, we have two facts, neither of which can be swept away, but both of which must be explained. Let us suppose, further, that we wish to concern ourselves mainly with the first fact, with the fact that some people do not perceive sacraments in a special way. It is clear that the mere fact that such perceptions are absent in the case of a given person does not, in itself, pre-decide anything about whether such perception exists or does not exist in general, and therefore about whether the object of such perception—the mystical what—exists. Nevertheless, such a conclusion is sometimes—erroneously—drawn; and we will show that, in this case, it leads to absurdity. With this aim in view, we will, for the time being, admit this conclusion; we will assert that, in principle, there exists neither a specific perception nor a specific nature of sacraments. Then, we will have to deal in one way or another with another fact: with the traditional theory of the specific nature of sacraments, which originated in the deep past and stubbornly continues to exist.

Whatever one's attitude toward the church, it cannot be so frivolous as to disregard completely her fundamental convictions—the convictions of millions of people of different educations and social positions, convictions that persist in the turbulent stream of time. Let it be the case that they are recognized to be erroneous and absurd; but even errors and absurdities, especially those which exist in space and time, have their causes which must be taken into account. To these convictions, one cannot apply "the method of not noticing."

"Perhaps it will be demonstrated," someone might say, "that this theory of sacraments is a result of historical influences on church doctrine, that it is a cultural inheritance." Let that be the case, but it is not an explanation. After all, we refused, in principle, to recognize that sacraments have a special nature. A genetic explanation only shifts the question to another time and another people, without touching on the essence of the matter or resolving the difficulty of explaining the creation of the church theory. In fact, if one were to deny unconditionally the existence of special perceptions in the life of the spirit when receiving sacraments, one could just as unconditionally assert that reflection on such perceptions is impossible. This does not in any way pre-decide whether the logical schema has an a priori character; it means only that prior to the experience a given possibility, a predisposition of the mind, has become actual. The notion of special elements is not obtained in the case of any combination of already-existing data that are different in principle from the first data. We can find eucharistic prayers that correspond to the blessing of the Jewish paschal canon; we can connect these prayers with the mysteries of Mithra, Dionysus, or the Orphics. But whatever the value of our asserting the historical continuity of one phenomenon or another, our assertion concerns only the form or shell of the sacrament; its mystical side, however, is absolutely underivable in this manner without mystical perceptions.

"But," someone might say, "in the spirit there may be given to us, prior to all concrete experience, the notion of the specific nature—a certain reflection prior to experience, so to speak, a purely logical possibility of schematizing the future experience." Let it be the case that in the spirit there is a notion or schema that is given actually prior to the presence of that of which it is a schema. Let that be the case. But then, if this possibility is unconditionally detached from concrete experience, it is impossible to understand how it could afterwards establish a connection with other concrete experiences, or sensuous data. In other words, it is impossible to understand how that which is general and nothing more, how that which is exclusively general and which also has a relation to specific content, could be applicable to the particular material content of sacraments, grace, which, moreover, is substantially different from that which is schematized by the given notion. It is impossible to understand why the theory of sacraments was developed with reference to some definite phenomenon, and not with reference to any other phenomenon; and since this question refers to all empirical data, it becomes in general impossible to understand what connects this general notion that is given prior to experience with any particular phenomenon given in empirical experience. It then becomes incomprehensible why the given notion cannot be grounded by anything we like; and this would mean that the matter of sacraments would not be able to find its way into the theory. For a notion to be applicable to a concrete thing, it must be attached to a definite concrete thing; but for the latter it is necessary that this concrete thing differ for the consciousness from all other concrete things, that it stand out from all the rest and be special, that is, that the consciousness apprehend in it some specific nature, if the general notion applied to it affirms the existence of such a nature.

In order for a theory to be applicable to experience, it is necessary that it have some correspondence to itself in experience; the experience must echo the theory, and this echo, this correspondence, must be experienced. In other words, the empyrean must be experienced.

Thus, the existence of a theory of a given sacrament as having a specific nature led to the conclusion that, if not in this sacrament, then in some other historical precedent of it, there took place an experience of the empyrean. This contradicts our fundamental denial of such a possibility, and we arrive at an absurdity. If that is so, then it is extremely probable that such cases of perception were noted and recorded in their time precisely as cases of something new compared to ordinary perceptions—as cases where other layers of reality broke into the consciousness through the empirical.

"But," someone might say, "the church doctrine of sacraments is based on simple trust in Christ's words. Christ said about the bread: 'touto estin to sōma mou'; and about the wine: 'touto estin to haima mou'[34] (Mark 14:22, 24). The Apostles had trust in him, and the early church had trust in the Apostles; and through the continuous handing down of the tradition this

---

34. "This is my body; this is my blood."

understanding of the sacrament has come down to us." This remark is just, but it contradicts the assertion we accepted earlier: that neither mystical experiences nor objects corresponding to them exist.

First of all, if Christ is a mere man (and that is what authentic empiricism asserts), there swirl around him all the doubts that would swirl around any author of a church doctrine of sacraments. If Christ was in error when he said the above-quoted words, it is necessary to explain the possibility of such an error; but that would assume that he, or someone who had influenced him, was not ignorant of mystical experiences. If Christ is the God-man, then the supra-empirical exists in him; then it is impossible not to believe in Christ, and the objection nullifies itself.

There can also arise the objection that Christ's words do not really signify a church theory of sacraments and that the church understanding is actually a later "layering" introduced by the Apostles or the church fathers. Let us suppose this too is true—that the church theory is the result of the development of an allegorical theory according to which sacrament is only a figure and the word "estin" is used in the sense of "signifies or serves as a sign of." Whatever the case may be, it would then be impossible to deny that, in the final analysis, sacrament nevertheless came to be understood as something more than a mere figure; such an understanding, as qualitatively different from the allegorical understanding, could not be a mere modification of the latter; and thus, in the evolution of the church doctrine, the introduction of a substantially new point of view had to occur somewhere. As such, it could not have occurred gradually for the given consciousness; it had to be discontinuous and sudden. There was a flash of a new understanding of the sacrament; and the one who first saw the flash was the one who created the new theory. And if that is what happened, we would have to repeat about him all that was said above.

To say that the church theory of sacraments was the result of the church's misunderstanding of Christ's figurative expression is to say nothing, since in order for such a misunderstanding to occur, into Christ's words there had to be introduced something which, in the opinion of the objector, they did not contain; but this requires the recognition that mystical perception and reflection on it were not absolutely alien to the spirit of the misunderstanding church.

Thus, though our aim was to do everything we could to reject the mystical character of the sacrament, we are compelled to accept mysticism in something else; and since a fundamental rejection of mysticism is impossible, we have every reason to accept it as what Christ and church tradition affirm, even if we ourselves have never personally experienced the sacraments and their mystical character.

III.

When the grace-bestowing essence of sacrament is given to the consciousness, consciousness perceives it as miracle. This miraculous character can be accompanied by amazement, that is, by certain empirical peculiarities that highlight and underscore the given phenomenon.

The ascetic literature contains many tales of such miracles; but before indicating why we attribute a great significance to these tales, we will describe the general character of these miracles.

They occurred, the ascetics tell us, during the performance or reception of sacraments, mainly during Baptism and Eucharist, especially the latter. The reason for this is absolutely clear: it is due to the everyday ordinariness, relatively speaking, of these two sacraments, especially in the monastic life.

Descriptions of cases of miracles clearly note the mystical perception. Thus, in one legend,[35] John the Chozebite, when elevating the Holy Gifts, "did not notice the Holy Spirit sanctifying them, as he had previously." This was explained by the fact that the eucharistic breads had, in error, already been sanctified. In another legend, a priest is judged for delaying the beginning of the liturgy and therefore violating the church rule. This is what the elder said by way of justification: "On Sundays I stand at the holy altar from midnight on, and do not begin the liturgy until I see the Holy Spirit descending on the holy altar. When I see that the Holy Spirit has descended, I begin the liturgy right away."[36]

In certain cases, mystical perceptions were clothed in the symbolic form of visions, whereas the above cases appear to refer to perceptions that are not symbolic. Here is a good example of this symbolic form. A certain elder, simple in his faith but great in his ascetic works, said that "the bread that we receive is not substantially the body of Christ, but only a figure (*antitupon*)." Two other elders tried to convince him, saying that this bread is truly the body of Christ, but the elder would not change his opinion: "I must have proof before I can become convinced." Then, after a weeklong prayer of the elder and the two others,

---

35. *The Spiritual Meadow* of St. John Moschus, ch. 25.
36. *The Spiritual Meadow* of St. John Moschus, ch. 27.

God heard them. When the week had ended, they came on Sunday to church.... And their eyes were opened. When the bread was placed on the holy altar, it appeared to the three brothers in the form of an infant. When the priest extended his hand to break the bread, an Angel of the Lord came down from heaven with a knife, slaughtered the infant, and poured his blood into the cup. As the priest broke the bread into small pieces, the Angel cut off small pieces from the infant. When they came forward to receive the sacrament, only the elder was offered the flesh with the blood. Seeing this, he was horrified and exclaimed: "I believe, O Lord, that this Bread is Thy Body and that this Cup is Thy Blood!" At once the flesh in his hand became the Bread, as is customary in the sacrament, and he received communion, thanking God.[37]

St. Macarius (of Alexandria, or the Younger) told of an even more terrifying vision he had seen. The brothers had started to receive Holy Communion. As soon as some of the brothers extended their hands to receive the Holy Gifts, Ethiopians, as if forewarning the priest, put burning coals on their hands; meanwhile, the Body of Christ offered by the priest was transported back to the altar. In contrast, when the more worthy brothers extended their hands to the altar, the evil spirits ran away in great horror. He also saw that an Angel of the Lord stood at the altar and that, like the priest, he extended his hand toward the altar and participated in the offering of the Holy Gifts.[38]

We find something similar in the tale of the elder who, because of his ignorance, celebrated a heretical form of the liturgy. The warning of a brother had no effect, since he saw angels officiating at the service. But they told him that his brother was right, and he started celebrating the correct service.[39]

In certain services the mystical nature of the sacrament was signaled by extraordinary empirical phenomena. For example, there was the case when, to test the correctness of the faith of a certain northern heretic, an Orthodox believer threw a piece of this heretic's communion bread into a red-hot vessel, and it burned up at once, whereas a piece of the Holy Gifts of the Orthodox Church was undamaged.[40]

The Alphabetical Patericon (1491) tells the story of a secretly baptized

---

37. *Remarkable Tales of the Asceticism of the Saints and Blessed Fathers*, translated from the Greek, 4th ed. (Moscow, 1871), 93–96.
38. *The Lives of the Desert Fathers*, compiled by Rufinus, ch. 29.
39. *The Spiritual Meadow*, ch. 199.
40. *The Spiritual Meadow*, ch. 29.

Jew who was persecuted by his relatives because of a fragrance emanating from him, which told them that he had become a Christian. By the special action of grace, the baptized Jew did not burn up in the red-hot bathhouse stove into which he had been placed by his persecutors, and so on. *The Spiritual Meadow*[41] tells how from pieces of the Holy Gifts thrown by heretics into a fire there sprouted stalks and ears, and this miracle produced such a powerful impression in Seleucia that "city-dwellers and villagers, native inhabitants and strangers, travelers on land and on sea, men and women, the old and the young, youths and elders, the rich and the poor, the powerful and the powerless, the educated and the ignorant, priests, virgins, and ascetics, widowers and married men, rulers and common people—all exclaimed: 'Lord have mercy!' and everyone cried out in his own way, glorifying God. Everyone thanked God for this ineffable and unfathomable sign. Many started to believe after this miracle, and joined the holy, catholic, and apostolic church."

Most frequently, in the legends mystical perceptions related to the sacraments are connected with the element of fire. The fiery sanctification of the Holy Gifts performed by St. Sergius brings to mind the sanctification of the apostles by tongues of fire: "And there appeared unto them cloven tongues like as of fire, and it sat upon each of them" (Acts 2:3). In some legends a tongue of fire is sent to interfere with an insufficiently reverent treatment of the Holy Gifts; and it therefore has a destructive effect. Thus, for example, a heretic called Isidore became enraged when he learned that his wife had received Holy Communion in an Orthodox Church. "Grabbing her by the throat," he recounts, "I forced her to regurgitate the communion. Picking it up, I threw it in different directions and finally it fell into the mud. All of a sudden, before my very eyes, lightning raptured away the Holy Communion from that very place."[42]

Similar descents of fire were recorded in cases when the liturgy was performed inappropriately and illegitimately. Here is one such instance, which occurred in the town of Apamea in Syria. Outside this town children were tending to lambs in a pasture, and they started to "play at liturgy." "One of them played the role of the priest; two others were deacons. They found a large smooth stone, and began their game: on the stone, as on an altar, they placed bread and wine in an earthen pitcher. The priest stood before the altar, and the deacons on two sides of it. The priest pronounced the prayer of the

---

41. *The Spiritual Meadow*, ch. 79.
42. *The Spiritual Meadow*, ch. 30.

holy elevation of the Gifts, and the deacons ceremonially waved their belts." The boy-priest knew the prayers and recited them loudly, as prescribed; during the liturgy the other children stood before the altar. "When all had been done according to church regulations and the boy-priest was about to commence breaking up the bread—suddenly a fire fell from the sky, burned up the Gifts, and vaporized the stone. Terrified by this unexpected occurrence, the children fell to the ground and could neither stand up nor scream." Their parents, who had gone out in search for them, found them in an unconscious state; and only the next day were they able to tell what had happened. The parents and the children, together with a crowd of people, went then to the place where this had happened. "Signs of the fallen fire were still visible there," which were also seen afterwards by the local bishop who built a church there.[43]

The Patericon tells about similar incidents where children performed the sacraments of Baptism and Eucharist. We will present, however, another story involving St. Athanasius. "When he was pope in Alexandria, St. Athanasius . . . saw children playing at the seashore. They were imitating the bishop and everything that is prescribed to occur in the temple. Looking attentively at the children's game, *he saw that they were performing certain sacraments.* Astonished by this spectacle, he summoned the priests and told them what he had seen. He then sent them to summon the children. The children came" and explained, among other things, that "they had baptized several men cast out by Athanasius, whom the children had elevated above themselves as their bishop. The bishop asked the children to describe the baptism in detail and found that they had done everything according to regulations. After consulting with his priests, the pope decreed that those whom the children had baptized did not require a second baptism."

We could present more examples, but there is no particular need to. We will move on to a number of theoretical considerations, which we present in a rather fragmentary form.

IV.

If one of the goals of the scientific-philosophical worldview is a "responsiveness"[44] in relation to every aspect of reality—a bookkeeper mentality con-

---

43. *The Spiritual Meadow*, ch. 196.
44. Dostoevsky's expression. (Florensky's note.)

sisting in the possibility of having in the consciousness every detail and "calculating" every side of it, then the goal of scientific "experience" (with this word understood in the broadest sense) is the splitting of the elements and aspects of reality, the underscoring and highlighting of them. However, in order to perform this labor of splitting, this fragmentation, the consciousness *must have* that on which it operates, and this thing on which it operates is *something that is given in the spirit*. This thing is not given to us all at once; it is worked out and revealed by a special subconscious process that can, most succinctly, be called "popular experience." To be sure, the terms "scientific" and "popular" are not taken in a sense where scientists have only scientific experience and the "people" have only popular experience. That is not the case, for these two experiences are inseparable; it is just that the first type of experience is dominant when reflection is the foremost factor; whereas the second type is dominant when contemplation and activity dominate.

Thus, scientific experience presupposes popular experience, and this clarifies the nature of the latter. The task of scientific experience is to underscore and separate. The task of popular experience is to provide the most full-bodied experiences, to provide material that, as much as possible, is *not* underscored or separated.

But this material cannot be concrete reality itself, since reflection cannot be focused directly on the infinitely diverse. Consequently, being neither reality nor abstract schemata, this material must be a *typical representation of reality in the spirit*.

This representation must be such that it permits the application to itself of schemata of reflection; that is, it must contain a certain unity, completeness, and limitedness (*peras*), yet at the same time it must possess the possibility or potential of the whole fullness of definitions of a reality that is never exhausted but is ceaselessly being exhausted; and in this sense this representation must contain a certain limitless multiplicity, incompleteness, and boundlessness (*apeiron*).

Integral in itself, it must have a multiplicity of roots through which the life-giving juices of reality flow into it; and being *part* of reality, it must in a certain sense contain *all* of being; actually *finished*, it must also be potentially *limitless*.

This makes clear that this representation must contain features of a work of art; it must be a living, juicy, organic type of reality which, if you will, unfolds in the spirit as the *idea* of reality, with the difference that in a work of art an idea is given to the consciousness as something finished; whereas here the idea is discovered by the consciousness.

This representation reminds us of the mixed and confused imagery of dreams—living poetry or poetic life. It is not by chance that Karamazov's Devil remarks: "Sometimes a man sees such artistic dreams, such a complex and vivid reality, such events or even a whole world of events tied together with such intrigue, with such unexpected details, from your highest intellectual functions down to the last button on your shirtfront, that, I swear, Leo Tolstoy himself wouldn't be able to invent all this; and yet such dreams are very often dreamt not by writers but by the most ordinary people, by clerks, newspaper humorists, village priests."

Ovsianiko-Kulikovsky[45] has called works of art an *induction* of a few observations of their creators. If we accept such a usage of this term, the representation of reality we have been discussing can even with greater reason be called an *induction*—an induction of a thousand generations and millions of experiences. That is why the experience of the people is "popular" experience par excellence, contains inexhaustible material for scientific processing, and is an undistorted (though often symbolic or even conventional) drawing of reality. No matter how absurd *this* experience might seem, the pride of hyper-reflection must humble itself before it: science must delve dispassionately into popular wisdom, which, because of its integral unity, is always ahead of science. Popular wisdom holds the key to more than one riddle of the world; and if we recall the history of science (e.g., the theories of meteor falls, or of phenomena of the subliminal consciousness and occult activities of the spirit) we cannot fail to be astonished by the thoughtless and ubiquitous disregard of the leitmotifs of popular wisdom.

But reflection can be applied only to "popular" experience, not directly to the experience of the people. The question is: How do we transpose the latter into the former? If we approach the works of the people with methods of rationalistic thought, it is clear that we will find in them nothing but words that express concepts; and as such they can be nothing other than a result of reflection, nothing other than part of the scientific-philosophical lexicon of the environment in which those works arose.

Thus, looking through "scientific" spectacles, we will see nothing except good or bad science; and it must be asserted in advance that any given science can see only that which is *not higher than it*. The experience of the people, on the other hand, is for the most part inferior in its scientific value to the experience of science, and therefore to approach it with *such* methods and without keeping the goals of history in view—is to lose time.

---

45. Dmitry Ovsianiko-Kulikovsky (1853–1920), Russian critic and scholar.

But if for reflection a word is only the sign of a certain schema, a concept; for the direct pre-reflective relation a word, at least in its connectedness with others, is more than just an instrument for calling forth a schema in the consciousness; for science there are, properly speaking, no words, but only terms, but a term and a word are different things. A word has a dual nature. It is a word in the proper sense and, as such, it can be called supra-rational—a miniature work of art. But it is also a term, something rational. Precisely this feature of the word[46] makes it possible to express with given words that which is absolutely inexpressible by them if one looks at them from the point of view of words-terms—reflection. Thus, the content of speech can outgrow its terminological meaning, which is the only thing reflection can grasp.

But do our hearts not burn and find repose in sweet serenity when our eyes fall on Ruth's astonishingly simple words to Naomi: "Intreat me not to leave thee, or to return from following after thee: for whither thou goest, I will go; and where thou lodgest, I will lodge: thy people shall be my people, and thy God my God: Where thou diest, will I die, and there will I be buried: the LORD do so to me, and more also, if ought but death part thee and me" (Ruth 1:16–17).

Will fragrant spring not warm our hearts, will the bashful wind not caress our ears, will our whole being not inflate like a white sail when we hear the shepherd's calls?

> Rise up, my love, my fair one, and come away. For, lo, the winter is past, the rain is over and gone. The flowers appear on the earth; the time of the singing of birds is come, and the voice of the turtle is heard in our land. The fig tree putteth forth her green figs, and the vines with the tender grape give a good smell. Arise, my love, my fair one, and come away. O my dove, that art in the clefts of the rock, in the secret places of the stairs, let me see thy countenance, let me hear thy voice . . . (Song of Solomon 2:10–14)

Let us imagine that we are reading words like these or, even better, the words of some mystic, such as Isaac the Syrian, and we try conscientiously to understand the experiences described, but we approach the words with reflection. What will we see then? Nothing, except that which is known to the scientific worldview *now*—that is, nothing except physiological and

---

46. We will not dwell on this feature here, for that would make it necessary to consider the theory of symbols. But that would require a special work. (Florensky's note.)

empirico-psychological processes. The mystical experiences will fall apart into optical, thermal, acoustic, muscular, and general-somatic sensations and into naked assertions of the *specialness* of this complex of sensations. However, the latter, that is, the pretension to specialness of experience, will remain completely unjustified and will even clearly contradict the total fragmentation of the described processes into "ordinary" sensations. This analysis is right in its own way, but that is the case precisely because science does *not* have the means to capture mystical experiences, and instead of them it catches concomitant processes—what remains in the hands is not the essence, but foam; not the pearl, but mud. But as soon as we approach the work in a different way and look at it directly, its *supra-terminological* content is revealed to the spirit: in simple words, in terminologically insignificant words, something infinitely dear and fragrant, like a baby's half-forgotten smile, awakes and looks out at us—he has just opened his clear little eyes and is stretching his little arms from his bed toward the pillar of golden dust that has broken through the curtain . . .

Myth is the extreme example of supra-terminological literature. For scientific analysis, authentic myth, as a whole, is an authentic collection of words—a primordial, half-meaningless philosophy of primitive thought. This (if we make a certain qualification in view of our contemporary myth-creation)[47] is really so; but, for the direct consciousness, myth, as the symbolism of the profoundest experiences projected onto the empirical, is the foundation of all knowledge of reality.

Legend, too, is analogous to myth. That does not mean that the "material" or "plot" of a legend is necessarily an invented combination of commonly observed events. On the contrary, it seems to me that the overwhelming majority of legends must be accepted *en toutes lettres* and understood tautegorically;[48] it must be recognized that everything narrated in them is real. Only the essence of the legend is narrated, however unexpected its plot; whatever novelty a legend may present for the scientific worldview, its key is not in the plot. The plot's importance is secondary; it is a projection of mystical perceptions on concomitant empirical phenomena which can be ordinary or extraordinary, but in any case which, in themselves, have the significance only of signs, *sēmeia*, *signa*. The main thing is the perception of

47. We find a remarkable and incomparable example of new myth-creation in the "poetry" of Andrey Bely, which bears an indelible imprint of myth. (Florensky's note.)

48. A word used by Schelling. Formed analogously to "allegorically," it is derived from *tauta agoreuein*—"to say the same thing." "Allegorically" means figuratively; "tautegorically" means literally. (Florensky's note.)

miracle, and an authentic legend (which is always religious in character) is a narrative about a miracle whose specialness is highlighted by signs.

Considering a legend without reflection, we can often capture those experiences that are contained in the shell of the plot; moreover it is not that important whether this shell was generated at the moment of the perception of miracle as a necessary screen for the projection of the mystical, or whether it was created later, gradually.

Without discussing this last question, we will note the fact of the remarkable uniformity of the plots of legends. This is usually attributed to the existence of a few prototypes giving rise to the various legends. Whatever the case may be, the application of the uniformities of symbolism to experiences of a similar kind indicates that there is some connection between that which is symbolized and that which symbolizes. Often that is why, even without experiencing a legend, it is possible to gain a great deal from it using a symbolism studied once and for all, in which definite external phenomena, definite signs, are projections of experiences corresponding to them, which too are definite and known beforehand.

The Goal and Meaning of Progress

Before reading my theses, I must make the following remarks: first of all, these theses are part of a larger work,[1] and so it may appear that they are being stated here without sufficient preparation. Second, I am forced to use terms connected with historical categories, such as "Protestantism," "socialism," and so on, but it would be a mistake to regard them as indicating historically known facts. I am using these terms to designate certain schemata that have been realized more or less fully in the corresponding historical phenomena; however, even if these schemata have not been realized anywhere, that does not take anything away from my theses. Their purpose is to permit a dialectical examination of certain principles.

* * *

The dialectical development begins with the notion of obligatoriness. I pay absolutely no attention to what elements compose this notion or to how it arises. My point of departure is the fact of the existence of this notion in the human spirit.

1. Obligatoriness is conceivable where there exists a set constrained by a real (potential), simply given unity, i.e., by the condition of interaction of separate parts of the set (*principium relativius*). A set constrained by such a unity is the condition of obligatory activity (of activity that should be).
2. The goal of obligatory activity is the establishment in this set, taken in

---

[1]. This work has not been identified.

its real constrainedness, of an ideal (actual) unity, appearing as obligatory; and, conversely, the destruction of this unity constitutes the goal of nonobligatory activity (of activity that should not be).
3. This actual unity can be conceived in two ways:
    a) Either as the consequence of the activity of the elements of this set, determined by nothing but the nature of these elements, i.e., as the result of the non-ideational, self-asserting activity of these elements or of the structure of their life.
    b) Or as a goal limited in its absoluteness by nothing but the nature of the elements of this set, i.e., as a task directing the activity of these elements.
    a′) In the first case, this actual unity is *ens rationis*—an imaginary, apparent unity established by the unconstrained activity of the elements, with this activity produced spontaneously, solely in virtue of the presence in the elements of the power to produce it. The unity is the result of the abstraction of the perceiving mind, the notion, and, as regarded as an immediate given, the idol.
    b′) In the second case, this actual unity is *ratio entis*, a real, genuine unity, establishing, without constraining in any way the freedom of the elements, their activity; determining this activity ideally, solely as a consequence of the truth of this law of activity. The unity is the cause determining consciousness, the idea, and, as regarded as its own truth, the ideal.
4. The possibility of one or the other of these forms of actual unity cannot be denied. Action according to goals, in conformity with moral laws, points to the possibility of the second form of this unity, whereas "statistical" unity, as the lawlikeness of mass phenomena, points to the possibility of the first form. The formal similarity of the laws governing totally different mass phenomena (e.g., the laws of the kinetic theory of gases and the laws of sociology) is a direct indication of the origin of these laws and is reducible, in the final analysis, to the fundamental theorems of probability theory, which examine the regularities of internally unconnected mass phenomena.
5. The unity of the law determining activity, i.e., the second type of law (*ratio entis*), is the principle of the hierarchical order of society; for its general tendencies it can also be called divine-human and theocratic. We can indicate the following attempts to implement this principle more and more deeply:
    a) *Imperium Romanum*. This is the principle of the external, compul-

sory law, which therefore negatively determines the activity of the elements of society, i.e., the juridical principle.
b) Catholic all-unity. This is the principle of the internal law, which therefore positively determines the activity of the elements of society, i.e., the principle of authority.
c) "Spiritual Christianity" (Quakerism, etc.). This is the mystical or divine principle, which therefore unconditionally determines the activity of the elements of society, i.e., the unconditional principle.

The general characteristic of the hierarchical order is internal harmony, diversity in unity.

6. The unity of the law determined by activity, i.e., the first type of law (*ens rationis*), is the principle of the anarchic order of society; for its general tendencies it can also be called human-divine and anthropocratic. We can indicate the following attempts to implement this principle more and more deeply:
   a) Protestantism. The principle of the absence of hierarchy in spiritual life.
   b) Republic (according to the type of republican system exemplified by the first French Revolution). The principle of the absence of hierarchy in juridical life.
   c) The socialist commune. The principle of the absence of hierarchy in economic life.

The general characteristic of the anarchic order is internal disharmony, uniformity in fragmentedness.

7. The consistent implementation of the first principle, the hierarchical one, leads to theocratism. Here, all of life is determined from within, by subordination to universal truth, and the whole lies in total law-governed unity.
8. The consistent implementation of the second principle, the anarchic one, leads to absolute anarchism. Here, all of life is determined from outside, by the collisions of different interests, and the whole lies in total lawlike unity.
9. Anarchism, when it is consistent, must reject all norms, since it seeks only a natural harmony of egoisms and as the means to the unity of society it chooses the constraint conditioned by these collisions. But with its

rejection of norms it inevitably leads (if it is consistently implemented) to a society where every member is insane: rejection of all norms constitutes an agreement consenting to the degeneration of the individual life. Growing collective insanity with the corresponding growth of the external law-governedness of society—that is the final result of anarchism if it is allowed to develop fully. In fact, the more spontaneous and disorderly the life of the individual elements, the greater the disharmony and fragmentedness of this life due to the absence of norms, the more precisely will the laws of probability theory operate. Self-annihilation will be the result of the anarchic self-assertion of society. A part of society—individuality—desires to be the whole, resulting in the annihilation of that part in order that the whole exist.

10. Of the two possible principles, the hierarchical principle remains. According to this principle, every member of society acts voluntarily to maintain and preserve a certain social law, a certain norm accepted by all and by every individual as the unconditional truth and the unconditional good. This free subordination to such a law, in conformity with the qualities of the nature of every member of society, leads to a voluntarily established differentiation of the social positions of the members of society, for differences in the nature of the individual members of society lead to differences in the methods by which the unconditional law is realized. Moreover, differences in the nature of the members necessitate that every member stay in his place, since he cannot be replaced by any other member of society. This is the basis of the only possible coordination of the members in the unity of their relation to the one unconditional law. This is exactly what hierarchy is. The unconditional law (the only law to which one can freely subordinate oneself) and the unconditional truth are conceivable only when one acknowledges that only the Unconditional Entity, God, can be the bearer of this law as permanently existent, and not just evolving, in human society. Thus, the hierarchy we are discussing can be defined further as government by God, theocracy. But government by God in the capacity of the unconditional Truth requires total freedom in the subordination of every member of society; it requires total freedom in the subordination to him in the capacity of the Truth. If that is the case, theocracy unconditionally excludes all coercion. Thus, in order to realize theocracy, every member of society must unconditionally subordinate himself freely to the Truth. This is the basis of a new definition of hierarchy as an all-human society and, further, as a universal society.

11. Theocracy is the unconditionally desirable order of society, but there is one circumstance that makes it unconditionally unrealizable: the perverseness or love of evil that characterizes man. The love of evil, existing in different degrees of intensity in all human beings and manifested in some as unrestrained active evil, is a love that does not allow human beings to recognize the realizability of the desirable theocratic order of society. By love of evil we mean the tendency of human beings to do evil not for the sake of profit but for evil's own sake—to do evil unselfishly, so to speak, in order to deride and revile goodness and truth; to hate goodness and truth solely because they are goodness and truth; to hate holiness solely because it is holiness. We know that this is possible, that it is an undeniable psychological fact. Even if it not fully expressed in every man, this tendency is undeniably dominant in some, and it will never permit such "underground men" to become reconciled to the theocratic order. If theocracy were ever realized, such men would do everything they could to destroy it; and therefore, in order to preserve the social order, their activities would have to be restrained. But this would violate the fundamental principle of theocracy, namely the principle that all the members of the theocracy subordinate themselves voluntarily and freely to its unconditional law. Even if just one of its members is compelled by force to harmonize his activities with the goals of the theocratic order, such an order would not really be theocratic. People say that there is a progress of goodness, and this is indisputable. But we are still far from an identity of social life with goodness, precisely because the progress of goodness has its double—the progress of evil. The growth of the wheat is accompanied by the growth of the tares. The goodness increases, so does the hatred of it; as the means of goodness develop and are improved, the means of evil also develop and are improved. Culture is a rope with which one can save a drowning man or strangle one's neighbor. The development of culture benefits evil as much as it benefits goodness. Meekness increases, but so does cruelty; altruism increases, but so does egoism. Evil does not decrease as goodness increases; rather, it is the same as with electricity: every appearance of positive electricity is paralleled by the appearance of negative electricity. Thus, the struggle between good and evil is not extinguished; it becomes fiercer. This struggle can neither end nor, apparently, fail to end.
12. Thus, if anarchic society is possible but self-annihilates in its logical development, and therefore cannot, in view of the ideal requirements of humankind, be regarded as desirable; then theocratic society is desirable

but, developed to its logical conclusion, cannot be regarded as possible because of man's empirically given nature.

13. Thus, we can conceive two logically consistent forms of human society: theocracy and anarchy. But man's nature makes the first horn of the dilemma, theocracy, impossible; while his requirements make the second horn of the dilemma inadmissible. The first of these possibilities we cannot realize, although we wish to; the second possibility we do not wish to realize, although we can.

14. Thus, the conceivable forms of a normal society are either inadmissible or unrealizable. If that is the case, absolute pessimism seems to be the only conclusion that can be drawn. No normal society exists or can exist, and consequently there should not exist any actions aimed at the realization of such a society; that is, there should not exist any goal-directed activity. But since, subjectively, our activity must be goal-directed whereas, objectively, it is meaningless and not directed at anything, or (which is even worse) directed at the undesirable anarchic order of society, at that which should not be—it follows that one should abstain from activity. Absolute ataraxy should be our only activity.

15. But by our very nature we cannot live in absolute ataraxy; ataraxy and life are mutually exclusive. We have arrived at the affirmation of ataraxy. Negation of life is death and the way to death is suicide. But suicide, too, is a goal-directed act and, as such, it contradicts ataraxy. We are entangled in contradictions.

16. We cannot accept a normal society, but at the same time, with our very life and even with our renunciation of life, suicide, since it is a manifestation of life, we cannot fail to denote positively and to affirm with our actions a normal society, or fail to denote negatively and to destroy with our actions the same normal society. Either way, this shows that, nevertheless, we accept it. But while accepting in some sense its existence, we are nevertheless compelled to reject all conceivable forms of its existence. Thus, while being compelled to deny its presence, we are compelled to accept it by the logic of reality.

17. We cannot accept a normal society. Nor can we deny its existence. If we wish to act (and we can absolutely not refrain from acting), we must accept the possibility of a normal society, but when we begin to accept this possibility, we are also compelled to deny it. However, life could not continue if this contradiction were absolutely unresolvable. But life continues, we act, and consequently somewhere in the depths of our spirit we know that this contradiction is resolvable and already resolved.

If that is the case, we are able to transfer this resolution into the domain of consciousness as well, for if a contradiction is resolvable, its terms cannot be absolutely mutually exclusive; and in that case, the contradiction is not absolute for the reason either. Consequently:

18. The fact that we accept the possibility and the necessity of a normal society, this fact and postulate is a necessary condition of life itself. But how is this postulate possible? If both assertions—both the possibility and the impossibility of a normal society, both its necessity and its nonexistence—are justified, and we have seen that both are justified, then these assertions must be opposite but not contradictory. This is possible, however, only when they are true not unconditionally, but conditionally, in a certain relation, when both are justified with a certain qualification. Consequently, our assertions about a normal society implied some condition, which was omitted in our further discussion; and this omission led to a number of contradictions. In order to disclose this implied limitation, we must go back a little.

19. Why was the anarchic society regarded as undesirable? Because the rejection of all norms leads to the destruction of society. Moreover, the rejection of all norms will *eo ipso* paralyze the very striving to establish an anarchic society, for such a striving is defined normatively. Further, why was the theocratic society regarded as impossible? Because man's present nature will not permit the realization of such a social order. Consequently, both assertions are justified only when they refer to human nature and human life.

20. If that is the case, we, being compelled to recognize the desirability and possibility of a normal society, must conceive it not with reference to the life and human nature known to us, but with reference to some other life and nature. Otherwise, as experience has convinced us, we will be entangled in contradictions. Thus, a normal society refers not to the human nature and human life known to us.

21. However, we desire a normal society for the people known to us. We cannot reject unconditionally their nature and life, since we do not desire a normal society that has nothing to do with those who need it, who struggle and suffer in an effort to achieve it. But it seems that we are establishing a normal society without these people. We get a strange contradiction: both this life and not this life; both this human nature and not this nature. The normal society comes to depend, again, on seemingly contradictory propositions.

22. For the same reasons we must set aside this apparent contradiction by

introducing limits into the aforementioned propositions, i.e., by limiting the essence and the form of the appearance of the life and nature. The normal society refers to this life and this nature, i.e., to this essence of theirs; and if it refers to this essence, it refers to every essence, for essence is identical to itself. The normal society refers not to this life and nature, for it is excluded by them; this means that it refers not to this form of their appearance, not to this form of the existence of that essence we have just spoken about.

23. Thus, in our demand for a normal society we are compelled to conceive a self-identical essence of life and of the experientially given human nature as well as a second form of the appearance of this essence, replacing the first, where the second form must be qualitatively different from the first.
24. The transition from the first form to the second is a change; consequently, a qualitative change in the form of life is a necessary postulate, resolving the contradiction of the normal society.
25. But the qualitative change in the form of appearance cannot be gradual; it is conceivable only as a discontinuous change, without intermediate stages.
26. However, this life advances in space and time; consequently, regardless of the nature of the other form of life and human nature, the moment of change must occur in time, since it must also be the end of the temporal, the end of this form of life.
27. From this follows the necessity to conceive as temporal the end of this form of life and therefore the end of history, when, in one way or another, a qualitative change in the nature of man and the form of his life will occur.

In conclusion:

28. Thus, the temporal end of world history, occurring at a specific moment of time; a qualitative transformation of human nature and human life; and the advent of a normal, obligatory order of society (the order that should be)—all this is a necessary postulate of all activity, whether it is directed at realizing a normal society or at obstructing its realization. The realization of such a social order is conceivable only after such a transformation.
29. We have indicated the necessity of the transformation of human nature as a condition of the possibility of a normal society. We have shown

that we cannot fail to conceive of such a society as long as we live. But here a question arises: This society is necessary, but in virtue of what is it possible?

The Prize of the High Calling

*An Appreciation of the Character
of Archimandrite Serapion Mashkin*

... tes aretes apsamenos kai tes akros filosofias geusamenos ...

(Isid. Pelus. Ep. CXVI, I. 1)[1]

I.

"Not duty and not happiness, but to love God"—that is the fundamental maxim of behavior. To be in love with God, to be drunk with God, *amor Dei intellectualis*—that is what truly molds a person. Monoideism is necessary for the life of a true person. "Monoideism is a condition of the personality, but it is so only if the object is infinite; in the case of finite objects, monoideism becomes a form of insanity, the one-sided ravings of a madman."

That is what the late archimandrite Serapion Mashkin thought and that is how he lived. Vladimir Solovyov, who resembled him in many ways, thought and lived the same way, as did thousands of other philosophers who, perhaps, did not record a single one of their insights. All these philosophers, going deep into themselves, encountered the theocentrism of being. For all of them the fuss and bother of life concealed an organized whole. For all of them the planets and comets of our world described not capricious arcs and arbitrary zigzags, but moved in defined orbits around the one Sun.

It seems that the idea of the Infinite grabbed these philosophers and

---

1. "... having touched virtue and tasted the peaks of philosophy ..." (Isidore of Pelusium).

The title is from Philippians 3:14.

flung them with amazing rapidity into the heights of contemplation; that in multiplicity it showed them the unifying Force and the multidiverse fullness; that it allowed them to see in the Unity "the fixed axis in the flight of phenomena," blinded them with its beauty and then lowered them back into the world so that they could infect the latter with the faithful love for God, so that they could show it the finger of God, the imprint of the ideal. And each of them who has resided in the heights truly seems to be an "origen"—one born in the heights; like their sublime predecessor, Origen, each of them seems to have been "born in the heights," a skylark living in the world, yet not of the world; a skylark soaring and vanishing from the field of vision. Each of them has poured out his trills from the pure heights.

Growing vigilant and listening attentively to the ringing of these heavenly church-bells, both Father Serapion and Vladimir Solovyov with meek smile asked those around them:

My dear friend, can it be
That you do not see that all that we see
Is only a reflection, a mere shadow
Of what eyes do not see?

My dear friend, can it be
You do not hear that the vain din
Of daily life is only a distorted
Echo of triumphant harmonies?[2]

And it seemed that both of them, with heads inclined slightly and like white marsh birds listening to the rustling of the reeds, were about to fly away from this world, to fly up to the heights and to stay there forever.[3]

2. The first two stanzas from an 1892 poem of Vladimir Solovyov. It is given here in the translation by Boris Jakim and Laury Magnus, *The Religious Poetry of Vladimir Solovyov* (San Rafael, CA: Semantron Press, 2008), 50–51.

3. Here is a brief chronology of Father Serapion's life: Vladimir Mikhailovich Maskhin was born in 1855 into a well-to-do family of the gentry in the Kursk province. After attending a naval academy and serving in the navy, he audited classes in the natural-science department of St. Petersburg University. Starting in 1884 he entered Panteleimonov Monastery on Mount Athos as a novice and lived there for six years under the direction of elders. His spiritual director on Athos told him to return to Russia, foretelling that he had a mission to fulfill. In August 1892 he received permission to audit lectures at the Moscow Theological Academy. In October 1892 he was tonsured into monasticism, receiving the name Serapion. Later that month, he was ordained a hierodeacon, and in May 1893 he was ordained a hieromonk. In

And both of them flew away . . .

II.

Russia has not had a single major philosopher in the Western sense, not a single philosopher-scholar or philosopher-investigator, not a single thinker along the lines of Descartes, Hume, Kant, or Hegel. Philosophy as a cabinet occupation, as an occupation of the "mind," has not taken root in Russia, just as it did not exist in antiquity. Our philosophers strive to be not clever, but *wise*; not so much thinkers as *sages*.

I do not know if this is due to the Russian character or to the influence of historical conditions, but there is no doubt that the philosophy of the "head" has not thrived in our land. Starodum's phrase, "a mind, if it is nothing but a mind, is an utterly inconsequential thing,"[4] seems to find an echo in every Russian; and when we show honor to Western scholars or philosophers and make use of the sweet fruits of their labor, we still gaze with secret contempt at the cabinet work that was required to grow those fruits and never refrain from mocking the "German"—even if it's Hegel or Kant—for having sat his entire life in his cabinet. Moral striving, religious awareness, actions performed not only by the head but by all the organs of the spirit—in other words, life outside the cabinet is the only life regarded by us as completely serious and wholly worthy. Furthermore, every scholarly discipline unstoppably strives to embody itself in life, in the active domain, and is anxious to demonstrate its relation to religion, morality, politics, and social activism. Even mathematics and gnoseology make this leap to the domain of "life." In the final analysis, all the threads converge in the single knot of religion, since in Russia even atheism is religious in its own way and even our positivism is metaphysical. In Russia every large personality becomes interested in questions of religion, especially in religious practice, positive or negative.

The Skovorodas, Khomiakovs, Tolstoys, Dostoevskys, Solovyovs, Trubetskoys, Serapions, Merezhkovskys, Rozanovs,[5] et al. appear to be exceptions from the general mass only at first glance. But if we look attentively, we immediately see that they are homogeneous with the whole Russian com-

---

1896 he was awarded the degree of Kandidat of theology, and in 1897 he was named father superior of Znamensky Monastery. In 1900 he was removed from this position and sent "to rest" at Optina Monastery, where he died on 20 February 1905. (Florensky's note. Abridged.)

4. Starodum is the hero of Denis Fonvizin's play *The Minor* (1782).
5. Litany of Russian religious writers.

munity, even with our social-democrats and our positivists. They all exhibit the same ardor, the same religious fire (though they believe in different gods), the same ideal of the philosopher-sage embodying his ideals in life, and the same demand for fullness of content and breadth of generalization, for sweeping theoretical conceptions, dizzying *aperçus à vol d'oiseau* (bird's-eye views), and the immediate and uncompromising embodiment of a theoretical social order. The striving for absoluteness is inextricably connected with the Russian spirit. If this striving does not find an outlet in religion, it will become a destructive force in other spheres of activity, and the finite forms of the latter will collapse under the pressure of this infinite striving. The scientific, the conditional, the useful does not satisfy the Russian spirit, which always tries to find a metaphysical, unconditional, theoretically finished basis for things of *practical* utility. Every proposition, like some gas, yearns to expand limitlessly, to occupy a maximally large volume. A simple generalization becomes a universal and necessary truth; a convenient order of social life becomes an absolute requirement, prepared to destroy everything on its path in order to attain its goal.

No, cabinet philosophy does not take root in Russia.

III.

The ancient idea of the sage, so vividly portrayed in Lucian's *Life of Demonax*, was given its supreme expression in the patristic conception of the monk as Christian philosopher. The gnostic[6] of St. Clement of Alexandria is a contemplative philosopher and ascetic, realizing in his life the Truth he has found and investigating the Truth, livingly preparing his entire being toward this goal. Other holy fathers have the same view of the philosopher.

Having ripened and been torn away from its native tree, blown by the wind of migration, the seed of this ideal found its best soil in the Russian loam and black earth; in our land, the ideal of the philosopher-monk, the contemplative ascetic, the gnostic was acclimated and produced succulent fruits. The Skovorodas, Solovyovs, and Serapions are known to us because they left written works. But who knows how many unknown gnostics we have had? An attentive gaze continually turns up new contemplatives, who can be found everywhere in Russia. This is the national ideal of the "living soul," characterized by a combining (uncommon in the West) of mysticism

---

6. In this case, one who seeks spiritual knowledge.

with rigorous logic, of the giving of oneself to God with active love, of religious tradition with political progressivism—in other words by a harmonious union of philosophical speculation and practical activity. Russian mystics are therefore the least reliable of men from the point of view of government; no government, except that of God, will satisfy their demand for absolute truth; they are organically, with their entire being, anarchic in relation to *all* authority, because, just as organically, they are conscious of themselves as being members of the kingdom of God.

But of all these philosopher-mystics it seems to me that the one who most strikingly expresses this ideal is Father Serapion Mashkin, the most pure-hearted in his sincerity, the most absolute in his metaphysics, the most radical in his social thought, the most audacious in his doubts, the most neglectful of external things, the most consistent in his life—in other words, the most faithful servant of his Lord (if it is possible for a human being to make such a judgment).

IV.

Father Serapion's exceptional honesty of thought and his inner freedom, familiar to all who knew him personally, compelled him to speak and write with extraordinary sincerity. Every word of his works is therefore permeated with the most authentic experiencing of what he is discussing, and like a purse of rough leather every one of his clumsy sentences conceals gold coins of blinding brightness. Like a peacock's feather, which radiates bright metallic colors in its smallest parts, Father Serapion's works are, in their tiniest details, a product of *personal* creativity, are grounded in personal experience, feeling, and thought; and so, even if one denies their metaphysical value, they will doubtless preserve a profound psychological interest as material for elucidating the character of the late sage, as the most intimate yearnings of a noble soul crystallized in the cool of profound solitude, as the very life of this exceptional man.

This sincerity of thought will become understandable, even predictable, if we observe that for Father Serapion philosophy was not just a profession and writing was not just a literary exercise. No, it was the satisfaction of a deeply personal need, a satisfaction *contrary* to external conditions, not thanks to them; it was a work dedicated to the Lord, a service of God and of humanity, a feat of moral-religious ascesis, invariably accompanied by prayer and the calling of the name of the Holy Trinity. Father Serapion's sincerity is "sealed" and "certified," so to speak, by the sign of the cross placed here and there in his manuscripts. This sign, together with the prayers often interspersed in or concluding his mathematical or philosophical investigations, creates a completely original atmosphere of seriousness, conducive to the development of abstract thought.

Of course, exclamations of prayer, in and of themselves, do not prove that much. But when we see, for example, that the fruit of many years of extremely intense mental labor, which resulted in acute neurasthenia in the author, ends with the words

Glory to God, glory to God, glory to the true God
By our Lord Jesus Christ

we cannot fail to experience such a prayer with veneration. Father Serapion's prayer becomes even more fragrant when we learn that he regarded it as a "method of philosophizing." The whys and wherefores of this are not important for us now. We are concerned with a psychological fact, and the important thing for us here is that this is a sincere opinion, whether or not it is a justified one.

"Christian philosophy," says Father Serapion, "is the philosophy of the critical human spirit, illuminated by Christ's mystical light." Philosophy becomes possible after reason is prepared by asceticism. "The true Christian is the true philosopher," but in order to *express* this philosophical content, technique is needed. Philosophy must be preceded by absolute skepticism, which does not spare any given, even the given of logical laws. This skepticism finds resolution only in the mystical contemplation of the Holy Trinity. "In a higher ecstasy, not distinguishable from religious philosophizing rooted in prayer or logical analysis with the co-presence or the mystical contemplation of that which is analyzed, a Christian ascends to the eternal moment." But to accomplish this, one must enact a "living ascesis grounded in truth." "This ascesis is the art of arts, the technique of techniques, the art of life in God, the true philosophical art, the state of ascetic self-denial."

On Father Serapion's lips the acknowledgment of the necessity to prepare oneself for philosophizing was not just an empty word. Having ascetically retrained himself on Mount Athos under the guidance of the elders there (chiefly, Makary, as I recall), Father Serapion then spent his whole life performing the ascetic feat of active love, prayer, and self-discipline. He wondrously combined complete inner freedom with precise adherence to the church's ordo. He served the "hours" in his room or cell with the precision of a chronometer every three hours, day and night, and no obstacles could impede his fervor. If it was his turn to do the censing, he would leap out of his room (in the Moscow Theological Academy) and, without saying a word, imperturbably serious, and wearing his liturgical vestments and with censer in hand, he would fly into the rector's apartment, or into the kitchen, or into any other place where there were people; and after having censed, he would disappear just as silently.

This immersion in prayer, combined with his exuberant temperament, would sometimes make him do strange things. Sometimes, leaving the sanctuary to cense the Academy church, he'd cover with clouds of incense nearly every peasant-woman he encountered on his way, which would significantly delay the progress of the liturgy. When he was reprimanded for this, he'd answer in his usual good-natured rapid-fire manner: "Well, I had to cense. It's the image and likeness of God, after all. . . . It's the same thing as an icon." And sometimes, immersed in the censing of the icons, he'd leave the church, because he'd remember there were icons in other places too. Someone had to be sent to find the overenthusiastic hierodeacon and bring him back. Finally, a special companion was assigned to Father Serapion, who would walk with him and keep him from getting too carried away.

In the last years of his life he prayed even more than usual. The weeks before his sudden death were a period of particular religious fervor. He would often fall prostrate and remain frozen like that. During this last period, just as throughout his entire life, Father Serapion would gaze fixedly at the Savior's countenance, trying to grasp some feature in him and to transfer it to himself. He would always carry a Gospel in his pocket, and when he was at leisure or in a conversation, he would rapidly turn the pages, uttering "right, left, right, left," and find and reread the passage that he had chanced to remember. His "gazing" at the Savior's countenance and his zealous and constant prayer were for him not the formal fulfillment of a duty; and, in general, Father Serapion did not recognize any formal duties. On the contrary, both the gazing and the prayer constituted the very element of his soul, the medium that fed his spiritual life. Like Vladimir Solovyov, at one time he had intimate knowledge—so intimate that his spiritual equilibrium was perhaps shaken!—of persecution from the Devil (as he himself characterized it). Among Father Serapion's papers we find profound descriptions and subtle characterizations of Evil and of how it touches the soul; these are the most authentic descriptions of this kind I have ever read. The only deliverance from the attacks of these powers was found by him in Christ. It's as if Father Serapion would run up to him and grab his feet. This allowed him to pass through the layer of evil. He would then see visions of Christ and of the saints, and his spiritual (from the universal-human, not psychiatric point of view) equilibrium would be restored.

We have no intention, of course, of investigating here the degree to which all these persecutions and visions were objectively real. They are important for us solely from the subjectively psychological side; it is important for us to know the state of Father Serapion's soul and to use this knowledge to show the importance of prayer for him. But, of course, a psychiatrist could interpret this inner struggle as a psychic disorder that had been repressed in its initial stages. This is what Father Serapion said about these attacks of evil:

> Some saints even asked God, for the mortification of their sins, to send demons against them. In the struggle with them the victor is crowned by the Lord and learns to hate sin. Satan is absolutely repulsive, there being no words to express the degree of his foulness, which can drive a person into a mad frenzy; and this teaches a person to know the power of the Lord's Cross and of the Savior's love. An ascetic learns to see his sin: egotism, the fullness neither of evil nor of good, the madness of evil and the wisdom of God.

Father Serapion also wrote the following:

> Even until now the Lord continues to teach the world. But His teaching is now of a different kind. He comes to His disciples, Christian philosophers, secretly, not bodily but spiritually, and inspires them, giving them His inner intuition, which implicitly contains discursion. Using this intuition of the Lord, a disciple writes what is written here. I, archimandrite Serapion Mashkin, am this disciple, the lowest slave and servant of the Lord. I am His slave, but in what sense? The Lord is not a master of slaves. For Him, all are free: "where the Spirit of the Lord is, there is freedom."[7] I am His slave in the sense that, having come to know Him in part and to love Him in part, I am still the slave of my bodily passions. Seeing that I cannot willingly free myself of them, I ask the Lord to hold my mouth in "with bit and bridle,"[8] to bridle me like that donkey on which it was pleasing to Him to ride into Jerusalem. In other words, if it cannot be done otherwise, I ask him to place my feet forcibly onto the path to Him. And the Lord grants my request, guiding me in different ways: by sicknesses, by health, by a sudden enlightenment of my mind, by permitting the demons to

---

7. 2 Corinthians 3:17.
8. Psalm 32:9.

attack me and thus cleanse me of sinfulness. Could I have written what I have written without help? And I have written a new geometry and a new mechanics and resolved an *epochē*.⁹ I do not want to boast, but must write this. I write this for the sake of the truth, which I cannot conceal and do not wish to conceal. The Lord guides me because I thank Him for everything and accept everything that He sends me. I pray with His prayer: "Our Father which art in heaven, Hallowed be thy name. Thy kingdom come. Thy will be done in earth, as it is in heaven," I praise and thank Him. Glory to Him. Amen.

V.

In this way, Father Serapion's life with God flowed on in complete trust. It would have been extremely astonishing if his life with God were not reflected in his life with people, and, indeed, the two were in total harmony. At one time possessing considerable wealth (up to 200,000 rubles, it was rumored, though I can't vouch for this), he fulfilled the gospel commandment with literal precision and spent his monastic period almost in poverty, having given away his wealth to the last kopeck, retaining only his philosophical-religious and mathematical library. When Father Serapion was still a student at the Moscow Theological Academy, on certain days of the year he would receive a shipment of money (from his mother, apparently) and all the scroungers would get wind of it: a large company of them would flock around him and his money would soon melt away in his hands. When he didn't have money, he gave away his clothes, his boots, everything he had. Once, we are told, he stopped showing up at the Academy. A search party found him in his cell, dressed only in his undergarments. When asked about it, he replied that some scrounger had penetrated into his cell and gotten his hands on his boots and outer clothing, and now he couldn't go out into the street.

When people would find out about his charitable giving, Father Serapion would become very embarrassed and mutter something to the effect that the gospel says quite clearly "Give to him that asketh thee,"¹⁰ and that there was no other way to interpret this except literally.

In the last period of his life, when he was sent "to rest" in Optina Mon-

---

9. The state of absolute suspension of all judgment, resulting from consistent unresolved skepticism. (Florensky's note.)

10. Matthew 5:42.

astery, he was without any income or resources. His cell-companion Father F. related tearfully that Father Serapion's days passed in such poverty that he often had no money to buy stamps or "a little tobacco." Father Serapion never asked anyone for anything. According to Father F., Father Serapion received from home not more than twenty-five rubles during a period of a year and a half. But in a communal monastery, like Optina, it was hardly possible to live without one's own money. If we take into account the fact that much of this meager sum was immediately given away to the needy and to scroungers and that some of it was used to buy books, we will get some idea of how difficult life was for Father Serapion. He was even pitied by monks who were not known for compassion. Lacking money, Father Serapion began to give away his last possessions; and when he had given most of them away, he began to give away his meals. He once went for a walk and returned in his undergarments; embarrassed, he admitted that he had given his clothes to someone.

This extreme self-sacrifice is clearly reflected in his last will and testament. There is not a single word about his works or about his personal affairs! There is a touching concern for people he barely knew, and his cell-companion is not forgotten.

I have spoken to many of Father Serapion's acquaintances, and they always mentioned his kindness and generosity. But human ingratitude, which had shown no concern for the sage during his life, was not stung by his death. He died and was forgotten. If you go to his place of burial, you will see nothing but a little collapsed hill covered with grass; there is not even a wooden cross there or little fence around his grave, and no one performs the customary memorial services. In the monastery many remember him only as the kind and eccentric archimandrite Serapion, and, as they do so, they often ask discreetly: "He was crazy, wasn't he?" When I asked to see his grave in the small Optina graveyard, I was met with some confusion: the brothers did not know where it was. Finally the graveyard watchman, a lame monk, led me unsteadily to the barely noticeable little green hill and conjectured that I must be a relative of the deceased. As if one had to be a relative of a sage to come and kiss the blades of grass on his humble grave and to shed tears onto this ground which was already saturated with the autumnal tears of the somber sky—to shed tears for one's own grief and for human heartlessness! My guide looked at me compassionately and wobbled over to the side, leaving me to my Nikitinesque thoughts.[11]

---

11. That is, thoughts similar to those inspired by the verses of Ivan Nikitin (1824–1861), a poet of melancholy moods.

By no means do I blame Optina or my alma mater, the Moscow Academy, for not understanding his "living soul." But the lack of elementary gratitude is strange, for one could have fashioned twenty graves with the legacy left by Father Serapion.

"They buried him like a dog," bitterly remarked one of the brothers close to him. I, too, wanted to say that, but I did not dare for fear of offending the memory of the deceased. "They buried him like a dog!" "Was there a single heart," I thought, "a single heart that trembled because of you? Was there anyone who saw the beauty of your soul and understood what filled your life and made you suffer, what made you sleepless at night and meditative during your daytime walks? Do your words—full of inexpressible sincerity and loaded with content the way a thick ear of wheat is loaded with grains—not lie buried in this monstrous heap of papers? Where will I find a publisher for these 2250 pages? Where will I find readers for you? You summoned me so many times; you set up a meeting with me this August to have a 'cup of tea' and talk about Infinity. And I have kept my word and come to you. Why did you leave, my friend whom I never met, bequeathing me your blessing to work on our common interests, but not the strength to do so?"

VI.

Somewhere in his papers Father Serapion speaks of his pride, which he was able to control only with Christ's help. Indeed, it would have been improbable if a nature so gifted and so conscious of its spiritual power were not beset with pride. It was perhaps the acute self-observation of pride in his soul that provided the philosopher with material for one of the finest pearls of his system: the metaphysical conception of Evil grounded on metaphysical pride. Pierced by Father Serapion's gaze down to the deepest recesses of its being, pride, from the psychological surface of consciousness, plunged to the metaphysical roots of being and became, in its new aspect, an essential element of reality.

But, having understood the essence of pride, Father Serapion condemned it at its very root and struggled fiercely against it, "tormenting his tormenter."[12] However, I do not know much about the heroic period of this struggle, since it took place in the "prehistoric" time covered neither by the documents in my hands nor by the oral testimony of those who knew

---

12. Quotation from Ephrem the Syrian.

him. In the "historic," post-Athos period, Father Serapion appears to us as already full of deep humility, which grows from year to year and attains its fullness in the last (Optina) stage of his life. We learn this from the direct testimony of Optina old-timers. His high moral rectitude was acknowledged even by those who strongly disliked him for his political radicalism and for his somewhat "gnostic" tendencies (à la Origen and Solovyov) in the domain of philosophy and religion and his thirst for absolute knowledge. Father E., who thought that Father Serapion suffered from "spiritual delusion," also proclaimed that he had mastered the two fundamental monastic virtues: "humility and the absolute renunciation of possessions." I will not try to harmonize this juxtaposition: on the one hand, "delusion"; on the other, "humility and the absolute renunciation of possessions." But the fact that a person so hostile to Father Serapion was compelled to recognize his "humility and absolute renunciation of possessions" tells us much about Father Serapion's successes in his struggle with himself.

I recall hearing about an episode in the Academy that seems anecdotal. A monk who was tonsured at the same time as Serapion asked to be ordained a hieromonk.[13] Fairness demanded that the same honor be accorded to Serapion. But when this was mentioned to him, he requested, alluding to his unworthiness, that he be allowed to remain a hierodeacon.[14] The rector insisted. Serapion then fell down at his feet and lay on the floor, announcing that he would not get up until his request was fulfilled. The rector did not know how to respond to this ultimatum, so he lay down on the floor too, and in this position the rector and the student continued their negotiations.

It would be a great error to interpret this episode as an instance of the usual monastic reverences, petitions, and apologies, as an instance of the complex ceremonial that sometimes conceals fierce pride, spite, and other "refuse of human emotions." On the contrary, the extraordinarily humble and meek Father Serapion often violated traditional etiquette. Who does not know, for example, that fear of speaking the truth, the desire for a cushy situation, and the toadying up to those in power have received their stereotypical "grounding" in pseudo-Christian "humility" and the abstention from having one's own opinion, especially with regard to political radicalism? Who does not know that the most vicious reaction is often based on the acknowledgment of one's intellectual weakness, on the impossibility of forming a correct opinion of life, and on a Jesuitically distorted theory of

---

13. A monk who is a priest.
14. A monk who is a deacon.

the ancient "obedience"? But it was precisely in this domain that Serapion stopped being humble and cast aside all etiquette.

Father Serapion acknowledged that nothing repelled him more than a deficiency of civil courage, and he, a man full of love and forgiveness, broke off, before my very eyes, all relations with a person he had long known who stood higher than he in the clergy and in society because this person exhibited this deficiency. Because she was marked by this deficiency he even considered that the Russian Church was not far from heresy, the heresy of caesaropapism. His honesty of feeling, his natural candor, his vital temperament, and his acute awareness of social injustice led him, in such cases, to flare up angrily, which made him many enemies and gave people reason to think that he was an odd bird, even crazy. I recall, for example, one of the stories told about him at Optina. This took place at the Vvedensky Cathedral during the liturgy on some feast day. Some governmental or synodal decree was being read from the ambo. An acute interest in everything that surrounded him compelled Father Serapion to grasp the exact essence of what was being read; and so, unconsciously, he kept moving closer and closer to the reader until he was almost on top of him. Having paid close attention to what was read, he understood that it contained something quite foul. Here, he spat energetically, turned around, and left.

For the same reason he abstained from performing the liturgy. I also heard the rumor that he was officially prohibited from performing this function, but I don't know if it was true.

The brothers at Optina told me about another typical incident: after the assassination of the Grand Duke Sergei, one of the Optina brothers encountered Father Serapion, and something like the following dialogue ensued:

"What a calamity! Oh, what a calamity," the brother said to him.
"Yes, what a calamity," Father Serapion agreed.
"How horrible! How could they have failed to protect him?" the brother continued.
"Yes. How could they have failed to help him to escape, to hide him?" Father Serapion replied.

The two misunderstood each other utterly. The brother was grieving for Sergei, while Father Serapion was sorry that the murderer, Kaliaev, did not escape.

Of course, Father Serapion, who never hurt a fly, had only a theoretical attitude toward assassinations. We are not interested here in his theoretical convictions regarding any specific issue. We are mentioning such incidents solely in order to describe Father Serapion's personal psychology—in order to demonstrate his honesty and decisiveness in the public realm, combined with a profound personal humility. One must be fair to the Optina brothers in one thing. This peculiar little world, including representatives of all worldviews and from all the corners of Russia, has a tolerant attitude (compared to other domains of Russian society) toward unusual opinions and is hard to astonish. Thus, despite his radical opinions, Father Serapion lived in harmony with the other brothers, and they (with a few exceptions) loved him, especially the simple monks who came to the tranquil monastery from peasant huts.

The joining of political radicalism with mystical asceticism in his personal life, as well as the joining of the results of natural-scientific studies with data from the Bible, was very natural for Father Serapion. He admired the French Revolution, and it was rumored that he had connections with Freemasonry in his youth. But, at the same time, he thought that a secular republic was necessary only for non-Christians, whereas Christians should form a theocratic kingdom, an approximate realization of which he saw in the monastic republic of Mount Athos.

VII.

Our discussion of the traits of Father Serapion's psychology as regards his relation to God and to people must be complemented by some considerations concerning his sense of nature.

"The evolution of nature, proceeding from what is simple and homogeneous to what is complex and heterogeneous, is written in two divine Bibles: Moses's Bible and the great book of nature. In both cases this is the writing of God."

For Father Serapion such statements are not random platitudes or formal-logical deductions from certain other propositions. Rather, they are expressions of his personal experiences and of the profoundest yearnings of his soul. It is well known how much he loved nature, a love that was surpassed only by his love of God. This was not an esthetic infatuation with nature's forms, colors, sounds, and smells, but a religious love; and I think it was less intermixed with esthetics than Solovyov's love, for example. This is not a criticism of Solovyov, of course, but it is important to underscore that, here as well as in many other respects, Father Serapion's relation to Solovyov resembles Nesterov's relation to Vasnetsov;[15] that is, Father Serapion's mysticism is more refined than Solovyov's, enabling him to penetrate deeper into the phenomenality of the phenomenal. In his view of nature as a "purgatory of sin," Father Serapion therefore stands closer to the patristic literature than does Soloyvov, whereas the latter stands closer to hylozoism.

Personal feeling, nature and his religious interest in it, had a profound effect on Father Serapion's metaphysical system, where cosmology plays a very great role. It was also quite natural that this interest, together with the realization that a philosopher had to be knowledgeable about the natural science of his time, should compel Father Serapion to study for four years in the natural-science department of St. Petersburg University; and tracking the progress of science as well as he could given his external circumstances, and reading widely, he came to feel pretty much at home among the problems of physics and of the other sciences, especially mathematics.

There is, as yet, nothing out of the ordinary here: people of religion sometimes do take an interest in the natural sciences. But their prejudice when it comes to goals and their polemical intentions often compel them to approach the propositions of natural science defensively and to criticize them with the same methods they use to criticize the propositions of metaphysics and religion. Auxiliary hypotheses, working theories, and methodological schemes are then transformed in the eyes of such Don Quixotes into apocalyptic beasts; and condemning these beasts to slaughter, these knights of La Mancha go at them pitilessly with tin swords. Meanwhile, the spirit of science remains uncomprehended and therefore unharmed.

But Father Serapion occupied himself with science not because of any polemical intentions but because he wished to clarify for himself the *truth* of science. This enabled him to have a free attitude toward this truth and to assimilate it (though many things had to be illuminated in a substantially new way). For example, he wholly accepted Darwinism, regarding it as the only correct theory of evolution; likewise, in the realm of phenomena he accepted the particle mechanism in physics and chemistry and the psychic-processes mechanism in psychology, although he had his own version of these mechanisms. But this freedom in the acceptance of natural-scientific data was not conditioned by uncertainty when it came to religious data; in his system, the two sides were in harmony.

15. Mikhail Nesterov (1862–1942) and Viktor Vasnetsov (1848–1926) were prominent painters at the time Florensky was writing. Florensky regarded Nesterov as a subtle religious painter, while regarding Vasnetsov, a folklorist and romantic, as a cruder kind of painter.

The seriousness of the mathematical and scientific knowledge possessed by Father Serapion is clearly attested by the fact that in places his works are almost inaccessible to people who are not well acquainted with such subjects, and this inaccessibility becomes especially great when he inserts into his text whole treatises dealing with special, e.g., mathematical and physical, questions. Here, Serapion the philosopher cedes his place to Serapion the scientist, and with vertiginous boldness the latter sketches ideas of unheard-of novelty, ideas which, in their creator's opinion, were destined to change fundamentally a whole series of disciplines: mathematics, mechanics, physics, etc. Of course, in the present essay I will not try to expound or evaluate these original ideas. I will note only that even if for some reason the significance ascribed to them by their creator is rejected, they can still be very useful in connection with narrower problems of mathematics, molecular physics, etc. It is indisputable that the kernel of these special ideas is of great value, and the only thing that can be debated is the size of this kernel.

But Father Serapion's main interest lay neither in these special questions nor in philanthropy or social well-being. The center of his seekings was to formulate a universal worldview, encompassing all the domains of human interest. He had a constant vision of "integral knowledge," as did Solovyov and Origen, and his task was the creation of an all-embracing interconnected system.

As an example, here is an extract from one of his letters to me (from December 11, 1904), dealing with actual infinity (the italics are mine):

> ... the foundations on which we stand are different. I wish one thing: that, God willing, you decide to visit me this summer at our tranquil Hermitage. It is tranquil and beautiful in its spiritual organization, in its grace-bestowing "silence," so dear to agitated souls. Moreover, in the summer our monastery is beautiful outwardly too: its nature is a miracle. It is not by chance that the Grand Duke Konstantin Nikolaevich and his entire family spent two summers in the vicinity (at the estate of a nearby landowner). The woods, the meadow, the river: ... we would go strolling and bathing, and then have our cup of tea and discuss the *universal system of philosophy*. The value of such a discussion gives me hope that you will not neglect us but will instead come to visit us. Come, Pavel Aleksandrovich! You will not regret it! You have mathematics, I have philosophy. Together, we are a force to be reckoned with. And now is exactly the time when a *new* system is needed. The old systems have outlived their time and there are no new ones; and the needs of our contemporary society are so great.

I await you. But let it be according to God's will. Let it be according to His Holy will. But may God allow it if it advances the good.

VIII.

Until his very death, Father Serapion toiled mightily to develop a system that would begin with absolute skepticism and that, after considering all the fundamental problems of humanity, would end with a program of social activism. After a stubborn and bold labor of thought, he produced a highly original system, which he attempted to write down several times. Somewhere in his papers he recalls that even in childhood he was drawn to the fundamental problems of the origin of the world, of God, and so on, and that even then he attempted to express on paper his solutions to these problems. His first serious attempt was his Kandidat thesis written in 1890–92, when he was thirty-nine to forty-one years old (I have not seen this thesis).

The second attempt, a grandiose one, was a work submitted as his Master's thesis and dated 1900, when Serapion was the father superior at Znamensky Monastery. This version is titled differently in different places. On the cover we find: "Archimandrite Serapion (Mashkin). An Essay on the System of Christian Philosophy." This title has been crossed out, and written above it we find: "An Essay on the System of the Teaching and Works of Jesus Christ (Christian Philosophy)." The original title is repeated on the first page, with the epigraph: "he measured the city with the reed . . . according to the measure of a man, that is, of the angel" (Rev. 21:16–17).

As we have said, in *this* version the work was submitted as a Master's thesis to the Moscow Theological Academy. Professor Aleksey Vvedensy examined it and returned it, suggesting a number of corrections, some of which concerned purely external defects (the manuscript's length, its repetitions and lack of clarity), and some of which were substantive in character. Father Serapion began to revise the work, and he made the manuscript extremely difficult to read with his numerous crossings-out, over-writings, reconstructions of previous texts, additions, and insertions of entire notebooks. For some reason, however, he did not submit this version, but began to develop his system in a completely new way, according to a new plan and with a new title: "(monk) Zavulon Mashkin. System of Philosophy, 1904"; and on the following page: "Archimandrite Serapion Mashkin. *System of Philosophy: Attempt at a Scientific Synthesis.* In Two Parts, 1903–1904."

This last version is highly compressed and at times distinguished by an elegance of exposition—by the same severe elegance that distinguishes Spinoza's *Ethics* or Kant's three *Critiques*. Expounded more *geometrico* and much more abstractly than the previous version, this last version demands constant intensity of thought from the reader, and this intensity must be even greater because of the multitude of quasi-mathematical symbolic formulas concisely embodying entire metaphysical theories and forming the basis for further speculations. Unfortunately, this second version was never finished: its second part survives in the form of fragments, many of which are almost impossible to read because of the author's indecipherable handwriting. It is very doubtful if this second part can ever be reconstructed.

Optina Monastery was bequeathed all of Father Serapion's papers, including the two versions of his system, rough drafts of his letters, and some individual notes, though there are very few of these. I am now publishing a portion of these letters and notes,[16] regarding them as characteristic of Father Serapion and as shedding light, at least in part, on our spiritual environment.[17] Optina Monastery has authorized me to be the editor of the most valuable of this material, and I will publish it in extracts as soon as a publisher is found. I also hope to publish a detailed and systematic exposition of Father Serapion's views and his biography.[18]

---

16. Florensky published "Letters and Notes of Archimandrite Serapion Mashkin" in *Voprosy religii* 1 (1906): 174–83; "The Prize of the High Calling" was published in the same issue of that journal.

17. In order to avoid misunderstandings, I must state *en toutes lettres* that I am far from being in agreement with the entire content of these letters. (Florensky's note.)

18. The systematic exposition remained unpublished, though Florensky did publish a brief biography: "Data towards a Description of the Life of Archimandrite Serapion Mashkin," *Bogoslovsky vestnik* 2–3 (1917): 317–54.

Questions of Religious Self-Knowledge

Letter I.[1]

"My speech and my preaching was not with enticing words of man's wisdom," writes the Apostle, "but in demonstration of the Spirit and of power: That your faith should not stand in the wisdom of men, but in the power of God" (1 Cor. 2:4–5). Christian faith is grounded not on reasoned arguments, not on explanations, not on proofs only, but, first and foremost, on the power of God. All that has its foundation not in the power of God, not in the experiential knowledge of God, is human, only human. That's how it was in fact when the Christian community had within it a multitude of obvious bearers of the Spirit. At the present time many people regard this as nothing more than a half-forgotten fairy tale; all hopes have been transferred to the works of man, and many people do not even suspect that the foundation of faith is in the *power of God* and that the goal of Christian life is the *acquisition of the Spirit*, of spiritual power.

"The Lord has revealed to me," Seraphim of Sarov once told a friend of his, "that when you were young you ardently desired to find out what the goal of our Christian life consists in and that you repeatedly asked many great spiritual persons about this. . . . But no one gave you a definite answer. They told you: go to church, pray to God, keep God's commandments, do good works—that is the goal of Christian life. Some were even angry with

---

1. This essay consists of a series of letters, published in the Orthodox magazine *Khristianin* (see the Translator's Introduction). The epistolary form is common to Russian religious writers in the early twentieth century, the most famous example being Florensky's own *Pillar and Ground of the Truth*.

you that you were filled with a curiosity not pleasing to God, and they told you: do not seek what is above you. But I, humble Seraphim, will explain to you now what this goal in fact consists in. Prayer, fasting, vigilance, and all other Christian works, however good they may be in themselves, are not the goal of our Christian life, although they are indispensable means for attaining it. *The true goal of our Christian life consists in the acquisition of the Holy Spirit of God.* Fasting, vigilance, prayer, charitable giving, and all other good works done for Christ's sake are means to the acquisition of the Holy Spirit of God."[2]

But one does not see the acquisition of the Spirit among Christians; one does not feel the power of God within them. They are Christians in name only or, at best, only in their convictions and works; but, in reality, they seem to lack the power that faith gives. But that is not yet the most terrible thing. The most terrible thing is that they have no understanding of the idea of the acquisition of the Spirit and, in fact, do not wish to have any understanding of it; they do not regard such an understanding as a valuable thing to have; they do not understand that, if it is bereft of real power, Christianity is a salt that has lost its savor, a lamp that has gone out. They do not see that the power of Christ that acts in a Christian is not a luxury but the most necessary thing, that the power given to a Christian is not a figurative expression but a genuine reality. Christianity is being undermined and destroyed not by unbelievers but by believers who godlessly diminish and reject the Lord's promise that a believer's words will have the power to throw a mountain into the sea.

That is the general picture of our contemporary state of affairs—at least as it is seen from the side. However, one should not think that these negative aspects are all there is. We believe and are convinced that beneath these warm ashes one can find the fire of true faith. But one must carefully rake through them before one can find, hiding in hidden places, the spiritual phenomena of the contemporary Christian world.

The most decisive test of faith is the investigation of the "sacraments," this word understood in the broadest sense as the designation of all the visible and earthly things behind which the invisible and heavenly is pre-eminently hidden. In theory, sacraments are sources of the deification of the creature, hearths of fire from which Divine heat propagates—the primary points where a new, special, creative power enters our reality, transfiguring

---

2. From St. Seraphim's conversation with N. A. Motovilov, as recorded in S. Nilus, *The Great in the Small.*

man and, through him, all of reality. That is the theory. But is that the reality? This question, posed so directly, must evidently be answered in the negative. The most reliable places where one should expect to find special Divine powers turn out, evidently, to be insufficiently reliable. For many people the sacraments seem to be nothing more than sources that have dried up. From all sides we hear that the sacraments are nothing more than ceremonies that, at best, signify images, remembrances, signs. We hear that in baptism a man does not acquire anything new compared to an unbaptized man: baptism seems to mean nothing more than a ticket of admission to the community of Christians. One who partakes of the Holy Gifts introduces into his body only a piece of bread soaked in wine (Tolstoy's assertion). Many think that marriage in a religious ceremony is in no way superior to marriage in a civil ceremony. Priesthood is regarded as nothing more than a type of employment, a job. Unction is regarded as mockery of the dying person. The same thing is said about other religious actions as well. Making the sign of the cross is regarded as no different from any other movement of the hand. That's what people say. And those who consider themselves believers often calmly confirm all this in the depths of their souls. How can this be? If sacraments do not represent something special and new compared to all other phenomena, wherein lies their power? If a sacrament offers no advantage to the soul or body of the one who receives it, what is it for?

By repeating what every believer hears very often, we foresee indignation from two opposite sides. One side will shout angrily: "Why tempt God with your trials? It is sinful even to repeat such things!" The other side will mock: "In our age of automobiles, X-rays, and so on, is it possible to speak seriously of sacraments?" Leaving unanswered the mockery of the second side (they will be answered by the facts reported by our readers), we will remind the first side of the following words of the apostle Paul: "Examine yourselves to determine whether you are in the faith; examine your own selves. Surely you must know that Jesus Christ is in you, except if you are reprobates?" (2 Cor. 13:5).[3]

We believe in the truth of Christianity and are therefore certain that it will withstand every examination, and we are not afraid for this truth. But the questions arising around us compel us to examine ourselves in order to determine whether we are all in the faith or whether we are "reprobates"— that is to say, not what we should be. It is urgently important to clarify how believers experience the sacraments. It is priests—the believers who are in

---

3. The KJV has been modified.

the most frequent contact with the sacraments and who participate actively in the performance of the sacraments—who are preeminently given the task of illuminating with their guidance this dark domain of religious psychology.

The editors of the magazine *Khristianin* plan to offer its readers several articles on the psychology of sacraments and in general on Christianity as a religion of power and the Spirit, something our theologians are reluctant to speak about. It is not our intention to write a history of the sacraments, though that would be easy to do, given the abundance of published works on the subject. Nor is it our intention to develop a historical survey of the psychology of sacraments, although such a survey would conform more closely to the essential tasks of the present age. It is relatively easy to find out what our predecessors thought and taught about the sacraments. But we, believers of the twentieth century, face a much more difficult problem (and this is a strange problem indeed!): we need to find out what we ourselves think about the sacraments—what *contemporary* Christians think and teach about the sacraments, and how they experience them. After all, Christianity is not an archeology but living life, continuously developing in the entire organism of humanity, leaving dying organs, but then quickening others that have become numb. And in our souls too (except if we are "reprobates"), Christ is continuing the spiritual work that he accomplished in the souls of the Christians who came before us.

That is why it is our intention to discuss these questions with our readers, in a *sobornost* with them, trying to find out how believers understand the power and meaning of the sacraments and how this power expresses itself. But, of course, what is interesting is the answer given by living reality, by everyday experience, not the answer given by books. And the answer given by life will be valuable even if these convictions and impressions born of experience diverge drastically from the statements of the dogmatic handbooks. The editors, inviting such an exchange of opinions, ask the readers temporarily to forget the dogmas and to speak candidly about what we can find nowadays in the consciousness of believers. For example, in the opinion of our readers, does baptism produce any change in those baptized (especially in adults) and how does the performer of the baptism experience or feel it (*feel* it, not think about it)? What does the performer of the Eucharist experience at different moments of its performance? What does communion signify? Is it true that the sanctified Holy Gifts are the Body of Christ? If they are, can this be proved in any way? What does a church marriage signify compared to a civil marriage (here it is particularly important to rely on confessional practice)? What is the power of unction? Does the sign of the cross have real power? And so on. It is impossible to foresee all the questions arising here. Anyone who understands our general idea will see that we are inquiring about the power of Christianity in general and are therefore asking where this power reveals itself. But the fruitfulness of the answer depends on how honestly and truthfully life itself is described. What people have thought, seen, and experienced—that is the material out of which, by our common exertion, we must build our spiritual renewal. Thus, the most important thing for our preliminary self-knowledge is to clarify the powers that are present. We can do this by describing particular cases: "this is what I experienced, saw, or felt at that time"; "this is what I observed"; and so on. We invite our readers to perform the difficult and excruciating communal work of religious self-knowledge. What is needed is the complete and naked truth; any attempt to embellish the present situation will only slow down the new creativity and harm our work. The present situation is very dire: we are speaking not of the political situation, which can always be remedied, but of the religious situation, which can turn out to be irremediable. We must count our fleet honestly and check our ships carefully. If we do not, the next storm may send us to the bottom. And it is already advancing toward us.

Letter II.

Before making any substantive declarations about the question of the sacraments, I think it necessary to invite the readers to send in their thoughts and observations. Thus, the present letter will be devoted wholly to material received from readers. First there is the narrative contributed by a provincial priest, N. E. B. This narrative, titled "Meetings," was recorded by me under N. E. B.'s dictation in a very nonliterary and conversational style, since I felt I didn't have the right to make corrections that would provoke suspicion and lead to the charge of tendentiousness. I will not draw any conclusions from this narrative, and besides, it sufficiently speaks for itself. I will only say that I know the priest N. E. B. to be an irreproachably sincere and righteous man who is surrounded by a true aura of priestly power. As far as "material proof" is concerned, I have personally seen a photograph of the narrative's heroine, V. V. P., her verse, and several letters from her and to her.

As for the two letters appended later, the answer to them was already, in part, given in Letter I, and will be clarified in what follows. Meanwhile, I wish to offer my profound gratitude to the priest D. G. T. for the sincere tone of his letters. They strike me as very rich in content despite their extreme terseness.

Meetings

During the Dormition fast of 1901, I confessed the sisters of the ———sk Dormition convent. The confession was still going on when a girl sixteen or seventeen years old entered the church; she was very lightly dressed, with a small woven shawl thrown over her shoulders, despite the rather cool August weather. When I finished the confession of the sisters, she went up to me and asked me to confess her.

At first, even before she had uttered a word, I felt an extreme heaviness. The girl felt the same heaviness weighing on her. I had guessed the most important thing that her soul was asking. On her part, the girl felt the heaviness weighing on me. I felt that I was nothing here, that I was an instrument and that my I was disappearing and being replaced by some other power that was controlling me; I was only an observer of what was taking place and it was clear to me, an observer, what effect this higher power was having here. The girl felt what was happening to me. I said almost nothing to her about religion.[4] But after the confession she became a Christian, even though formerly she had in no wise been a believer but had only aspired to the truth. The confession permeated all of her, and in an instant she was reborn, as it were. The partaking of the Holy Gifts had a particular effect on her, as she wrote later in her diary. Each of us was split in two, as it were; each of our I's was split in two. One of my I's had fleshly eyes and saw an ordinary person in the girl. My other I saw her Guardian Angel.[5] I felt that this girl had something important to tell, but at this time she didn't tell me anything and it didn't enter my head to try to get anything out of her. The girl didn't tell me anything during her confession, but only repented of her sins. The confession had such a startling effect on me that I walked around like a halfwit.

V. V. P. (that is what we shall call her) told me about her parents, her background, and her life in general when later I invited her into my home, where my sister was visiting. After conversing with my sister and me, she asked me to pray for her and left for the convent, where she was given refuge. Afterwards she took a steamboat home, back to her mother.

---

4. As clarification it should be noted that the priest N. E. B. is, in principle, against instructing and admonishing people who are being confessed, for during the performance of this sacrament he regards himself only as a *witness* and does not consider it appropriate to introduce his purely human conversations and reflections into the action of grace. (Florensky's note.)

5. N. E. B. was unsure whether he should call the girl's second I her Guardian Angel or her purified spiritual center. This is understandable given the close connection between the two concepts. (Florensky's note.)

In the middle of September I unexpectedly received a letter from her in which she shared with me her joy that she had become a "Christian," as she phrased it; that now no persecutions, whatever form they might take, frightened her, and that life in Christ had become everything for her. At almost the same time I received a letter from her mother in which she asked me to persuade her daughter to "stop her insanities" and be like everyone else, instead of shunning the society that should be natural to her. Soon after this letter the mother herself arrived and asked me to give a statement to the authorities at the high school her daughter attended to the effect that she had come to me at the convent at such and such a time to receive communion; this was needed because it was rumored that people had seen her at a fair at that time, and because in general she was being slandered and her reputation was being harmed. I gave this statement, parted with the mother, and heard nothing of V. V. P. until the beginning of April 1902. I did not write to her, and indeed in her letter she did not ask me to. At the beginning of April 1902 I received a lengthy letter in which V. V. P. gave a fairly clear and detailed account of the state of her soul and of her life from the time she fled her parents' home up to April 1902. She wrote that she clearly noticed intrusions of the evil spirit that tried to make her doubt herself as she had before (she had never known such intrusions before); but she did not give in to these doubts, although sometimes she wavered. The attacks of the evil spirit became so frequent that she couldn't bear it, and she decided to write a letter, promising to visit me in the summer; she wanted to do this secretly so that her parents wouldn't find out, because they feared my influence on her. The attacks of the evil spirit were felt to be from "outside": she experienced its presence outside, not inside her, and she felt "its soul-freezing breath" (her words).

In July of the same year I received a brief letter in which she wrote that she couldn't come to see me because of many obstacles, in which she again clearly saw the action of the evil spirit, without giving examples this time. Meanwhile, her inner heaviness became so intense that she couldn't find the words to express her soul's torments. From that July to Holy Thursday of 1903 she wrote nothing and did not send me any address. On Holy Thursday, after reading the twelve Gospels I was leaving the church, when I saw a girl of about nineteen or twenty standing at the side, but I didn't recognize her. She came up to ask me some questions. From her questions I could see it was V. V. P. After spending the night in the convent, she came to see me in the morning to give me a brief account of what had happened to her during the time we had not seen each other.

She asked me to confess her on Holy Saturday so that she could receive communion in the convent church on Easter; and she explained that she now felt how great was the power of the sacrament of holy confession and of holy communion. She explained to me that the attacks of the evil spirit had intensified during this time because she had not received these sacraments, since she didn't want to seek another confessor but couldn't come to see me. It also became clear how great was the power of prayers before the altar: at first, fulfilling her request made at her first visit, I prayed for her, but then I almost forgot to pray for her and prayed for her only on certain special occasions, which I remembered well. In her little book the girl recorded the hours and days when her soul felt light and good. The times corresponded. She also showed me a fairly large notebook that she called her diary and in which she described her whole life from the moment she had any memories of herself up to her second visit to me. V. V. P. told me that this time her mother did not try to interfere with her visit, but even advised her to go sooner. Her mother, who had looked upon me with such disapproval because she thought I was the one who had destroyed her daughter's former convictions, invited me to visit her now, which I did in early May 1903. This change of opinion was explained by the fact that V. V. P. had read her diary to her mother; but at that time the mother made every attempt to react sarcastically and mockingly to what she heard, because she viewed her daughter as someone obsessed with fantasies.

V. V. P. then made her confession and received communion. The miraculous power again acted upon her and upon me, and this time it was more intense. Both of us also palpably felt the power of the evil spirit, whose interference caused the confession to be interrupted twice and as a consequence to take an hour and a half. A few times the girl felt that she was unable to make her confession and even wanted to leave; on my part I felt I could not read the prayer of absolution because the purification of her soul had not been completed, the main thing had not been said, although the girl had confessed all her sins without concealing anything. It was felt that the repentance had not gone down to the depths of her soul. A few times I became very weary as if I was performing an extremely strenuous physical labor. *The girl had not even told me anything in particular; it was the enemy amusing himself.*[6] She had confessed everything; the confession was very sincere, but nevertheless she was saying that she

---

6. N. E. B. asked me to emphasize this part. (Florensky's note.)

was unable to confess. It was a strange feeling, which to this day I cannot understand. It was as if she was speaking against her will. I was the first to feel that the burden had been lifted, and without delay I read the prayer of absolution, after which her soul became wholly renewed. She experienced the same degree of joy as at her first confession, in August 1901.

When I came to see them, in the town of N., another strange event occurred. V. V. P. was waiting for me at the dock. But in spite of the fact that there weren't that many people there, and we had exchanged letters arranging a meeting, we were not able to find each other, in spite of a lot of searching. I went alone to her home, as did she; when we finally met and started conversing, we both felt and simultaneously announced that this was due to the evil spirit.

V. V. P. and I began a regular and fairly frequent correspondence, which lasted from the middle of May to August. Suddenly she stopped writing until the middle of October and around October 20 she came to visit me deeply distressed, as if she had experienced a great grief. She told me a very painful story,[7] again connected with her being persecuted by the evil spirit. After this, our correspondence went on uninterrupted, though it became very infrequent, and between May 1904 and early May 1905 it stopped completely. That May I encountered V. V. P. in a wondrous fashion. At that time I was unemployed and living temporarily in the town of Ks. But a certain business compelled me to make repeated visits to the town of K. On one such visit (which took place on April 30 or May 1, 1905), as I was returning to Ks. from K., my intention was to take the first steamboat going up the Volga from K., but some power held me back, even though I had resolved to board this steamboat and had made all my preparations. There were no obstacles but I felt in my soul that, instead of taking this steamboat, I must take the steamboat of another company, and the power that restrained me become so strong that it possessed me fully; it was as if my will no longer existed, as if it had disappeared somewhere. It should be noted that the other company's steamboat would arrive in Ks. at a very inconvenient time (nearly at midnight) and wouldn't depart from K's port for a very long time. But that didn't stop me, and I left the dock and went to wait for the other company's steamboat. When I finally boarded the steamboat, I saw an aged man, nearly elderly, accompanied by a girl, apparently his daughter. The girl and I immediately recognized each other. The girl turned out to be V. V. P. and the man was her father.

---

7. N. E. B. requested that this story be omitted. (Florensky's note.)

During the journey she told me about the state of her soul and about her life; and among other things she told me about the chance event that had unexpectedly compelled them to take this steamboat. She also told me that, in the course of the past year, she would repeatedly sit down to write to me but some power would inspire in her an unfriendly feeling toward me and she would abandon the letter; this power would then leave her and her friendly feeling toward me would return; and this would happen repeatedly.

From that meeting until the present time (February 1907) I have had no news of V. V. P. I don't know where she lives and I haven't received any letters from her, even though I gave her my address and she promised to write and to send me her diary.

I will now describe the contents of this diary. V. V. P. grew up in a family of the nobility. Her parents have lost much of their wealth, but at that time they were prominent in society. In childhood she had many wondrous visions, and when very young she showed poetic talent. These visions kept her early faith from disappearing completely. Her parents, especially her mother, tried to bring her up as a nonbeliever; and from her birth until she started school (and it was officially impossible to continue doing this), they did not take her, and did not allow her to be taken, to church for prayer. In her home there was not a single icon and not a single book that referred to any religion. All their acquaintances held the same views as the parents. The only believer near her was her nanny, who would secretly take her to receive communion, but that happened very rarely. Unfortunately, she was placed in a high school where all the teachers, even the religion teacher, were either indifferent or openly hostile toward religion. I don't know how old she was when a kind of split occurred in her, which was partly caused by her waking visions. She wondered why people were divided into believers and nonbelievers, but she couldn't figure it out, and there was nobody to ask, and when she did ask, she wouldn't receive a satisfactory answer. The confessions she was required to make in the school did not seem to have any effect on her, but after communion her reflections about religion (often forgotten in the meantime because of the busyness of life) would come back each time with greater force; and these reflections, causing an increasing agitation in her, made, in the end, her environment unbearable for her. This life became repulsive for her, but she could find no way out of it.

Things dragged on that way until she was sixteen years old. Once during summer vacation her younger brother—who was strongly infected with the spirit of atheism and who had just started attending a technical high school—began to sneer at religion and at anyone who believed. Their mother nodded in agreement. This revolted the girl so much that she decided to run away from her parents' home, if only temporarily, though having no idea where she could go. She chose a day when her mother wouldn't be home (at the beginning of August 1901); and so with nothing but the clothes she was wearing (and she was dressed very lightly, because it was almost nighttime), she left her parents' home in the country, where she was living temporarily just with her mother, since her father was in the hospital then. The girl went straight ahead, not knowing where she was going. When she came to herself, she saw she was near a big road leading to a village with the closest river-port to her home. Lost deep in thought, she stopped and seemed to hear an *inner* voice say: "What are you doing, mad girl? Go back." She was ready to obey this voice, but suddenly, frightened of something, she ran ahead, not realizing what she was doing. But some hostile power suddenly stopped her and, all her energy drained out of her, she sank to the ground. And the girl exclaimed involuntarily: "Lord! If you exist, show me what the truth is and make it possible for me to know it." And the girl clearly heard not an inner voice, but one coming from *outside* her: "It's now or never!" This voice emboldened her, filling her with a kind of special energy she had never felt before; and she boldly walked ahead on the road to the port, paying no attention to the deepening twilight.

Two priests lived in that port village. The girl was possessed by a resolve to sail on a steamboat, but again she had no idea whither; and here she remembered that she had left home without any money, and that the only thing of value she had with her was the gold bracelet on her wrist. Her instinct was to ask one of the priests for help, but the wife of this priest greeted her sternly and V. V. P. lost all desire to ask her for help. She then went to the home of the other priest and asked him to lend her some money, keeping the bracelet as a surety. The priest, refusing to take a surety, trustingly gave her the money, seeing from her dress and her speech that she was a person of the upper classes who could not fail to inspire trust. After taking the money, she went to the dock. Two steamboats were docked there, which were due to leave at about the same time, one up the Volga, the other down it. This confused her and made her indecisive for a brief moment. For some reason her eyes were drawn to the steamboats' itineraries, and she saw that the town of K. was highlighted, eclipsing all the other stops. She took this as a sign from above and bought a ticket to K., not knowing what it was: whether it was a town or a village, what province it was in, or how far away it was. She had just enough money for the ticket, and had not a kopeck left over. The weather became bad. She had to travel in third class with all its discomforts, something she had not been accustomed to in the course of her pampered life. After arriving in K., she asked at the dock, again instinctively, without thinking about it, whether there might be some retreat here where she could pray. A peasant told her that there was a monastery for men about eight miles from town, and he showed her the road there. She set out, experiencing a horribly heavy feeling. Midway she stopped suddenly. It seemed to her that she was going to the wrong place and she asked a peasant who was riding by. "What idiot told you there's a monastery eight miles away and that it's for men?" the peasant said. "There's one that's two and a half miles away and it's for women." And he offered to take her, especially since he had to pass by this monastery anyway. He left her off about half a mile from the monastery, and she arrived there exactly when I was confessing the sisters.

I've already told about the confession. V. V. P. returned home by steamboat. Although she had hardly eaten anything, she experienced a state of such bliss that she felt neither cold nor hunger nor tiredness. This joyful mood was friend and dress and food and everything for her. She would have joyfully suffered for Christ if it were required.

It happened that her steamboat did not go directly to the port she needed, and she had to get off at an intermediate port and wait several hours for the next steamboat. There were almost no people at this port, and those who were there soon departed, leaving her to wait alone. This was early in the morning, between five and six. The port-master eyed her suspiciously, because she was dressed lightly, wearing her woolen shawl, although the weather was cold. He made a foul proposition. When it was rejected, this man, calm and restrained till then, was transformed: his face became evil and bestial and he tried to grab her and drag her into the cabin where he lived. "What are you doing, you madman? You call yourself a Christian, and I too am a Christian, and I even received communion yesterday," she shouted. She then directed an inner prayer toward God, asking him for help and firmly believing that he would intercede for her. And a miracle occurred. As if guided from above, she extended the index finger of her right hand and touched the chest of this man, who was so strong and towered over her as if she were an infant. This powerful figure staggered, and if the outer wall of the cabin hadn't supported him, he would have fallen on his back. He felt God's power and asked her forgiveness. Meanwhile, people were gathering to catch the steamboat which was about to dock, and V. V. P. boarded it and returned home. At home, new trials awaited her. While still on her journey she read in a newspaper that she had disappeared from her home, and it was not too subtly hinted that she had run away with evil intentions. Meanwhile the authorities at her school heard the rumor that, at that very time when she was in K. confessing and receiving communion, she had supposedly been seen in places forbidden to students, and so the authorities wanted to expel her. When it became clear where she had been, the sisters of the monastery and I were asked to submit a declaration stating that, at the time in question, she had been staying in the monastery for a religious purpose.

In conclusion, let me describe some of V. V. P.'s visions.

When she was only five years old, soon after the death of her little brother, she had a vision. She was sitting in the living room with her mother, the curtains on the windows were lowered, there was deep darkness in the street. Suddenly the little girl extended her hands toward the window and said to her mother: "Mama, Mama, look: my little brother is in heaven. He's stretching his hands out toward us. He's radiant like the sun . . ." And so on. The mother became frightened, raised the curtains, and tried to show her that there was nothing there and that it was night now, but the little girl joyfully moved toward the window and confirmed that she saw her radiant brother.

After she became religious, she had many visions, two of which were particularly remarkable. One came in a dream, the other when she "seemed" to be awake (she said that when she had that vision she was "outside herself"). In the dream she saw herself sitting in a dungeon. The windows had thick iron bars. A winged youth (resembling an angel depicted on icons) flies up to the window, breaks through the bars, and flies into the prison. At this time the girl is praying before an icon of the Mother of God with a silver cover. Grasping her by the shoulder, the angel exclaims angrily: "To whom are you praying, you mad girl?" She says: "To God." The youth rips the cover off the icon and instead of the Mother of God the girl sees something poorly defined, but she senses that Satan is depicted there. "Your mother is to blame for this," the angel says, and hearing these words, the girl wakes up.

When she was "outside herself," she saw the following. She was looking at the sky. In the distance, feathery clouds were gliding rapidly toward her as if blown by a strong wind. Above the clouds and in the midst of them some sort of Being was sitting, surrounded by a blinding radiance. As the clouds got closer, she saw that these were not clouds at all, but winged beings, resembling angels as depicted on icons. The Being surrounded by the radiance was Christ himself. Toward these winged beings two angels were flying, which from afar had appeared to her to be feathery clouds; gliding rapidly, they were taking up to heaven a young girl, the vision resembling an icon that depicts the soul separated from the body. The Savior rose to his full stature, and this girl, supported by the angels, made a deep reverence before him. Then everything disappeared.

Letter to the Editor of *Khristianin*:
Regarding Letter I. of Pavel Florensky's "Questions of Religious Self-Knowledge," I wish to say the following to him:

In the Name of the Father and of the Son and of the Holy Spirit.

(As I say this, I make the sign of the cross over myself.)

The content of the letter struck at my favorite theme: A Christian's religious-moral improvement is accomplished by means of two powers acting hand in hand—by the power of God and by the Christian's own power (or effort). Without the power of God none of a Christian's efforts or virtues will bring him to the measure of the maturity of Christ's accomplishment; on the other hand, if the power of God acts on a Christian without the latter's heroic exertion, it will return to its source unreceived and unignited in his heart. *Your world will return to you.* The efforts of individuals and of communities directed toward the establishment of the kingdom of God on earth by *purely human* collective exertion in the name of love, truth, equality, and so on—these efforts are the greatest ailment and error of this age. The leaders of this age are Father Petrov,[8] Leo Tolstoy, and those like them. To use a colorful expression, Father Petrov is hopping on one leg, and it's even his left one. His right leg, i.e., the power of God, has withered, and therefore he has hopped his way (and will continue to hop his way) to complete impotence and failure, which is what happened to Tolstoy.

Desiring, with the majority of my contemporaries, to become better in the sense and spirit of the gospel and desiring that my contemporaries also ascend into the understanding of truth, I constantly seek to grasp hold of God's power and call out: "My help comes from the Lord who created heaven and earth. The Lord is my strength and my salvation. Let

---

8. Grigory Spiridonovich Petrov (1868–1925), priest, advocate of Christian socialism.

the strong man not boast of his strength, let the wise man not boast of his wisdom, let the rich man not boast of his riches . . . but let him be praised who understands the Lord and does works of righteousness. Christ is my strength, God, and Lord, the holy Church sings piously, glorifying the Lord," etc. etc. . . . and all that is performed, sung, and read in the Christian Orthodox liturgy. I encounter here the holy sacraments; I find here the answer to the question, Where should I seek God's power and how can I constantly keep it near myself and always warm? Without doubt this is accomplished where it is accomplished. He who has been baptized in water has received God's power and received it in abundance (superabundant grace). He who bears the stamp of the gift of the Holy Spirit, in him that stamp can never be effaced. He who has partaken of the Holy Body and Blood of Christ has, without doubt, been united with Christ, and it is so with all the sacraments. It is useless to try to prove and explain this, i.e., to try to prove that God's power has descended upon a man and is preserved in him. This is not proved; it is felt. It is transmitted to others not through explanation but through inoculation: those who seek it and go towards it, or those who are guided to it by others, they are inoculated with it. The objection will be raised that some approach the sacrament with faith and fervor whereas others approach it without faith and coldly, as something that is required, but my answer to this objection is that however one approaches it, one nevertheless approaches the sacrament and is acted upon by it. If someone has approached it, he must in fact have some faith and fervor, and at the very least he is not against the sacraments. Here it is a question not of faith or unfaith, but of the degree of faith and perhaps of the degree of unfaith. But it is not for us to measure the degrees of faith and fervor and the degrees of the spiritual help and effectiveness of God's power. God alone will measure this.

Two powers always participate in the action of a sacrament—God's power and man's power. The first is invisible, the second is visible, and God's power will not act if man's power does not act. If the priest does not thrice immerse in water the one being baptized, while pronouncing the name of the Holy Trinity, the person will not be baptized and the Holy Spirit will not enter into him and give birth in him to a new spiritual Christian life. If the priest does not perform the liturgy, or does not bless the bread and wine in the liturgy while pronouncing certain words, the sacrament will not be enacted, the bread will remain bread and the wine will remain wine. Our God and Lord Jesus Christ and the Holy Spirit does not enact sacraments for man without the participation of man; or, as it is said, he does not save man without the participation of man. But it will be asked: Why does God need man here? Can God not just send down his power and save man without man's participation? I will answer: man is needed for the same reason that God is needed: the Son of God was made *man*. I feel (not know) that there is a profound connection here between the whole Orthodox and Gospel doctrine and all of God's work concerning man's salvation: God's wisdom is shrouded in mystery here.

Mr. Florensky's letter vividly expresses our contemporary pessimism or—to put it in an Orthodox way—a sense of hopelessness, a despairing sense that contemporary Christian society (or, more precisely, Orthodox Christian society) is bereft of the efficacy of God's power, fails to live the gospel life, suffers from a deficit of faith and morality, does not possess the spirit of Christ's life, is left with nothing but empty form and ritual, and so on. This is all a lot of nonsense; whether evil-intentioned or due to ignorance or thoughtlessness, it is pure nonsense, a superficial view implanted, most likely, by the insane press (which nowadays multiplies like poisonous mushrooms in foul weather). People take it upon themselves to judge matters outside their competence: they judge the state of Orthodoxy though they are far from Orthodoxy; they judge the sacraments though they do not recognize them; they judge the Liturgy though they do not participate in it. This depresses me greatly. Meanwhile, I, a sinful priest (together with many holy archpriests and priests), bemoaning my sins and errors, am gladdened by our Orthodox common Russian people, because of their pure faith, their virtues, their piety; it is not I who teach them, but rather they—my parishioners, who are not only my parishioners but also my spiritual children—who teach me. They teach me not only their virtues but even the subtle dogmas of faith. And I am amazed that these simple, uneducated peasants know the Scriptures without having studied. I am amazed by how they think about Christ, the Holy Trinity, the Empress of Heaven, and the sacraments. The most learned theology cannot give a comparable definition of the truths of Orthodoxy.

Amen, amen I say, that they are taught by the Holy Spirit, descending on their hearts and imprinting his seal by anointment in the holy sacraments. "The anointing which ye have received of Him abideth in you, and ye need not that any man teach you" (1 John 2:27). This is hidden from the eyes of the wise and rational, who say blasphemously: faith is weak; there is no gospel in the life of Christians, and so on. Florensky writes: "one does not see the acquisition of the Spirit among Christians;

one does not feel the power of God within them." Approach and look, is my answer to him. Scrape away the ashes, and you will see the fire, which always tries to hide: that is the nature of Christ's fire. I have much to write on contemporary questions and even more to say to those with whom it is necessary to speak. But I have little talent when it comes to writing for publication, and I do not regret that. My work is a higher one: to serve the sanctuary, to illuminate my parishioners with the holy sacraments, to pray and to converse with them to the extent of our faith and knowledge of God.

May God keep me from leaving the service of the sanctuary and of my parishioners and becoming a contributor to our newspapers.

However much Florensky might desire to clarify the sacraments in *Khristianin*, he will never accomplish this. The sacraments are clarified and assimilated through the performance of the sacraments; Orthodoxy is clarified by an Orthodox life, not by books.

Therefore there is a reason experienced archpriests and priests have told us, and tell us, to pray to God, go to church, and receive the holy sacraments. It is not known whether or not St. Seraphim spoke against this. If he did, the one who heard him and tried to convey what he said (I have read about this) failed to understand Father Seraphim and was not able to convey what he said. But an inquiring believer who is not satisfied with the advice "go to church and pray to God," and who desires to have a more profound conversation with his pastor, must find a pastor and spiritual father who will satisfy his needs and heal his ailments. Our Orthodox pastors are constantly maligned but, as always, they shine their light on all those who are within the church. Yes, on those who are within the church, but they do not shine their light on those who flee from the Holy Church—on the newspaper scribblers who do not seek light from pastors, but wish to shine their own light on them.

Our contemporary religious intellectual, weak, nervous, and, sensitive, wants to ascend in one step the ladder from earth to heaven, from sinfulness to saintliness: he jumps up but falls down on his head and is smashed to pieces (Father Petrov, Tolstoy). That is not how things should be done. One should establish a firm footing on the first step, and then climb cautiously, without hurrying, onto the second step, and so on. One who desires to believe and to have knowledge of his faith, must begin, for example, with the cross: he must put a cross around his neck and never take it off; he must learn to make the sign of the cross correctly; he must read the simple and usual prayers, and so on. It will be explained to me that a cross around one's neck and prayer mean nothing without faith, without an understanding of the cross, without the ardor of the heart. My answer is: wear the cross without faith, without ardor of the heart, without awareness, and this little thing will teach you about the great thing. Once a person puts on a cross, crosses himself, and obeys others, this is already a faith in the cross, an obedient, childlike faith.

Regarding the hopelessness glimpsed in Mr. Florensky, I will say that he himself suffers from presumption, and in relation to others, even in relation to the entire Christian community, he suffers from hopelessness. (I write this not to denigrate him but to help him know Christian hope.) This, too, is a contemporary ailment that is common to our religious intelligentsia. One cannot fail to observe that faith is growing stronger at the present time, or at least that the search for faith is growing stronger, and that the faith and love of the intelligentsia are even boundless. But the third (or rather the second) virtue, hope, is either absent or very weak in the believing and loving intelligentsia, and that is why these two pillars of piety—faith and love—are unconnected and perilously unsteady. Join together Christian faith and love with Christian hope and you will get stability and groundedness.

I ask the editors and Mr. Florensky to forgive me for sending a rough manuscript. I write not for publication; I am only giving my impressions and thoughts on contemporary questions. I am not a literary man. Signed: Priest D. G. T. of the Church of the Transfiguration of the Savior in the town of T.

February 16, 1907.

* * *

In another letter, which, however, does not deal with our question, the same writer writes, among other things, the following: "In my letter to you I posed a very serious question—the question of Christian hope and of the harmonious action of two powers in salvation (making it possible to walk on two feet without limping). I repeat this now. I recommend that you occupy yourself with these questions; you will find the definition of Christian hope in Philaret (in his Catechism). When you have some free time, write to me about the results of your inquiries."

Two More Letters

I.

The editors received an anonymous letter, signed "A monk." The fact reported in this letter can be interpreted in different ways, depending on one's general view of the sacraments and of the sacrament of repentance in particular. But the letter is typical: behind its simple words one feels hopelessness and the coldness of despair, which causes one to grieve both for the author of the letter and for oneself. Several of its artless sentences deeply affect our consciousness. The secret sores of our churchly life are revealed. But let the letter speak for itself. Here it is:

> In *Khristianin*, issue number 1, P. A. Florensky poses the question: What is experienced and felt by those who perform and receive sacraments?
> I will tell what I personally experienced as regards the sacrament of repentance. This was long ago, when I was only thirty years old (I am now sixty-five) and had just been tonsured and ordained as a hierodeacon; the liturgy required a great deal of preparation. There were times when my conscience said: "It's necessary to confess; you can't partake of the Holy Gifts the way you are." My cell was next to the confessor's cell. I'd leave my cell, go up to the confessor's door, stop, and my thought would say: "It's not necessary, don't bother him, we're not in a fast, after all." I'd stand there for a while and go away: "No, I don't need to bother him." And I'd return to my cell. But my conscience would say: "What are you doing? How can you serve at the liturgy? Go and confess." Again I'd go up to the confessor's door, and my thought would say again: "Don't bother him. It's awkward." And I'd stand there for a while and go away again, but my conscience would keep saying: "How can you approach the Holy Gifts?" And after a long struggle, I decided at last to say a prayer and to enter his cell.... When I left it, I felt as if I had taken off a tremendously heavy fur coat. I felt as if I could fly—I was so light and my heart leapt so joyously from the fullness of some inexpressible lightness. It's impossible to express this in words.
> Such is the power of the sacrament of repentance.
> This happened more than once. But, alas, it happened long ago.
> A monk.
> Forgive me for being illiterate.

II.

Here, also, is a letter from a village priest, who is a personal acquaintance of mine:

> I apologize for sending my letter so late. In *Khristianin* you have been publishing letters from readers on the question of the sacraments. Even if my letter is the last one, I cannot be silent about several incidents that I witnessed in my practice in connection with the sacraments of confession and communion offered to sick people.
>
> I must first say that I have always believed in the power and efficacy of the holy sacraments. The incidents I am going to describe have served to confirm me in my belief.
>
> The first incident: I was summoned to the village of Dubininskaya to give communion to a sick peasant (P. V.). He had formerly been a confirmed drunkard. I had told him many times to abandon his vices, but to no effect. He continued to sin. But now he had become sick, and so sick that, by the time I arrived, he could no longer speak, though he was still conscious. After the pre-communion prayers, I started confessing the sick man. I told him that this was God's way of punishing him for his sins; he nodded as a sign that he agreed with me. I summoned him to reform his life and leave behind his past sins. I told him that, if he repented and made it his firm intention to stop sinning, God might open his lips and raise him from this sickbed. P. V. prayed and, looking at the holy icons, he was clearly summoning God's help; his eyes expressed the holy intention not to repeat his sins. I finished the confession, gave him communion, and told his family members: "Let us pray, brothers and sisters, for our dear sick one." I then started to read the prayers that are customarily read over sick people; I read with deep faith and almost with tears. Guess what happened? The moment I finished the prayer, the sick man started to speak. He said to his wife: "Give this *polotentse*[9] to the Father and let him hang it on the icon of the Mother of God in our church." After this, the sick man started to recover rapidly until he became completely well. I told him to confess and to receive communion again in church; and in church, before the holy cross and the gospel, he repented publicly of his sin of drunkenness and vowed to abstain for half a year.

9. Small tablet icon.

That is how the healing of a sick parishioner occurred before my very eyes. I explain this healing as due to the action of the holy sacraments of confession and communion and of the prayers for him of the believers.

The second incident happened in a neighboring parish. Because the priest there was absent, I was summoned to the village of Svatkovo to give communion to a sick youth (sixteen or seventeen years old), Vasily Shirshanin. The woman who had come to get me said that the sick youth had lost the power to speak, and thus she asked me to go to him as quickly as possible. I got ready quickly and rode off.

The sick youth had truly lost the power to speak, and until my arrival he had been unconscious. He lay on a bench; I went up to him, took his hand, and said: "Vasya, get up, I am going to give you communion." And—miracle of miracles!—the sick youth got up at once and started speaking. I began to confess him at once and gave him holy communion. After that, he fell again into unconsciousness and died in that state.

From this incident it can be seen that the Lord, not desiring the death of a sinner, wanted the sick youth to be cleansed of his sins and to be united with him in the holy sacrament of communion. And thus he visibly, so to speak, confirmed the salvific nature and necessity of the sacraments for every man.

The incidents I have described are not a product of my imagination, but the absolute truth. I affirm this before all the saints. Alexander Sokolov, priest of the village of Buzhaninovo (Vladim. Province, Aleksandrovsk. District).

Dogmatism and Dogmatics

*To my uniquely cherished friend,
Sergey Semyonovich Troitsky*[1]

Honored Attendees!

I apologize beforehand for the polished tone of the thoughts I am about to express—a tone that accords poorly with the author's ignorance. I found it necessary to pose in a somewhat stylized way the problems I confronted, to highlight them emphatically. The reason for this is not an overconfidence that forgets about the nuances and half-tones of thought, but a fear of getting lost in a series of "althoughs" and "on the other hands." A lack of time thus impels the author to formulate things more sharply than he would have wished.

> Ye worship ye know not what . . .
> But the hour cometh, and now is,
> when the true worshipers shall worship
> the Father in spirit and in truth. . . .
> God is a Spirit: and they that worship him
> Must worship him in spirit and in truth.
>
> John 4:22–24

---

1. Sergey Semyonovich Troitsky (1881–1911) was perhaps Florensky's closest friend. He was married to Florensky's sister, Olga.

Speech read on January 20, 1906, at a meeting of the philosophical circle of the Moscow Theological Academy.

I.

To worship God "in spirit and in truth," "en pneumati kai alētheia"—that is the demand of the twice-born. A renewed consciousness can no longer be satisfied with the mere givenness of God; it also demands that he be justified. Man desires to worship God not only as a fact, not as an all-shattering power, and not even as his Protector or Master; this Power and Protector can be an object of worship only in its Truth, in its justice as the Father. Prior to the justification of man, one seeks the justification of God; prior to anthropodicy, one seeks theodicy.

Anthropodicy and theodicy! These are the two elements that constitute religion, for the latter is based on the idea of the salvation, the idea of the deification of man's entire being. The first of these elements is, in the main, a *Sacrament*, a mystery, i.e., a real descent of God down to humanity, God's self-humiliation or *kenosis*. But before this salvific and purifying (cathartic) Divine self-humiliation (a self-humiliation that justifies man before God) can be received by humanity, it must fulfill the second of these elements— the justification of God. This aspect of religion is, in the main, a teaching, a dogma, and it therefore represents humanity's ascent in contemplation toward God, humanity's magnification or deification, its theosis (but only in contemplation). But we are speaking now only of the final element, of the necessity of God, of the dogma that establishes God's right to demand the justification of man.

The man who can say "the Sun of Emmaus has gilded my days"[2] or who has at least experienced the multiply reflected shining of this Sun—this man will bow down neither out of fear nor out of self-seeking, nor out of gratitude. He will bow down only out of pure veneration of holiness. "Thrice Holy," received from the heavenly powers, is the most characteristic hymn of the new man: he directs the wail "have mercy!" toward the Being that God is conscious of as the Holy Being, the Being strong in its holiness and therefore immortal, again because it is holy. The word "Holy," pronounced each time this Being is addressed, is not an attribute equivalent to the other attributes; it is much more central and fundamental in the characterization of the Good Being and conditions the possibility of the other attributes for the consciousness.

Whether God is a punisher or a benefactor, one will not bend one's knees before his unjustified power, before a might that is not recognized to

---

2. From Vyacheslav Ivanov's poem "*Mi fur serpi amiche*."

be the other side of his holiness; and not bearing in himself his justification, he will necessarily be subservient to the commands of inexorable Fate—that is the lot of everything that is nonabsolute. Then, Prometheus, the Titans, and all the other heroes who rebelled against God in the name of Truth and Goodness—these heroes become infinitely dear to all those illuminated with the "Light of Christ" and blessed by the "Good News." This apparent rebellion against God is revealed before healed eyes to be the bearing of God in oneself; and the transformative Prometheus, who suffered out of love for humanity, a crucified god with lanced side, turns out to be—in his rebellion against God—a precursor of Christianity. But it is only through the yearning for the coming Christ that this prematurely awakened consciousness can find refreshment from its feverish agony and break through the circle of this mirage of delirium; only the self-proving ray of Tabor will illuminate the tormenting darkness; only the heat of Emmaus will "ignite the heart." The power of the imaginary heaven-dwellers burns and consumes the Martyr, but the demand for truth rises with glorious divine and divinely given flames.

> Who is the bearer of God? Who is the rebel against God?
> Terrible, O terrible, is the gods' approach and their kiss!
> Having embraced the god, he fights the god;
> Having embraced the flame, chosen by the flame,
> He sinks in the flame with his audacious spirit—
> His dust of the earth is burnt![3]

Let us recall the idea of deification, which is like the fixed polar guiding star in the spiritual sky of the Christian ascetic—this idea that fully possesses the ascetic and attracts like a magnet his iron will. Let us recall the titanic challenge to Caesar from the Great Cappodocian: "I am commanded to become divine and cannot bow down before a creature."[4] Do we not hear in these words a terrible theomachic thunder, which is an echo of the ancient thunder that led Prometheus to the shores of the full-watered Phasis, to the hoary precipices of the multi-peaked Caucasus? Do we not hear the crashing noise of Mount Pelion being piled upon Mount Ossa? But that which had been lawlessness for the mythological consciousness became an obligatory

---

3. From Vyacheslav Ivanov's poem "Tantalus."
4. Basil the Great's response when commanded by the Roman emperor to accept Arianism.

requirement, a duty for the Christian consciousness. This was the great spiritual revolution brought into the world by Christ; this was the legitimization of man in his Jacobian relation to God.[5]

A new duty appeared in the consciousness—the duty to worship God "in spirit and in truth." Whatever might have been the attitude toward Christianity of men of the new times, this duty encircled every soul with such strong roots that it was no longer possible to return to the past. Men who were on the road to Damascus and whose eyes were blinded by this sudden lightning of renewal, these men were organically no longer capable of accepting God as a simple given. The new men became Prometheuses; and until it becomes certain of God's person, until it sees him with its own eyes as Holy, the reborn consciousness will remain without God. Contemporary man will be tormented by the phantasmagoria of Sheol; he will fall irresistibly into the bottomless "outer darkness"; he will cry out of the depths unto the Lord, whom he does not know, but he will not be able to worship a Lord whose law consists perhaps only in power, who is perhaps an idol and usurper. Is it not this depth of Christian consciousness that sometimes produces the most zealous Sauls and the most frenzied atheists? After Christ, the "Unknown God" becomes a Great *contradictio in adjecto*, a Despot, a Powerful Destroyer of what is divine in man. The Christian temple can be dedicated only "to the Known God," as is inscribed above the doors of a certain cathedral.[6]

"To the known God," to the God known by us as God, as Absoluteness, as Spirit, as Holiness and Truth. That is the initial formula of the Christian worship of God. The demand for "knowability" is an original and permanent demand of the redeemed person. "Ye worship ye know not what," Christ tells the Gentiles. "But the hour cometh, and now is, when the true worshipers shall worship the Father in spirit and in truth ..." And as if revealing that this prophecy is already being fulfilled, in his last discourse he notes the change in consciousness: "Henceforth I call you not servants," the Lord tells his disciples. "For the servant knoweth not what his lord doeth: but I have called you friends; for all things that I have heard of my Father I have made known unto you" (John 15:15).

True worship of God is inaccessible to the pagan consciousness because paganism does not know the Object of its worship, views it slavishly, externally, and unfreely, and therefore does not have the power to penetrate into

---

5. Allusion to Jacob wrestling with God.
6. Florensky has in mind the Uspensky (Dormition) Cathedral of the Trinity Lavra of St. Sergius.

its inner essence—into the Person of God: "No man hath seen God at any time" (1 John 4:12). In contrast, the mysteries of God are communicated to the Christian consciousness: the Christian knows the Father, whom he worships, and therefore his relation to him is that of a friend and son, not that of a slave; his consciousness penetrates inside the person of God and is not satisfied solely with the manifestation of God's powers. "He that hath seen me hath seen the Father" (John 14:9). The ancient theomachy could not be satisfied with the contemplation of God's powers, which are immanent to the world and therefore alien to the divine principle in man. Christianity elevates consciousness above all that is immanent to the world and brings us face to face with the transcendent Person of God. And therefore the fundamental given of Christianity turns out to be the fundamental unknown of non-Christian theomachy.

This duty—to worship God as the Truth—is fulfilled in man's direct experiences of God, because only in them can God be given as a reality; and only in this reality itself, and not in any concept invented by us, is God's essence revealed, his essence which *implicite* contains the data for his justification. Only standing face to face before God can man with his illuminated consciousness grasp God's truth and bless God for all things. "But the great mystery here consists in the fact that the transitory earthly countenance and the eternal truth touched each other here. Jointly with the earthly truth, the action of eternal truth is accomplished."[7] And when this "touching of other worlds" is accomplished, the stunned heart will suddenly tremble and be riven with ineffable joy. And it will sing its ardently exultant hymn to the Lord, thanking and praising, and weeping for all things—especially for those things that seem horrible and foul to the unilluminated consciousness: "For God hath concluded them all in unbelief,[8] that he might have mercy upon all. O the depth of the riches both of the wisdom and knowledge of God! How unsearchable are his judgments, and his ways past finding out! For who hath known the mind of the Lord? Or who hath been his counselor? Or who hath first given to him, and it shall be recompensed unto him again? For of him, and through him, and to him, are all things: to whom be glory for ever. Amen" (Rom. 11:32–36).

God will then pierce the misty miasmas of the unredeemed consciousness with a luminous ray, and the freshening wind will disperse the suffocating fog of the ancient myth. God will gaze at us like the Father, like the

---

7. A musing of Father Zosima in Dostoevsky's *The Brothers Karamazov*.
8. The Russian translation of this text has "disobedience," not "unbelief."

bright sun through a cloud-free, washed-clean atmosphere. The imaginary theomachy will turn out to be a search for the Father; and Prometheus will throw himself down on his knees before this Father who has been found. "You are holiness and goodness, our Father. I humble myself here before you, stung in my heart with your love. I desire what you desire, for I know that my own will and my own thought will yield nothing as good as your will and thought, my Father. I obey you—not because you are strong, not because you crush and break me. Rather, I see your justice, O Lord; I see your truth. It is not you who demand that I put my trust in your will; rather, it is I myself who give myself in joy. I waver and pray that the cup of my earthly humiliation, of my earthly kenosis, pass me by. But, making an effort to conquer my weakness, I say: Let your will be done, not mine, for I know your truth and your holiness."

That is what Prometheus will say. That which before could have been torn out of him neither by the horror of theomachy, nor by Zeus's lightning bolts, nor by the all-powerful tortures of crucifixion, he now gives like a child to the Heavenly Father, having gained knowledge of his truth in the prayerful experience of purified consciousness.

II.

However, both history and everyday experience attest that the experiences of prayer, these wavering and extremely fluid elements of consciousness, are, by themselves, insufficient for life in its entirety. This is true even for the esthetic domain, where the external has so much significance. This is what a poet-philosopher says:

> O, my poor verses, the poem of my love—
> Has your charm died so rapidly?
> Or is my heart today closed to yesterday's feelings?
> Where is their former freshness? Did it ever live in me?
> How everything has changed, how cold my theme has grown!
>
> But in you my love and life once lived,
> O my poor verses of yesterday![9]

---

9. From M. Guyot's poem "My Verses of Yesterday" (in I. I. Tkhorzhevsky's translation). I have abbreviated this poem.

Dogmatism and Dogmatics

But this is even truer for purely inner religious experiences.

> I caught this thought on the road and used the first poor words I could find to bind it so that it wouldn't fly away. But now it has died because of those cruel words and is hanging and dangling from them; and looking at it, I can barely remember why I felt such joy when I caught this bird.[10]

That which is clear today, so often becomes obscure tomorrow! That which is decided with finality and absolute clarity in the experience of a moment, becomes an eternal question again in the hours and minutes of another day, when the heart is again dark. The experiences of prayer are too fleeting, too ephemeral; and this is true not only for ordinary people but even for the greatest saints. These experiences must be given a structure; a skeleton of concepts and schemata must be created to support their living flesh. This is where reason plays a legitimate role.

A concept, having no intrinsic value, acquires conditional value through its connection with the experiences it schematizes, just as an unstable experience is differentiated, shaped, fixed, and stabilized through a concept that schematizes it. Direct interaction with experiences is replaced by operation over concepts, and the advantage gained is the same as when writing is introduced into the domain of thought or paper currency is introduced into the economic domain. Experiences are reduced to a common denominator and become comparable to one another. The unstoppable retreat of the past is arrested by the accumulation, growth, enrichment, and diversification of experience. Finally, we acquire an orientation in the winding recesses of our spiritual life; this is something like a geographic map that enables us to reproduce previous experiences and to firmly retain their boundaries in our memory. All this makes a system of concepts and schemata absolutely necessary for us.

History gives us the same palpable sense of the need to schematize experiences. The satisfaction of this need constitutes the whole history of science and philosophy, theological as well as general-cultural. What does the history of the Ecumenical Councils represent if not a stubborn, indefatigable attempt to create a system of concepts and schemata that would stylize and clearly and with certainty delineate the appropriate experiences of spiritual life, while doing this as economically as possible, i.e., using as few terms as possible? To unite the greatest fullness of schematized material with the least complexity of the schemata that are united into a single structure—that is the task which

---

10. From Nietzsche's *The Gay Science*. I have translated the translation used by Florensky.

confronted each of the holy fathers. Many a theologian of that great epoch of the dogmatic disputes tried to construct such a system, but the inevitable result was a one-sided system incapable of embracing the fullness of the church's spiritual life. And so it was necessary to turn to conciliar reason, to the supra-individual collective consciousness and organization of the church, to her supra-personal *sobornost*. The fullness of experiences corresponding to the latter makes it possible to avoid one-sidedness and to create a system of concepts that embraces as simply and economically as possible the totality of the church's spiritual life, the totality of her spiritual tasks and strivings at a given moment. Truly, one is amazed by the purely mathematical precision and expressiveness of the Christological formulations, where it is impossible to change a single concept. The system of schemata is so compact and of a piece that if we touch any part of it, the whole edifice collapses. Likewise, what does the whole history of science and philosophy represent in its formal aspect if not an unceasing attempt to develop a series of concepts that unify as economically as possible a particular scientific material?

III.

What is needed is a "dogmatics," this word used in the broadest sense as a system of fundamental schemata for the most valuable experiences, something like a concise guide to eternal life. First of all, this refers to the religious domain in a more narrow sense. The contemporary consciousness seeks formulas avidly and in a great agony of spirit.

> Behold, the days come, saith the Lord GOD, that I will send a famine in the land, not a famine of bread, nor a thirst for water, but of hearing the words of the LORD: And they shall wander from sea to sea, and from the north even to the east, they shall run to and fro to seek the word of the LORD, and shall not find it. (Amos 8:11–12)

The throat grows parched and all one's insides burn; more and more unbearable becomes the agonizing thirst for dogmatics. But . . . instead of dogmatics we have dogmatism.

People will ask me: "What about Sylvester, the two Filarets, and Makary?[11] What more do you need? Are you seeking new dogmas?" I hasten to

---

11. Allusion to the authors of standard Orthodox dogmatic handbooks: Bishop Sylvester

reassure all my Orthodox and non-Orthodox listeners: I accept the content of this dogmatism and I am not speaking of the creation of new dogmas; rather, I am complaining about the fact that people are ignorant of the old dogmas, about the fact that it is almost impossible to grasp them as religious truths. If anyone asks me about the above authors, my answer will be: "How do you view our dogmatics? For example, how do you view Makary?"[12]

If for a moment my listeners stopped suppressing their spontaneous reactions, I foresee that their response to me would be an unending series of yawns, both non-Orthodox and Orthodox, with the latter predominating.

Let us not try to assign blame here. We are compelled to admit the fact that at the present time our system of faith-teaching has suffered as great a damage as it is possible for a spiritual value to suffer: it has become devalued for our consciousness. The salt has lost its savor; the light has gone out. The hearth has stopped warming the consciousness; the center of life has turned out to be outside of life. The one thing that is needful seems superfluous and unnecessary for the majority of people. Our dogmatic system seems boring, so boring that people do not even take the time to polemicize with it; those who praise it admit to themselves that dogmatics is good, but that it is not for them but "for someone else." In other words, it exists not for life, not for people, but for some unknown purpose.

The slight yawns produced in answer to my question about dogmatics are only a poor cover for the terrifying abysses of the contemporary consciousness into which the holiest and greatest treasures of the spirit have disappeared. But in our carelessness we do not notice this, and we have forgotten the task that has been entrusted to us. "Sanctify them through Thy truth: Thy word is truth" (John 17:17), Christ prays for us. "That they might know Thee, the only true God" (John 17:3), he says about us. And if Love Itself did not pronounce these words, they would sound like unbearable mockery to us: Do we really apprehend religion as the Truth? Do we really know God as the foundation of all truth and all certainty? And on our part, do we have any relation to the Living Center of our religion?

Let us not bury our heads in the sand of neglect, hiding like an ostrich from danger. Now, more than ever, is the time to clarify our relation to the

---

(Malevansky), author of *An Essay on Orthodox Dogmatic Theology*, 2nd ed. (Kiev, 1892–97); Archbishop Filaret (Gumilevsky), author of *Orthodox Dogmatic Theology*, 2nd ed. (Chernigov, 1865); Metropolitan Filaret (Drozdov), author of *An Extensive Christian Catechesis of the Orthodox Catholic Eastern Church* (1820); and Metropolitan Makary (Bulgakov), author of *Orthodox Dogmatic Theology* (Moscow, 1848–53).

12. Makary's handbook was probably the most commonly used one.

Christian worldview. It appears that the hour is at hand when it will no longer be possible to remain a semi-Christian and a semi-atheist, to remain neither hot nor cold, to remain lukewarm; when, *nolens volens*, it will be necessary to take a stand either for or against true freedom.

A number of deficiencies are pointed out—and justly so—in the "dogmatic handbooks" produced here in Russia, especially in Metropolitan Makary's handbook. These deficiencies must of course be taken into account, but to remove them would be like trying to put out a large building fire with two or three drops of water. It is true that these unfortunate deficiencies damage the architectonic integrity of the dogmatics, but is it worth lamenting them if it is more important to ask whether students of this dogmatics see its integrity and harmonious stateliness? Do they see how the parts are interconnected into a whole? Do they ponder on the dogmas, which are formulated with mathematical precision and are interwoven like a fine lace fabric? Or do they see this fabric as "woven out of errors and imaginings"? Do they understand the unity of the plan, the mutual conditionedness and interdependence of the different concepts and propositions which, like organs of a single organism, serve a single ordered whole? To my knowledge, all this remains in utter obscurity and dogmatics is regarded not as a system, not as a structure of schemata, but as a chaotic heap of texts and words.

There is also another necessary correction that must be stated, a more important one. But it too is insufficient. Namely, we have a system of Orthodox dogmas, but we need an orthodox dogmatics as a truly living religious worldview. In other words, to the system of dogmas a propaedeutic must be added.

I repeat: Neither the correction of particular deficiencies in the dogmatics nor its appreciation as an interconnected whole is, in itself, sufficient. There is a more serious circumstance.

Life flows on outside of our faith-teaching, and faith-teaching flows on outside of life. Here it goes without saying that I do not take life to mean any kind of economic or political movements. No, even much deeper strata of the spirit—deeply internal disturbances in the vastness of the spirit—turn out to be outside of faith-teaching. Another question is whether, on this path, the currents of life might not flow into the swamps of false mysticism and onto the sands of sterile positivism. But the fact is that even purely inner moral and religious life has pushed its streams into other domains. Furious waves of disturbed flow beat against the shores and tear at the roots of thousand-year-old oaks. Rushing by, this flow drags along beams from fallen structures, domestic utensils, and familial holy objects . . .

Having torn itself away from all living and intimate things, from all the things that are near and infinitely dear to us, from all the things that grip our heart with a painfully sweet yearning for the distances; and having lost the fragrance of personal religious experience, the system of religious concepts has stopped being convincing for those who reject it and attractive for those who accept it. It is not appropriate to speak here of believers and nonbelievers as synonymous with the Orthodox and the non-Orthodox. Nowadays we encounter believing atheists as well as nonbelieving Orthodox. Just as the latter, bereft of spiritual content, are prepared with ignorant indifference to accept any schema of a certain brand in order not to burden themselves with mental labor, confessing beforehand anything on which is written "*Avec approbation et privilège du Roi*," be it the Creed or someone's invention; so the former, tormented by the agonizing need to shape the flames of spiritual life and not knowing how to use already-existing schemata for this purpose, do not desire and are unable to accept them slavishly, to accept them without seeing their truth. And just as an "Orthodox" sometimes, directly or indirectly, makes the cynical pronouncement that "God is not important to me, but only cult is"; so an "atheist" sometimes admits shamefully that he needs God and only God, and that all the rest is tinsel and rubbish. But there is no God in our dogmatics. Tolstoy noted not without justification that many people believe not in the dogmas but in the fact that it is necessary to believe in them: a dead and empty form does not contain inner truth and is therefore an idol. We are helped here neither by the filigree finish of dogmatic concepts, nor by the system's profundity of content, nor by tradition. The system has become hopelessly boring and hopelessly unconvincing for the majority of people, and often even for those who sincerely accept the entire gospel. It would be too hasty, however, to blame those who sincerely admit they have fallen away. It would be more correct to examine whether any elements of the same mood are shared by many others who have not fallen away and then, admitting the sad truth, to clarify the cause of this coldness. Only by removing this cause can we have a living attitude toward the system of dogmas, this lace fabric of crystals formed over many centuries out of the tenderest and most fragrant exhalations of the soul toward heaven in the purifying cold of reason.

Dogmatics has been replaced by dogmatism. That is the key to solving the riddle of our coldness toward its beautiful but (for us) lifeless forms. In the contemporary consciousness dogmatics has lost its connection with living feelings and living perceptions. The body of the religious worldview has been separated from its soul. We concerned ourselves only with ourselves, not desiring to abandon our point of view even for a moment; and as a result we have forgotten how we came to this point of view. No wonder, then, that others cannot find entry into this grandiose Gothic cathedral, beautiful in its whole and in its parts but deprived of a porch and steps. Its numberless windows, covered with spider webs, give off a somber blackness; and passersby, looking away in fear, hasten to their domestic chapels. Meanwhile, the faithful, unable to find the exit from their own temple, roam pale and lifeless between majestic columns, gaze out of the arrow-shaped windows, and, instead of prayers, mutter with their powerless lips anathemas against the passersby in the street who perhaps (and this happens very often) desire to enter the temple to pray. Instead of accepting mutual aid in deciphering our own soul, instead of engaging in communal spiritual labor, we become angry with those who cannot break through the ice of our petrified dogmatism and, abandoned to the vicissitudes of fate, go their own way. Or we ourselves turn our backs to the infinite treasures collected by the preceding generations; we turn our backs instead of taking upon ourselves the accumulated sin and melting with the true fire of God-knowledge all the ice that shackles the great edifices of the holy fathers, our predecessors who had the holy audacity to inscribe over the door: "To the Known God." Yes, forgotten are the traditions of the holy dogmatists; forgotten are the testaments of the ancient Russian philosophers who built the temples of St. Sophia, the Wisdom of God, and strove to worship the "Known God." But what are the passersby to do? Where are the doorkeepers of the temple? What secret word will open for the passerby the doors of the majestic cathedral? Let us first try to be comprehensible and convincing for people of other camps; let us try not to be lulled into pleasant sleep by the approbation of those (and only of those) who think as we do, approbation often accompanied by portentous smiles; let us abandon the absurd habit of beginning an investigation with dogmatic statements. Not only are such statements not binding until they are proved in one way or another (the word "proved" being understood here in the broadest sense), but they are even absolutely incomprehensible, since they consist of terms that, in such an exposition, have no real content. Before speaking with someone, one should not only define one's terms but also explain them, that is, one should fill them with living concrete content by referring to what one's interlocutor has experienced or by infecting him with one's own personal experience, by sharing one's fullness with him. In the contrary case, one gets nothing but word-constructs, argumentation with words alone, which ends with one's opponent being defeated—with words. But at the very moment when, drenched in sweat, you are celebrating your victory and imagining that you have proved something to your opponent, he remains completely calm and utterly indifferent to his defeat. Your victory is so much smoke.

Let us set aside all empty talk about the usefulness of such exertions of proof for society, exertions that amount to nothing more than self-gratification. Let us look at the matter from the practical point of view.

Any argument that is unconnected with experience, untransparent for intuition, and unconvincing psychologically—any such argument, regardless of its provability, will be nothing more than a special variant of the *argumentum baculinum*.[13] One should not forget that people live, first of all, by the spirit, and only afterwards do they draw abstract conclusions from what they have experienced: theoretical propositions are only schemata or signs of actual experiences; it is the experiences that are the source, life, and goal of any theory. An argument in the domain of religion and morality has full validity only when it is convincing, that is, when the truth it tries to prove is discovered intuitively on concrete material, when a general proposition is embodied in a unitary feeling of truth experienced with one's whole being. If they are estranged from the life of the spirit, theories and systems hang suspended in the air and the rainbow colors of experience fade like the colors of certain sea animals that have been thrown onto the shore out of their native element, leaving a gray, boring mass of colorless schemata. The interrelation of concepts, their relative topography, easily visible in the living organism of a worldview, gets twisted up in lifeless, fibrous remains, in the same way that the crystalline colors of a jellyfish melt away when it has been thrown out onto rocks on the shore.

What would people say about mathematical computations that have no beginning or end? If you mechanically perform a sequence of operations without knowing what their goal is, what data they are based on, or what the signs used mean, your whole work will seem infinitely unconvincing to you, even though you do not find in yourself the strength to object to the operations at any single point of the process. Strictly speaking, not only are you unable to show the falseness of these operations, but you have no sense of their truthfulness either. That, in the best case, is the status of contemporary dogmatics, mechanically based as it is on the authority of Sacred Scripture and Sacred Tradition, a Scripture and a Tradition which (under the most favorable conditions) do not give us any reason to contradict them but which also do not make their truthfulness clear to the majority of people.

---

13. The argument of the cudgel, i.e., an appeal to force.

What truly convinces us in an argument is a power of proof that is more than a mere formal victory over one's opponent, a power of proof whose logic is grounded solidly in experience instead of being a kind of airship voyage through a domain of arbitrary invention, a domain of the imaginary, not of what has been really experienced. Our dogmatics lacks this power of convincing us, and the result is before our eyes. Some people go into a frenzy when arguing about some insignificant distinction of dogma or ritual (e.g., about the number of fingers to use when making the sign of the cross), but they are often uncertain about the most essential things. And it is hard to count the number of fundamental ideas once considered to be of vital importance that have become alien to the consciousness of the majority of people and are preserved in the dogmatic handbooks solely in order to lower the grades of young pupils and to question the Orthodoxy of grown people. The notion of evil, for example, has disappeared from the spiritual horizon, and the opinion that it is nothing more than an insufficiency of good determines everyone's relation to the world, although in conversations this hidden semi-Pelagianism or Pelagianism of the majority of people is covered up by a meaningless repetition of the church teaching. One can say with even greater certainty that the majority of people regard the whole cycle of eschatological ideas as only a means to condemn socialists of various stripes by showing that it is impossible to establish an ideal order on earth. There are many more such examples, but the crux is not in them. If we lack a *psychological* foundation, we find ourselves utterly powerless in the face of the childishly naïve but convinced attack of other worldviews, and it goes without saying that we are utterly without influence on others.

Rozanov says somewhere that "advice can be stupid or it can be smart. It is stupid if it is tied to the mood of the person giving it; it is smart if it is tied to the circumstances of the person requesting it.... Stupid advice is tied to the soul's pettiness, to boundless egotism, to an instinct of boundless soul-expansion that is deaf to everything else: the adviser desires to expand his soul and exclude all other heterogeneous souls. Wise advice, on the other hand, is tied to the adviser's extraordinary sensitivity, where he diminishes his soul and is boundlessly interested in the myriad of other souls and other lives."[14]

Every system of concepts aims to regulate the flow of experiences, to shape and differentiate this flow, to bring order and stability into it. In this respect such a system is similar to advice; and dogmatics, too, resembles

---

14. V. V. Rozanov, *In the Proximity of Church Walls* (Petersburg), vol. 2, pp. 97–98.

advice. Rozanov's words are very much applicable to dogmatics; and, using his terminology, one would have to call our dogmatics a system of "stupid" advice.

Our dogmatics is not easy to use. But one would distort my thought completely if one takes "not easy to use" to mean "useless." On the contrary, it is we who do not know how to use the infinite treasures collected over generations; it is we who do not know how to transmute the concentrated creativity of many centuries into our own flesh and blood. This is because we have forgotten how to approach the enchanted treasure that we see, but does not give itself into our hands.

I do not propose a new truth for the old place; rather, I demand a new place for the old truth, because the old place of consciousness is cluttered with rubbish.

IV.

We know perhaps that in a dogmatic system the parts support one another; we may even know *how* such mutual support takes place. But, knowing *how* dogmatics says what it says, we do not know *why* and *for what purpose* it says it; chiefly, we do not know *what* it says. However, for dogmatics to spring to life in our consciousness, we must know its *what*, its *why*, and its *for what purpose*; without this knowledge dogmatics turns into an intricate scholastic amusement with conventional signs, which in value is not superior to a game of chess. But from the meaning of the foregoing discussion we clearly see what dogmatics needs if it is to be full of life. The secret word consists in saturating the theological schemata with psychological content, in connecting them with what has been directly experienced, in transforming them into the nerves and bones of living life.

We encounter here a difficulty that often forces one to retreat. The great Georg Cantor says that "the essence of science lies in freedom." We say that the essence of our work lies in its freedom *kat' exochen*.[15] The reworking of a religious worldview, the creation of a propaedeutic for it, is possible only as a *free* creative activity originating in that which is directly observed in the spirit. This activity cannot be stopped by any conclusion placed in its path, and it does not fear any pain when an operation is necessary, when it is necessary to tear oneself away from all traditions, conservative or progressive,

---

15. Par excellence.

when one's duty consists in being ready to renounce all that is near and dear and in remaining for a moment in absolute emptiness and absolute unconstraint. To advance toward a goal while apparently going away from it; to work for the Truth and to be merciless toward it when it is not fully known as such, to lose in order to receive—all this requires a faith in the Truth and a love of the Truth so courageous that no obstacles can make one retreat.

To be sure, it does not follow that we do not have the right to use anything except that which is directly observed in the spirit. We have every right to be guided by ready-made schemata, but they must only be used as a preliminary scaffolding that allows a more rapid and efficient processing of the raw material. Speaking figuratively, we say that the schemata, in this case the dogmas, must have not the decisive voice but only an advisory one. The role of ready-made schemata is, at first, only probabilistic, and its value is conditional, even if, individually, we regard it as unconditional. This resembles the mathematical method of successive approximations, with the difference that here inner feeling compels us to foresee the result of the work. The material (guided by Holy Scripture) for the latter must consist in our own experience and the experience of others as it is expressed in ascetic and mystical writings, in imaginative literature, in art, and in music. Also needed is a complete review of the patristic literature, not in order to sniff out "confirmations" of one's views, but in order to determine the psychological data that compel an author to speak as he does, and not differently.

These direct data, combined with auxiliary data from the natural-historical sciences (the study of the physiological underpinnings of the phenomena of spiritual life), will be the basis for a convincing dogmatics of the future.

I will be asked: "But is it possible to prove a dogmatics? Is this not excluded by the very concept of revelation?" But take note: I do not mean formal and logical proof; the requirement I have put forth is that a dogma become intuitively transparent for a religiously attuned consciousness and that it be indicated how such a consciousness is to be approached. To accept or reject a dogma is done by an act of will, but we must clearly know what it is we are accepting or rejecting, because the act of will cannot consist in accepting or rejecting mere words. At the present time it is very common to believe not in the content of the formulas but in the formulas themselves, in words. The sons of the church will be truly faithful when they cease being tied to the church and at any moment are free to descend in their thought to the principles and motives of their faith and, having descended, are free to return, because that is what truth demands. The time foretold to the woman of

Samaria will come only when everyone will be able to see the faith-teaching in its entirety, from the soil in which it is rooted up to the complex peaks of its supreme conclusions and expectations.

To make this clearer, let us indicate the characteristics of a convincing dogmatics of the future, along with certain tasks for the near future. N. M. Minsky writes the following:

> In the eyes of the philosopher the whole world appears to be an equation with one unknown, which is God. The first part of the equation is the visible world of sensuous phenomena (understood in the broadest sense), the world of the creaturely, the conditional, the transitory; the second part is the world of thought-phenomena hidden in us, the determination of the unknown constituting the task of the life of all humanity. In the case of many or even in the case of two unknowns, in the case of polytheism or ditheism, the solution would be indeterminate, but an equation with one unknown, a universe with one unknown God, yields a precise and determinate answer. [Given such an understanding of the matter] it is not God but the knowledge of God that is dependent on the world. There are two possible methods of investigation here: one based on guesswork, proceeding from the unknown to the known; the other, the true method, proceeding from the known to the unknown. Since the known is the world and the unknown is God, in religious creativity it is possible to follow one of two paths: a path based on guesswork, proceeding from God to the world through the definition of God's essence, His attributes and properties; or the true path, proceeding from our human nature to God through the uniquely fruitful investigation of *what we know about God and how this knowledge arises in us*. The fundamental law of religious creativity can be expressed as follows: all judgments leading to the true knowledge of God have as their invariable subject our human, conditional I, and as their invariable object they have the absolute deity.[16]

That is the principle of the dogmatic work proceeding from man to the divine. But we would repeat the unforgivable error of all subjectivists if we limited this work solely to this principle. Truly, for the philosopher to the extent he is a theoretician, the object of religion is always only a predicate given for the conditional I of the philosopher himself. Truly, such a philoso-

---

16. N. M. Minsky, *The Religion of the Future (Philosophical Conversations)* (Petersburg, 1905), 150–51. (Florensky's note.)

pher can speak only of the divine, not of God. However, when living mystical experience takes him out into the sphere of trans-subjective reality, man and God change places and God (like all objects of the religious consciousness) is transformed from a predicate into a subject. At the same time, subjective conditional dogmatics is transformed into objective unconditional dogmatics. The gnoseological dependence of the knowledge of God on man is replaced by the mystical dependence of man on God.

But where is the bridge for this transition? In order to sketch a map of the road to the transition point, we direct the listener's attention to the following: we say a dogmatics must necessarily be based on direct experience, and first and foremost on the dogmatist's individual experiences. But the universality of the task requires a further expansion of the domain of the experiences. It is necessary to answer again the following question: Out of what kind of experiences and out of whose experiences is the dogmatics to be constructed?

The dogmatics must have universal significance. All people must have access to it. A serious doubt arises here. If, ideally, a dogmatics must be accessible to everyone, then the experiences on which it is based must, evidently, also be accessible to everyone; they must, evidently, be commonplace experiences, a common coin of the spiritual life. But everyone knows that the wider a domain of common experiences is, the more meager, colorless, and banal its spiritual content will be. Moreover, even if we select a sufficiently wide sphere of experiences, a sphere that everyone can accept, even then new people might arise tomorrow who are blind to these experiences.

Thus, ever dependent not on the value of the experiences but on the number of people experiencing them, always determined by external statistical conditions, dogmatics could never represent anything stable but was always tossed around by the slightest gust of wind—and this instability consisted not in an evolution of what was already possessed but in the constant possibility of a total "no" where "yes" had just been. There is no attempt to find a middle path between a willful relativism which amounts to absolute nihilism and a slavish legalism which replaces living life with dead formulas. This middle path cannot be attained by philosophy without religious experience.

The path that was found unsuitable is the *common-human* path—the method of the largest common divisor, reducible to 1, i.e., to the indifference of an empty unity in the purely formal data of spiritual life, which do not at all express life itself. What we need instead is the *all-human* path—the method of the least common multiple for all experiences in all their diversity.

That path was the path of the sifting out of all heterogeneous and disparate things. *This* path is the path of synthesis, the path of the gathering together of the whole fullness of spiritual life. But this gathering cannot be a mechanical heaping-together: in its essence, spiritual life is saturated with a personal character. Therefore, if on the *common-human* path the object of study was contentless man with the minimum of spiritual life, on the *all-human* path the object of study is the Bearer of the maximum of spiritual life. This is the Son of Man, *ho huios tou anthrōpou*, the Bearer of ideal humanity. Having experienced Jesus of Nazareth as the Son of Man, as the universal Man, we thus pass to a new phase of work. It is his experiences that constitute the true foundation of dogmatics. The experiences of Jesus of Nazareth are the bridge on which dogmatics can cross over from earth to heaven, from psychology to metaphysics. But this crossing-over does not happen all at once. At first, the universal Man Jesus is only the universal subject of the dogmatic consciousness: we concern ourselves not with what he is but with what he has. Furthermore, dogmatics, invariably regarding the divine *only* as a predicate, acquires the right to affirm the universal significance of its judgments even though these judgments do not yet have a metaphysical character. Henceforth it addresses not man but humanity, and it is therefore capable of touching everyone's heartstrings, of blossoming brightly in every soul. It addresses not *idola*,[17] not that which is separate and peculiar, not the caprices, random associations, or selfish calculations of one individual or another, but that which is eternal, all-human, holy, and selfless in every man. It addresses not that which deprives a man of his human image but that which makes him a true man. In other words, dogmatics begins to use *argumenta ad humanitatem* instead of the former *argumenta ad dominem*, and the *psychology of religion* phase is replaced by the *New Testament theology* phase. But this only the first change, one of form.

But this convergence in Jesus of self-consciousness with divine consciousness[18] leads to a new change in the dogmatic judgments. The conditional human I, which until now had been the invariable subject of all judgments, is supplanted by a new subject—God; as a result, all that is divine in

---

17. Florensky uses this term to mean "phantoms."
18. This brief essay is not the place to discuss this convergence in greater detail. According to St. Justin, Philosopher and Martyr, baptism makes us, who had been "children of necessity and ignorance," "children of freedom and knowledge." However, even after baptism we must still win our freedom and knowledge by a long ascesis, since we possess them not actually but potentially. And only after attaining freedom and knowledge will we receive the right to write on our cathedrals: "To the Known God." (Florensky's note.)

man becomes only the predicate of the new Subject. The judgments become metaphysical and refer to trans-subjective reality, and the *New Testament theology* phase is replaced by the *mystical gnosis* phase. It is only here that dogmatics begins in the proper and authentic sense. The sequence of phases can be approximately represented by the following table:

Subjective Series	Trans-Subjective Series
State of Consciousness	The World
Limited Personality	Man
The Divine in Personality	Deity
The Person of Jesus	Divine Life
The Son of Man	The Son of God
Jesus's Self-Consciousness	The Knowledge of God

That is the approximate plan of a work all of us must undertake—the development of an empirical[19] dogmatics. Only when a convincing dogmatics emerges will everyone, in full spiritual awareness, be able to resolve the dilemma of either/or in relation to Jesus Christ "come in the flesh" (2 John 1:7). Only then will it be possible to separate the wheat from the chaff.

---

19. An empirical dogmatics would correspond to all of contemporary science, which, too, is being developed on a directly given, empirical foundation. (Florensky's note.)

Orthodoxy

I.

The elements out of which Russian Orthodoxy evolved: Byzantinism, Slavic paganism, the cult of sun gods, and the cult of ancestors. The Russian national character. The baptism of Russia and its chief symbolic moments.

If we recall the early church, so simple in its organization and yet superabundantly filled with divine powers, and compare it to what is today called the Christian church, we will be amazed by the enormous change experienced by the church over the nineteen centuries of her existence, and we will also be confronted by the question whether this church—catholic[1] or other—has anything in common with Christianity. Indeed, Christ had "blessed are the poor in spirit," whereas we have a complex theosophic[2] system, the doctrines of the hypostases, of the natures of God, of unity, of trinity, and so on. The apostolic church had violation of the law, freedom from ritual, rite, and rule, whereas we have fasts, reverences, feasts, and innumerable rites. Christ told people not to speak much,[3] but we have six-hour liturgies, countless akathists, ektenias, stichera, and so on. Christ's disciples had freedom of movement and inner freedom, whereas we have veneration of tradition, strict conservatism, a readiness to die if a single letter is removed from the

---

1. Allusion not to Roman Catholicism, but to the catholicity (universality) of the church. Traditionally, the church is called "One, Holy, Catholic, and Apostolic."
2. Allusion not to Blavatsky-type occultism, but to the church's philosophical investigation of divine things.
3. See Matthew 6:7.

Creed.[4] At first glance, this comparison seems to justify Harnack's exclamation: "This official church—with her priesthood, with her liturgies, with all her sacred vessels, vestments, images, amulets, fasts, and feasts—does not have anything in common with the religion of Christ."[5]

It cannot be denied that Christianity in its present forms does not resemble the Christianity of Christ's disciples. But we will try to prove that the Christianity preserved by the church as she now exists is as pure and uncontaminated as any divine thing can be that has been poured into earthly vessels. First of all, the Christian teaching did not appear in the world with the purpose of transforming it immediately. The freedom of the world and of man presupposes that the forces introduced by Christ into the world will spread gradually over the latter, in proportion to their free reception and assimilation by men. But, in receiving the gospel, every country, region, and nation receives it *in its own way*. After all, John's Christianity is different from Peter's; Francis of Assisi's Christianity is different from the apostle Paul's. The same is true for different countries and nations. The Western world received the gospel in its own way, and the East in its own way. The full truth is something absolute and therefore it is incompatible with the world. In their essence, the world and man are limited, and therefore their reception of the truth of Christianity is limited; and since every nation and every man are limited *in their own way*, their Christianity also differs. That is the first factor that divided the integral truth and changed it.

Second, the community of Christ's disciples lived by the power of grace that directly poured out on them; present-day churches live by the same grace, which is proved by the continuing presence of saints in the churches, both Catholic and Orthodox, saints who in their spiritual life conform to the types of saintliness that were so abundant in the early church. The only difference is that in the apostolic church the powers of grace poured down in torrents and rivers, whereas today Christian life is diluted by such an enormous quantity of paganism even in the church, that one gets the impression that the powers of grace drip down on it like tiny dew-drops and that what once had come easily, is attainable now only through unbelievable toil. This toil which ascetics take upon themselves seems artificial sometimes, nothing more than an absurd contrivance; but there is no other way now to do this. What once was received just by contemplating the image of the living God-Christ, is now attained by disciplining one's will over many years. It would

---

4. Allusion to the Old Believers.
5. A. von Harnack, *The Essence of Christianity*, Russian translation (Moscow, 1907), 220.

not be difficult to revoke all present-day prayers, services, relics, and sacraments on the grounds that none of this existed in Christ's time. But would that make the way to God easier? We do not have the time now to discuss this in detail. We will only make one point: If we recognize religious life as the sole thing that saves us, we must study the experience of those individuals who attained the highest degrees of the religious life. And we must recognize them to be saints; but the saints followed the path of church *ritual*, partly leaving it only when they had attained the highest degrees of life.

Thus, the purpose of the whole complex apparatus of the present-day life of the church is to receive, preserve, and transmit to people the drops of divine power that are accessible to them. No one intentionally devised this apparatus. It evolved by necessity. The first Christians lived religiously twenty-four hours a day, and every act of their lives was performed for the sake of God. Their gatherings had, initially, the character of free, programless conversations, prayers, and hymn-singing; the only fixed points of these gatherings were the Eucharist and the reading of Scripture. As the religious enthusiasm cooled, the most inspired prayers and hymns composed at previous gatherings were deposited around these fixed points. These elements, too, became fixed; their number grew until these gatherings became established services, performed according to a definite program. There was another process, parallel to the first: gatherings that had occupied the Christian's entire day, now became services performed several times in the course of the day; and then the separate services (the hours, the matins, the vespers) gradually became compressed and unified for the convenience of laypeople until it became customary to perform and attend the service just once a week, the rest of the time being spent outside the church and without God.

That is how the present-day church evolved. In the past, inspired prayers were improvised; today, almost no one composes them and we have to repeat the old ones; in the past, God himself taught and blessed people; today, the only way he can be approached is through his words (the gospel) and through prayers and sacraments. Of course, we can cast aside the tested ways, methods, and approaches, and aspire towards God independently and with our own powers; but even the powers possessed by the early Christians would be insufficient for this; and as long as this remains the case, we must hold on to the only thing we have. If you don't know how to sing, sing along with others; if you don't know how to pray, pray along with those who know how.

But this "cooled" Christianity had its good side. Humanity's powers, incapable of achieving direct communion with God, began to manifest themselves in the domains of speculation, theology, and art. The unified white light of ecstasy broke apart into the multicolor rays of Christian poetry, science, theology, painting, and architecture. Since all these spheres are spheres of *human* activity, different currents arose, isolated from one another and often mutually antagonistic; different confessions arose—the Catholic, Eastern, and Protestant churches. These churches (especially Catholicism and Orthodoxy) are not richly creative but, naturally, see their main task as the preservation of the sacred tradition.

In this essay, our subject is not the Eastern Church in its entirety, and so we will not discuss the Orthodoxy of the Greeks, the Serbs, the Bulgarians, and so on. We will discuss only *Russian* Orthodoxy and, first off, we will consider the origin of the latter.

The Russian faith was formed though the interaction of three forces: the Greek faith transported to us by Byzantine monks and priests; Slavic paganism, which encountered this new faith; and the Russian national character, which received Byzantine Orthodoxy in its own way and reworked this Orthodoxy in its own spirit.

Byzantine Orthodoxy has the following characteristics: The tendency to view religion from a philosophical point of view is combined with a high valuation of ritual. Together with a developed theosophy, which uses philosophical terms to clarify the relations between the Persons of the Holy Trinity and between the natures in the God-man, as well as the notions of the church, salvation, immortality, and so on, Eastern religiosity has a profound respect for ritual, so that the performance of the latter is considered equal to or even more important than the fulfillment of the moral commandments. This importance of ritual and teaching leads to a conservative attitude towards them; preservation of the unchangeability of ritual and teaching becomes the main task of the church. The ritual and teaching are often incomprehensible to the masses, but nevertheless their *power* is clearly felt by believers. This contradiction engenders humility before the depth of the church's treasure and obedience to its protectors.

Meanwhile, ecclesiality entered life and permeated the entirety of everyday existence, becoming an inseparable part of the national character. For the Armenians, Bulgarians, Greeks, and Russians, ecclesiality is inseparable from nationality, so that "Orthodox" and "Russian" become synonymous. A second circumstance should be mentioned: Given the conditions of the formation of the Eastern Church, the concept of "Tsar" receives a sacred significance that is closely connected with the concept of the church. The divine Roman Caesar, the emperor of the world who has appropriated all the traits of an eastern despot, becomes the protector of the Christian church, the "bishop of her external affairs," and the implementer of Christian principles in the life of the political state. In this way, the idea of the Tsar is fused with the idea of Orthodoxy. The church becomes inconceivable without the Tsar.

That is the form in which Christianity came to Russia. Byzantinism entered the world of the Russian Slavs as an enormous force, and this for three reasons: first, because it was supported by the rulers; second, because it was an organized force; and, third, because it brought science, civil and church law, enlightenment. It was a source from which the Russian nation drank for centuries, having virtually nothing else. Nevertheless, Russian Orthodoxy differs from Byzantine Orthodoxy in virtue of the fact that, prior to the adoption of Christianity, the Russian nation had its own special worldview and its own special tribal character.

Like other pagan religions, the religion of the Slavs was based on a mystical relation to nature. This relation had two aspects: (1) Nature was regarded as the great begetter and religion took on a phallic character, becoming the cult of birth-giving powers. (2) The other inevitable element of nature that was venerated was death, engendering the cult of the spirits of the dead, the cult of ancestors. The religion of the ancient Russians contained both elements; and both elements were developed to such an extent that we find among the ancient Russians an entire pantheon of higher gods, who, to be sure, preserved their natural significance as thunder, sun, wind, and so on. Our greatest knowledge is perhaps of the cult of the sun gods of love, marriage, and fertility. Their popularity is confirmed by the large number of their names (Yarilo, Lado, Kostroma, Khors, Dazhd'-bog, Tur, and others). The Yaroslavl and Kostroma provinces are even named after these gods of love and merriment; phallic images have been found in Kostroma, and there is even a saying, "Kostroma is a merry place," i.e., a place of fornication. The cult of these gods survived the adoption of Christianity and continues to the present day, sometimes indirectly, in the form of numerous games and round-dances with the singing of indecent songs (indecent from the point of view of the intelligentsia); and sometimes directly, in the form of the honoring, mourning, and burial of a maiden representing Kostroma, or in the form of a scarecrow representing Yarilo. These data indicate the great role played in Russian religious plays by events related to childbirth and marriage. The annual rebirth of the sun and general awakening of nature (just like its autumnal dying) were accompanied by noisy celebrations with wreaths, flowers, dances, singing, and games. The stubborn, many-century battle waged by Christian priests against these celebrations shows how unrestrained and orgiastic they must have been; the religious authorities regarded these "games" as worship of Dionysus, as we learn from the following passages in the "Stoglav."[6]

"On St. John's eve, men and women and young girls gather for nocturnal bathing and indecent talk, and for demonic singing, dancing, and hopping, and deeds disgusting to God; young men defile themselves and young girls are deflowered." The "Stoglav" compares such deeds to "the demonic depravities of the Greeks," when they, the "Greeks," "raise a great howling and wailing, summoning the Greek god Dionysus, teacher of drunkenness." The common folk had a different view of such celebrations; even in our day, mothers readily let their daughters go to such "revelries" in order to "become brides." In this tolerant attitude toward love before marriage we perceive the ancient sense of the sacredness of such festivities, sanctifying that which, in another time and in other circumstances, would have been considered shameful and criminal.

These springtime and summertime celebrations of the sun and of the beings filling nature are only a particular example of the religious and mystical relation of ancient man to nature.

Let us now consider the cult of ancestors, of the souls of the dead, and of spirits in general as it existed in ancient Russia. The saying "he sat on the stove and prayed to the bricks" is ancient and profound. The ancient stove, synonymous with the sacred hearth of Aryan nations, was nothing at all like our contemporary stove used for cooking or like Dutch or other stoves used for heating. The Russian fireplace gives us some sense perhaps, though a weak one, of the ancient sacred significance of the stove as the hearth and religious center of family and home. The stove was the seat of the household gods, the spirits of the ancestors; its fire was therefore sacred and its ashes had healing powers. Even today, when moving into a new house, a peasant woman will bring ashes from the old stove, these ashes representing the household god. The souls of all those who had died lawfully were regarded as such protector-spirits. Even today, in the Penzensk and Saratov districts, Mordovian peasants bring food to the graves of the dead and say: "This is for you! This has been brought to you by a woman named _____ ; protect her animals and grains; feed her chicks; watch over her home." On the other hand, those who took their own lives turned into evil spirits.

Let us now consider the third "component" of Russian Orthodoxy—the

---

6. "Stoglav" (The Book of One Hundred Chapters) is a collection of decrees of the Russian church council of 1551 that regulated canon law and ecclesiastical life in Russia.

national character. But here we encounter a difficulty consisting in the fact that we have to define the character of the Russian Slav as it was before the adoption of Christianity. The present-day type of Great Russian is the result of Christian influences; and in order to define the Russian character as it was before the adoption of Christianity, we would have to have information describing the character of the pagan Slavs or we would have to subtract mentally from the present-day Russian everything that was formed in him by Christianity. The first path is closed to us, since history provides us with only meager information about the character of the pagan Slavs. It is possible to establish a few traits, though they tell us little that is specific: hospitality, gentleness of mores, a tendency to intertribal conflicts, and in general the dominance of ethical and religious principles over social and juridical ones.

The second method is not less difficult. A national character is not something stable and fixed. Thousands of causes determine it and change it noticeably even in the course of a single century. In particular, the Russian tribal character changed greatly with the migration to the Volga and Oka; the solitary struggle against a harsh natural environment produced traits in the Russian tribe that had not been present in Kievan Russia. However, even these traits are important for us, since, irrespective of the time of their appearance, they imparted very specific characteristics to Russian Orthodoxy.

Kliuchevsky has interesting things to say about the Great Russian character: The natural environment of northeastern Russia "often laughs at the most careful calculations of the Great Russian. The capriciousness of the climate and the soil deceives his most modest expectations; and having gotten used to these deceptions, the calculating Great Russian sometimes recklessly chooses the most hopeless and irrational solution, opposing to the capriciousness of nature the capriciousness of his own audacity. This tendency to taunt happiness, to bet against the odds, has become intrinsic to the Great Russian character." The brief, quick summers trained the Great Russian to exert himself strenuously, though briefly, and then to fall into a prolonged winter inertia. Solitary work did not foster the habit of collective toil; and therefore, taken separately, the Great Russian—self-sufficient, cautious, unsociable—is higher and better than "the Great Russian society." "In the struggle against unexpected blizzards and thaws, against unforeseen August frosts and January slush and mire, he became someone who deals with accomplished facts, rather than someone who takes precautions; someone who has trained himself to notice consequences, rather than someone who sets goals; someone who has taught himself the art of summing up results." "The Great Russian often engages in a kind of double-thinking: he always goes straight at his goal, but as he does so, he keeps looking around him; and his step therefore seems unsteady and wavering. After all, you can't break through a wall with your forehead, and only crows fly straight ahead."[7]

And, so, these are the three forces that interacted to form what we call Russian Orthodoxy. Byzantinism, a finished, complex faith-teaching with an elaborate and detailed ritual, was introduced into a thoroughly pagan country, with a people whose character was completely different from that which the Byzantine understanding of Christianity had produced.

The inception of the new faith, its first steps, no matter how random and accidental they might seem, have an important significance for the understanding of this faith. In order to complete this important part of our essay, we will examine these first moments of the birth of Christianity in Russia.

Even before the baptism of Russia there were Christians in our land, particularly among the Varangians. In general, constant relations with Christian Byzantium and with the West prevented Russia from remaining totally isolated and pagan. The baptism of Princess Olga shows that Christianity was, for Russians, not something absolutely hostile and unacceptable.

Everyone is familiar with the Chronicles' narrative of the baptism of Prince Vladimir and of his subsequent Christian life, but we will talk about it anyway. However legendary this narrative might be, it nevertheless has a number of elements that symbolically illuminate our theme. What did Vladimir seek in Christianity? He rejected Mohammedanism, even though it appealed to his sensual nature; he did not see in it the breadth, universality, and joy that he wanted: "There is no merriment in it, but only great sorrow and suffering." Nor could he accept the Jewish faith. He understood that faith is inextricably connected with the entirety of national life, and so the expulsion of the Jews from Jerusalem and their diaspora over the earth did not greatly recommend their religion.

Why did he choose Christianity? What did he find appealing in it? Three episodes of the Chronicles' narrative provide an answer. When a Greek theologian expounded to Vladimir the whole history of divine providence and of human destiny, he concluded by displaying a picture depicting the Last Judgment, the ineffable beauty of the kingdom of heaven, the joy and eternal

---

7. Abbreviated quotes from V. O. Kliuchevsky's Seventeenth Lecture of his *Course of Russian History*. The last sentence combines two Russian sayings.

life destined for some and the infinite torment of fire and of the "sleepless worm" destined for others. Vladimir sighed and said: "Joy to those on the right; sorrow to those on the left." What amazed him the most about Christianity is that it is a religion of absolute valuations, a religion of *judgment*, but also a religion of *salvation*.

When the envoys sent by Vladimir to investigate different faiths returned to Kiev, they told him about the liturgy of the Greeks, about its beauty, harmony, and angelic singing; and their conclusion was that God was visibly present in this liturgy—which perhaps hinted at that vision of the Infant Christ offered in the eucharistic sacrifice which they saw in Hagia Sophia in Constantinople. In other words, what the envoys saw was that the Christian religion had the power to transform the grotesqueness and randomness of life into divine beauty and harmony, and that at rare times, in the liturgy, it could really unite men with God.

After he became a Christian, Vladimir showed that he had wholeheartedly accepted the two aforementioned principles of Christianity: he began to build churches; to baptize his subjects, saving their souls from the power of the Devil; and to establish schools. But the biographers discuss in particular detail another aspect of his activity: "Vladimir's greatest deed was his giving of charity." "All the paupers were told to come to the Prince's court and to take what they needed—drink and food." For those who were too ill to come, Vladimir arranged special carts on which "bread, meat, fish, different vegetables, mead in some barrels and kvas in others" were delivered all over the city. Such charity was also distributed in the villages and countryside and, indeed, "throughout the Russian land."

That is the third element that Vladimir saw in Christianity: the fact that it is a religion of charity. He introduced Christianity without the approval and often even against the inclination of his people; but in the great work of choosing the Christian faith and baptizing Russia, he foresaw in a mysterious manner the destiny of Christianity in Russia. Vladimir died long ago but, even today, Orthodox believers stand horrified in some cathedral or monastery when, as Vladimir once did, they look at a picture of the torments of hell and yearn to be with those who are "on the right." In their humble little churches, as well as in the great cathedrals of the cities, they—like Vladimir's envoys—see half of the meaning of Christianity in the liturgy, in the union in prayer with the heavenly powers that serve invisibly in the temple; and when they leave the church, they remember its other half—charity.

II.

The Orthodox element. The church and everyday life. Democratism as the church understands it. The significance of ritual. Conservatism. The monastic ideal. Parish Orthodoxy. A glance at the priesthood. Everyday life; ecclesiality in everyday life. Pagan memories. Discipline in domestic life. Orthodox culture. Relation to the earth and to bread. Double-faith. Sorcerers.

In the previous section we examined the elements out of which the faith of the Russian nation evolved. Such a combination of elements had to result in something highly original and complex. And that is indeed the case. The Russian peasant, who is our most serious and sincere Orthodox believer, believes in God, the church, and the sacraments, but he also believes in the wood demon, the barn demon, magical incantations, and so on. And his faith in the existence of these spirits is just as strong as his Orthodox faith and just as strongly influences his behavior and worldview. He views mystically not only the world of the saints but also the world of nature, not only God but also evil spirits. Furthermore, for the peasant the religious domain is not limited to the church and nature; it includes a third sphere, that of everyday life, consisting in his agricultural labor, his family relations, his clothing, his eating and sleeping, and his daily routine in general. Thus, we will examine Russian Orthodoxy in relation to three domains: the church, everyday life, and nature—"nature" here meaning not only natural phenomena in the usual sense, but also the world of pagan elemental spirits.

For the Orthodox the church is not an external authority, as it is for Catholics. The Orthodox never put a high value on a church unity that is bought at the expense of the church's members losing their freedom, but they are far from sharing the Protestant conception of freedom, where the church becomes an empty sound. Catholicism tends to identify the church with the priesthood, to erect a wall between the priesthood and the laity. In Orthodoxy the church is inconceivable without the people, and the believing people are the church. This view is held by all the Orthodox churches, from the Armenians to the Greeks. In the seventeenth paragraph of the Encyclical of the Eastern Patriarchs of May 6, 1848, we read: "neither Patriarchs nor Councils could have introduced novelties amongst us, because the protector of religion is the very body of the Church, that is, the people themselves." Innokenty, the bishop of the Aleuts, said that a bishop is both the teacher and the pupil of his flock. When the priesthood is not sharply separated from the laity, we get (ideally) a unified and harmonious life of all the members of the church. Therefore, in the Orthodox Church, "every word inspired by truly Christian love, by living faith and hope, is a teaching; every deed bearing the seal of the Holy Spirit is a lesson; every Christian life is a model and example."[8]

Another aspect of the Orthodox relation to the church is the tendency to emphasize cult, especially ritual, instead of doctrine and morality. Quarrels, fights, drunkenness are lesser sins than the violation of fasting; violation of chastity is forgiven more easily than the failure to attend church services; participation in the liturgy is more salvific than the reading of the Bible; the performance of cult is more important than charitable giving. It is not by chance that the Russian people assimilated Christianity not from the Bible, but from the lives of the saints; that they are enlightened not by sermon, but by liturgy; not by theology, but by the veneration and kissing of holy objects. Minds inclined to elevate rationality and analysis are dismayed by the so-called ritual-worship of the Orthodox, but this dismay is due to a misunderstanding. Is it more useful for a sick person to study medicine than to take medication? Religion is not a rationalistic business; those who reject religion are dismayed not only by "ritual-worship," but also by religious philosophy, whereas those who regard religion as real must recognize that it consists not in rationalistic understanding and not even in knowledge, but in a real relation to God. Religion consists not in reasoning about divine things, but in the reception of divinity into one's being. For the believer the prayer in which God descends into the soul of the person praying is therefore higher even than the reading of the Bible; higher than the kissing of relics, out of which grace pours as out of an over-full vessel; more important than the acquisition of theological wisdom. The Eucharist, the reception of the Lord's Body into one's own body, is infinitely more important than any sermon, than the establishment of institutions pleasing to God, schools, hospitals, and so on. For the Orthodox believer, the formulas contained in the prayers uttered in church, the hymns sung there, the lighting of the icon-lamps and of the candles—all these acts are not mere words and gestures, but *sacramental actions*, i.e., formulas and acts that, despite their resemblance to ordinary words and movements, possess mysterious, mystical, supernatural power.

---

8. Slightly free quotation from Aleksei Khomiakov's "Some Remarks by an Orthodox Christian concerning the Western Communions, on the Occasion of a Brochure by Mr. Laurentie." See *On Spiritual Unity: A Slavophile Reader*, ed. Boris Jakim and Robert Bird (Hudson, NY: Lindisfarne, 1998), 57–62.

In its appearance, sanctified water does not differ in any way from ordinary water, but it chases away demons, heals the effects of an evil eye, and helps to cure all sicknesses.

This explains the stubborn conservatism of Russian Orthodoxy, which does not permit a single letter to be changed in Scripture or a single movement to be changed in ritual. It is precisely *these* formulas that have turned out to be salvific, and it is not known what the new ones will be like.

Perhaps, the following kind of reasoning operates here unconsciously. "Christ is risen!" is being sung in the cathedral. At this moment this hymn—with exactly the same words and exactly the same melody—is being sung in all the cathedrals, churches, and chapels of Russia. Our distant ancestors sang it in exactly the same way; the pious Tsar Aleksei Mihailovich as well Alexander Nevsky with his army listened to and repeated the same words. Furthermore, in the dark Roman catacombs the first Christians sang the same song in the light of copper and clay oil lamps. But the melody of the hymn, its music, is even more ancient; our triumphant song is sung to the melody of ancient Greek wedding hymns, which were sung before representations of the ancient gods. The deep, hoary past sounds in this hymn, but our inattentive ear does not perceive this; we do not listen, and even if we do, we do not understand. In front of the priest and the procession of the cross, a candle in a glass lamp is borne. This is a survival of the ancient custom of carrying a torch in front of the bishop in order to light his way through the darkness of the catacombs into an underground temple. Many of our liturgical rituals and symbols originated (in their external shell, in their body) not just in Christian antiquity, but even in ancient Greece, Phoenicia, or Egypt. Do we seriously believe that it is the task of the human mind—whose horizon is limited to several years, whose knowledge extends back only to yesterday—to change what for millennia has given life to men and united them with the divine world?

But Orthodox conservatism is not absolute. The Orthodox consciousness readily and even joyfully assimilates new things, but only if it clearly sees in them the mark of holiness. New, especially efficacious prayers, new (revealed) icons, and, finally, new saints are greeted with living joy and without any doubt if grace clearly rests on them. In this domain the Orthodox people are even too gullible, often accepting counterfeits as holy things.

Let us now leave these general characteristics of Orthodoxy and examine the details.

Orthodox believers regard as Christians both laypersons who live a family life and monks who have consecrated themselves completely to God, but nonetheless they regard the path of the monk as special and as more salvific than the path of the layperson. Thus, Orthodox believers who live in the world regard the monastery as the higher path, as the path destined for the elect. Even as in deep antiquity, so today too, the illiterate peasant receives nourishment for his religious feeling from liturgy and prayer. He visits elders celebrated for the strictness of their lives; he stands through long services at the monastery; he makes reverences before the relics of saints; in the refectory, he listens to tales of the lives of the holy ascetics, and these tales, together with accounts of holy places, are broadcast in the form of oral narratives throughout many villages and hamlets, reinforcing in the people the ideals of holy ascesis.

The peasant separates this Christianity of the monasteries and the saints from his own domestic (so to speak) Christianity, whose center is found in the parish church and the parish priest. Here, the parishioner is not very demanding; he does little to make his church beautiful and, in general, our parish life is not very developed. He is not upset when the deacon reads incoherently and is not completely sober; and all he requires from the priest is the performance of a few simple functions. He does not expect the priest to serve beautiful liturgies, or to deliver stirring sermons, or to organize the parish life, or even to give any particular moral guidance. The priest's role is to baptize, to marry, to bury, to celebrate prayer services on the meadows, to bless the bread for Easter and the fruits on Transfiguration Day. Of course, an energetic priest can interpret his duties more broadly and undertake to better the life of his parish by instilling higher moral standards among the parishioners, eradicating drunkenness, improving family relations, or opening a credit union. But none of this will be regarded as absolutely necessary, and a true Orthodox believer might even suspect a Lutheran spirit here and condemn such activity.

Let us now consider the second domain—everyday life in Orthodoxy. It is not by chance that peasants have the saying: "Without God, not a step." Even outside the liturgy and outside the church the Orthodox believer is surrounded by ecclesiality. In the church, however, he tends to forget human things and to live by what is divine, whereas outside the church his humanity comes to the fore and seeks God's blessing.

First of all, the Orthodox believer conducts his life according to the church calendar. On the one hand, he religiously observes the feasts, knows them all with precision, even the most minor ones; he observes all the fasts according to monastic rules, remembering when fish can be eaten and when only vegetables should be eaten. On the other hand, the peasants link particular agricultural and household duties to specific days of the year. The days thus acquire special names: for example, January 24 is "half-wintered, half-breaded Aksinya," i.e., half the winter has passed and half the food stored for the winter has been eaten; April 1 is "meatless cabbage soup"; April 12 is "Vasily, put the sled away and get the cart ready"; April 23 is "Egory the shepherd," i.e., the animals are let out into the field; May 5 is "Irina the planter," i.e., the cabbage is planted; May 6 is "Job the pea-planter"; May 23 is "Leonty the cucumber-planter," and so on.

Thus, acts of agricultural and domestic life are put under the protection of the saints. But there's more. All the moments in the life of an Orthodox believer are blessed by him either by a complex ritual or simply by the sign of the cross. First of all, the most important moments of his life—birth, death, marriage—take place before the face of God and are blessed by sacraments and services. The main role here is, of course, played by the church and the priest, but the ancient pagan rituals are not forgotten either. They are closely interwoven with the church rituals and are performed even today in many parts of Russia. Dozens of pages in ethnographic works are devoted to describing the marriage ritual in some northern province. Up to the seventeenth and eighteenth centuries, those rituals were particularly widespread, and the church authorities fought in vain against them.

The "Stoglav" says that "worldly weddings have musicians and entertainers who sing demon-inspired songs. And when they go to church to be married, the priest rides with his cross and in front of him are all the revelers hopping around in their demonic games."[9]

The less important events of life are also consecrated by the church—housewarmings, plantings, harvests, name-days, remembrances of the dead. The Orthodox accompany such events with prayer services, sprinkling with holy water, cross processions in the fields, the bringing of some specially venerated icon into one's home, and so on. These are special events in the life of the Orthodox, but even routine, everyday happenings are accompanied by prayer. Prayer precedes eating, sleep, all work, the "creation" of bread. Even when prayers are not said, the sign of the cross with a reverence is made.

It must be admitted, of course, that prayer and making the sign of the cross are often (and even in the majority of cases) done mechanically; in other words, at these moments the peasant's consciousness is not occupied with divine things. But even such mechanical prayer may excite certain sub-

---

9. Freely translated from the Russian.

conscious movements in the soul, the sum-total of which forms the type of the Orthodox peasant, as we see him in the remote places of our northern provinces. Strict observance of church fasts, obligatory attendance at liturgies, prayer before beginning any work—all this thoroughly permeates the life of the Great Russian, reinforcing it and making it sturdy and harmonious. The participant in such a measured, sturdy life feels himself at home in it, does not do things hastily; and the consciousness that he is performing a work that hundreds of generations have performed before him, makes him self-confident, dignified, and joyful. Furthermore, constant prayer produces a stillness in his soul and a particular gentleness, combined with profound seriousness. For the Orthodox, eating is a sacred act; he does not eat—rather, he partakes. When he enters another's home, he crosses himself before the icons, and this act creates in him a profoundly serious attitude both toward the home he has entered and toward the people who live there. To make this clearer, let us consider the external side of the life of a member of the European intelligentsia: he eats hastily, having a crudely materialistic relation to his food, reading his newspaper as he eats and preparing to rush off to conduct some business; he enters another's home as if it were a restaurant, store, or club; when he starts out on a long trip and the train departs, instead of crossing himself like the Orthodox peasant, who becomes intensely serious even if for only a second, the European hastily finishes the sweet roll that he bought at the station buffet and skims the evening paper. In all this we see, primarily, a lack of respect for that newspaper, for reading, for eating, for people, for every act of life, and often even for his family and for his work. That explains why, whereas among the peasants "who live in the past" there are many persons who could serve as models for an icon, because their faces are so strict, beautiful, and full of "style," the European physiognomy, on the other hand, startles one with its accidentalness, inexpressiveness, and absence of spirit.

It is customary to say that the peasants lack culture (we are speaking mainly about the peasants because they have most fully preserved Orthodoxy). This assertion is premised on the notion that only one type of culture exists—the European type. That is untrue, of course. Not only peasants, but even savages of all continents and parts of the world, possess deeply rooted and complex cultures. In particular, the Russian peasant, too, possesses his own culture. We mention this here because this culture has a religious character and can be called a culture of Orthodoxy. This is not a misuse of this word; the Orthodox themselves use it in this sense. From their point of view, someone is Orthodox not because he rejects the *filioque* and purgatory and recognizes communion *sub utraque*.[10] "He doesn't eat in an Orthodox way." "He doesn't dress in an Orthodox way." These are common expressions. An Orthodox believer is Orthodox not so much because he adheres to Orthodox dogma but because he does not eat before the Sunday liturgy, because he eats pies on feast days, because he does not sit down to a meal without crossing himself, because on Saturdays he steams himself in a bathhouse—in other words, because his everyday life is Orthodox in character and he is a child of Orthodox culture.

Nature is the third sphere toward which the Orthodox believer has a religious attitude. This domain merges with what we considered above under the heading of Orthodoxy in everyday life. Here, we will consider not only the relation of the Orthodox believer to nature in the narrow sense, but also his relation to agriculture. This category also includes the survivals of natural pagan forces in the form of wood demons, household spirits, and so on—forces that are part of the life of the Orthodox peasant even in the present day.

Grass, birds, trees, insects, all kinds of animals, and the earth itself inspire an unexplainable sympathy in the peasant. Listen to how the peasant talks with animals and trees, with things, with all of nature: he caresses, asks, implores, upbraids, and curses; he converses with it, is furious at it, and sometimes hates it. He lives in close union with nature, struggles with it, and humbles himself before it. All of nature and all things are alive and personal. Those innumerable beings—wood demons, field demons, household spirits, barn demons, mermaids, kikimoras, and so on—are doubles of things, places, and natural elements. They live their own lives, demand that people feed them, conduct the routine business of life, marry, eat, drink, sleep, quarrel, fight, weep, die. All things and events take on a special form. Food is no longer *simply* food; sickness is no longer *simply* sickness; clothing is no longer *simply* clothing; fire is no longer *simply* fire. Everything is simple and not simple. A whirlwind swirls along the road, but this is not simply wind. It is a witch celebrating her impure marriage with a demon. It is easy enough to be convinced of this. All you have to do is throw a knife into the whirlwind, and the knife will fall to the ground, bloodied.

It is a commonplace to say that the earth is the Orthodox believer's holy mother. The following example shows that this commonplace is filled with living and real meaning for the peasant. In the Yaroslavl district there

---

10. Communion "in both kinds," where both the bread and the wine are administered to the people during the Eucharist.

is a certain practice that is followed in the case of "prityka," an enigmatic sickness for which the peasants can find no explanation: a man who had been completely healthy suddenly, when working in the field, feels a pain in some part of his body. This is a sign that he is being punished by mother-earth for some infraction. In order to get better, one has to ask the earth for forgiveness. On the patch of ground where he felt the pain, the peasant must say, turning to the east and bowing down to the earth: "Forgive me, moist mother-earth, that I have offended you."[11] It is easy to imagine the kind of sacred and serious significance that agricultural work acquires.

The gifts of the earth, especially bread, are also sacred. Bread is a "gift of God"; it is an emblem of abundance and fecundity. Beginning a new loaf, a peasant proclaims: "Bless it, O Lord!" It is a great sin to handle bread carelessly, to roll balls out of it, for example. Conversely, those who do not abhor any bread, but eat it even when it is stale or spoiled, will never be struck by lightning, will not drown, but will live to a very old age without knowing want. There is no doubt that, since deepest antiquity, all activities related to the production of bread have been accompanied by religious rites. "Both before and after such activities, before mowing and harvest, a cross procession proceeds to the fields, with church icons and banners wreathed with fresh greenery and flowers; the priest blesses the grain fields, sprinkling them with holy water. On the Feast of the Presentation of Our Lord in the Temple, every master has a wax candle blessed, which he preserves carefully in the granary, and then carries out into the field when sowing begins, and also at harvest time."[12] "On the Feast of the Annunciation and on Clean Thursday, prosphora are blessed and tied to the seeders; in some villages the prosphora are dried, ground into powder, and mixed with the seeds prepared for the sowing; in the Chernigov district the custom is to have the seeds themselves blessed in churches."[13] Harvest, too, is accompanied by special rituals. In certain parts of the Ukraine the first sheaf is harvested by the priest. We do not have the space to mention all the rituals that relate to agriculture. The rituals mentioned above are typical ones (they are collected in volume 3 of Afanas'ev's *The Slavs' Poetic Views of Nature*).

If, leaving the domain of agriculture, we now devote our attention to other phenomena of nature, we will notice the following fact: the peasant's attitude toward natural phenomena is always religious in character, but in

---

11. See *Zhivaya starina* 6 (1896).
12. A. N. Afanas'ev, *The Slavs' Poetic Views of Nature*, vol. 3 (Moscow, 1865–69), 763.
13. Afanas'ev, *The Slavs' Poetic Views of Nature*, 763–64.

many cases it is not a Christian one. Thus, there is nothing Christian in numerous survivals of pagan religious festivals that accompany different moments in the life of nature: in such things as folk dances, games, the leaping over bonfires, the weaving of wreaths, and so on. For peasants the elemental spirits—spirits of water, of forests, of the home—are living personal beings. Are they beings of light or of darkness? In any case, they are not beings of light. When praying to a house spirit, no Orthodox peasant would ever think of invoking God or any of the saints. When the house spirits run wild (this happens in the spring when these spirits "change their skin," desiring to marry witches), peasants would never think of consulting a priest. Instead, they go to a shaman. But these powers are not always evil. The house spirits are usually regarded as good: they sweep the floor, feed the animals, keep watch over the house, warn the peasants of misfortune, provide them with abundance and wealth, and so on. The house spirits serve other functions as well. Here, for example, is the prayer of a peasant woman of the Smolensk district, addressed to all the elemental powers: "Our master and father, the house spirit, and our mistress and mother, the house spiritess! Our master and father, the wood demon, and our mistress and mother, the wood demoness! Our master and father, the water spirit, and our mistress and mother, the water spiritess! Our master and father, the field spirit, and our mistress and mother, the field spiritess! Forgive me, a sinner and unworthy (she bows in all four directions). Help me and save me from all manner of attacks and evil wishes. Give me good health!"

But more often than not, these spirits cause harm to people—they send sickness to people and to animals, as well as poor harvests. They are called foul spirits, filth, spirits of evil. And the peasant, conscious of himself as Orthodox and as a child of the church, feels that he is stronger than these spirits and rarely turns to the church to deliver him from them. True, he sometimes protects himself with prayer or sprinkles the corners of his house with holy water, but more often than not he goes to a sorcerer or shaman, a frightening man born of a woman but fathered by one of these elemental spirits, a man who never receives communion and who begins his incantations with the following highly significant formula: "without blessing myself I will stand and without crossing myself I will go," and so on. One should not think that those who consult sorcerers experience the same feelings as the Western Fausts who sell their souls to the devil. No, the peasant woman who seeks a sorcerer's aid does not feel this is a sin; afterwards, she will go to church with a pure heart to place candles and pray for her dead. In her consciousness the church and the sorcerer are different departments, and the church, which has the power to save her soul, is powerless to save her from the evil eye, while the sorcerer, who has the power to cure her infant of screaming fits, does not have the power to pray for her dead husband.

We must correct ourselves here. Such duality is very commonplace, but it must be said that sometimes, and even very often, one finds utter confusion in this domain. Peasants will often consult "persons of church rank" (anywhere from a starets to the woman who bakes the prosphora) when they are attacked by evil spirits or possessed by demons, or even when they have a toothache; or they will consult shamans who are not as dark and frightening as the ones I have described. The incantations resemble Christian prayers: "in the name of the Father and of the Son and of the Holy Spirit" is chanted; the formula quoted above is changed to "blessing myself I will stand and crossing myself I will go," and so on. There are even villages where the priest performs the functions of the shaman. Still, the Orthodox attitude towards nature has an element of enslavement, fear, subordination, and "superstition" in the sense of acknowledging one's weakness in the face of elemental spirits.

III.

Conclusions. The character of Russian piety. The suffering Christ. Separation between the Divine and the human. The Orthodox view of charitable giving. Irrationalism. Humility. Intimacy in the relation to God that verges on familiarity. Sectarianism. The Old Believers.

"*Noli me tangere,*" the resurrected Christ told Mary, even though later he allowed Thomas to touch his wounds.

In his *Pensées*, Pascal explains this apparent contradiction by affirming that we, Christians, must take part only in Christ's wounds and sufferings. If these wounds are interpreted to mean Christ's humiliation, his abjectness, his "form of a slave," the Russian people, in their religiosity, live with the suffering Christ, not with the resurrected and transfigured one. This does not mean that Russian Orthodoxy lives by some extraordinary sufferings and feats of self-abnegation. Just the opposite. Nothing is more alien to Orthodoxy than heroic deeds and effective gestures of suffering. God humiliated himself for us—he became a man and lived among people: "he shall grow up before him as a tender plant, and as a root out of a dry ground: he hath no form nor comeliness; and when we shall see him, there is no beauty that we should desire him. He is despised and rejected of men; a man of sorrows, and acquainted with grief" (Isa. 53:2-3). This is the Russian Christ, so similar to the humble Russian landscape, to the gray unsightly villages, to sick, drunk, ruined Russia. This is the Christ who is the friend of sinners, of the low and abject, of the poor in spirit.

"Orthodoxy," wrote Pobedonostsev, "is a religion of prostitutes and publicans, who will enter the Kingdom of Heaven before the lawyers and Pharisees."[14] Leskov and Dostoevsky understood Orthodoxy in the same way, and they are unparalleled in describing the deep essence of the people's faith. The power of God is manifested in powerlessness: if God himself came in a powerless and humble form, how can we despise powerlessness and humility? Perhaps, grace is revealed precisely in what is powerless and humble? Therefore, Orthodox believers never judge by appearances. They are in no hurry to be outraged and to condemn; inwardly, they even sympathize with the drunk, the poor, the tattered, the ignorant, and the outright foolish. They do not seek brilliance, magnificence, and power; on the contrary, they are wary when they see magnificence and power, which they always view as something "human, all too human." Orthodoxy is wholly opposite to the pagan and contemporary European view (expressed most powerfully by Nietzsche) that a person's value is directly proportional to the excellence of his external qualities—that the more intelligent, attractive, and powerful in body and will he is, the more divine he is. Orthodoxy's revaluation of values is even much more radical: it is not only dubious about such a direct proportionality between a man's value and his human qualities, but it even tends to understand this proportionality as an *inverse* one. To be sure, this tendency characterizes not only Russian Orthodoxy; it is the view of the whole apostolic church, although in the Western confessions it has been supplanted by pagan and positivistic valuations.

Orthodoxy carries this valuation into the domain of political activism as well. "Except the Lord build the house, they labour in vain that build it" (Ps. 127:1). Orthodoxy views the social and cultural process suspiciously; at best, it regards this process as a very relative and wholly human affair that has little in common with those mysterious, genuinely divine processes that are taking place in the souls of peoples. Perhaps, universal equality will be achieved one day, poverty and hunger will be eradicated, and international peace will be established, but "when they shall say, Peace and safety, then sudden destruction cometh upon them" (1 Thess. 5:3). Moreover, perhaps, suffering and calamities are more necessary for the world? Perhaps, if it

---

14. Imprecisely quoted from K. P. Pobedonostsev, *Moskovsky Sbornik* (1896), 201.

achieves prosperity, humankind will grow proud and forget God? Perhaps, satiety will put conscience to sleep, and a sorrow-free life and laziness will awaken unheard-of vices? Therefore, Orthodoxy does not chase after political activity and does not put a high value on social undertakings. Even in the sphere of church activity (e.g., missions and religious education), Orthodoxy displays not only ineptitude but also indifference. Evlogy formulated this view very precisely when he was ordained bishop of Lublin:

> Should one take up a sword and arm oneself with all the means of battle employed by the doctrines of other confessions which take pride in the enormous quantitative successes of their propaganda? But we hear the terrible words of the first shepherd: those who take up the sword shall perish by the sword. No, the power of true shepherding according to the spirit of Christ lies not in this: it lies not in the harmoniousness and strength of the external organization of activists, not in the breadth of their penetration into all the social spheres, not in the abundance of material means, not even in sickening spoutings of human wisdom. No, we, the holy apostle says, "do not war after the flesh: for the weapons of our warfare are not carnal, but mighty through God."[15] Our weapons include the armor of truth, the shield of faith, the helmet of salvation, the spiritual sword, that is, the word of God and prayer.[16]

This extract clearly expresses not only contempt of human means of struggle, but also the fear that one's human activity will be recognized as a divine work. This does not mean that Orthodoxy rejects all human works; it means, rather, that what it fears most is the confusion of God's works with that which is earthly. This is wholly opposite to Lutheranism, for which service in the church, sermonizing, and church philanthropy are all examples of the work of the church. Orthodoxy does not reject philanthropy: clothing the naked, feeding the hungry, and visiting the sick are all native Russian virtues, but their meaning lies solely in the fact that these are works of love and charity, not works of the reorganization of the world from "a vale of tears and weeping" into an earthly paradise. While the social activity and church philanthropy in the West aim to remake the conditions of life into more normal ones and therefore take on an impersonal and mechanical form (workhouses, the eradication of poverty, government pensions for the

---

15. 2 Corinthians 10:4.
16. *Tserkovnye Vedomosti* 5 (1903).

elderly, insurance), Orthodoxy, though fervently sympathizing with the suffering world, does not believe in the possibility of changing it by human means. Philanthropy in Russia, therefore, has a personal character: it is aid given to *specific* persons, without intermediaries and exclusively out of love for them, rather than being given with the calculation that it will change the conditions of human life.

The human world is incommensurable with the divine world; things that are small in the human world turn out to be great in the kingdom of heaven; the ways of the Lord are unfathomable. Human beings are unable to understand the meaning of the historical process as a whole, and this leads to two conclusions: irrationalism and obedience. Here, again, Orthodoxy is wholly opposite to Catholicism and Lutheranism. In those two we find faith in the human mind, a striving not only to attain knowledge of the divine but also to subordinate it to the laws of reason. We find this tendency not only in Lutheranism (whose essence consists in rationalism), but also in Catholicism. In contrast, in Orthodoxy we find faith in the most irrational and absurd things, faith understood as a rejection of reason, and finally an actual rejection of reason in religious questions and therefore a ready acceptance of facts contradictory and inaccessible to rational understanding, facts that make the rationalist fall into convulsions.

But once we accept that all things depend not on our human mind but on Divine judgment, that man proposes but God disposes, that in the end all things are in God's hands—it becomes our religious duty to humble ourselves before God, to renounce our human will and not to oppose God's will. That is the Christian's first duty. He must humbly do the work he is called to do and live like everyone else, not thrusting himself forward, not seeking to perform great works, and reasoning as little as possible.

If you are a government official, a military man, a teacher, strive to do your work well, get married early, love your wife and family. That is the sphere of your activity in which you can manifest all your abilities, but do not imagine that you are called to perform great works; do not struggle needlessly, do not hit your head against the wall, and all will be well. We can find a model for such a truly Orthodox life in Dostoevsky. His private life was one of everyday toil; in thrall to gnawing quotidian concerns, "he was overwhelmed by the petty cares of ordinary life, covered with the dust of commonplace prose."[17]

17. A. S. Volzhsky, "The Life of F. M. Dostoevsky and Its Religious Meaning," *Voprosy religii* 2 (1908): 123–92.

How far from God such a life seems! Does such an existence really have anything in common with religious life, or even with life itself, not necessarily religious?

Our preceding discussion has, I think, prepared us to give an affirmative answer to this question. Yes, answers the Orthodox believer. Christ, who lived among sinners and prostitutes, even now walks among us, in our petty ordinary life. It seems that, of all the Christian confessions, none is equal to Orthodoxy in its vivid sense of the *personal* Christ. In Protestantism this image is remote and does not have a personal character. In Catholicism it is outside the world and outside the human heart; Catholic saints see him *before* themselves as an example they seek to imitate to the point of stigmata, the wounds made by the nails. Only the Orthodox, not only saints but even ordinary pious laypeople, feel him in themselves, in their hearts. Let us recall the story of Father Kiriak as told by Leskov in "At the Edge of the World": when he was a child, Kiriak, hiding under a bathhouse shelf, prayed to God that he not be beaten for mischief he had done; and he suddenly felt a gentle coolness, and something stirred "near his heart, like a warm little dove." That was Christ. "The whole universe can't encompass Him, but when He sees a sorrowing child hiding in a bathhouse, He crawls up to him and dwells under his shirt."

This intimate closeness with God has nothing in common with Western exaltation and sentimentalism; on the contrary, for the Russian peasant these relations readily take on a character of good-natured familiarity. The peasant himself makes fun of this familiarity. "Father Forerunner," a peasant woman prays jokingly, "I am Pavlov's daughter-in-law and Ivanov's wife—have mercy upon me!" "He winked at one, nodded at another, the third will figure it out for himself," it is said about a careless prayer. The peasants live on familiar terms with the saints. "Nikola helps a peasant carry his load." He is the peasant's best friend: "Ask Nikola, and he'll tell the Savior." Therefore, the peasant does not consider it an insult to give saints nicknames that are not always respectful, such as "Awful Nose" for Afanasy, "Ivy Face" for Evdokiia, "Cabbage Head" for Nikola, "Raise Up Your Tail," for Akulina, and so on. This down-to-earth character of the peasant's religious feeling excludes not only religious romanticism but also sanctimoniousness. Even though the ordinary Orthodox peasant prays a great deal, he cannot stand those who say, "Hear, O Lord, my truth!" He cannot stand hypocrisy in religion.

Our brief description of Orthodox piety shows, we hope, that the Russian Orthodox religious instinct has happily avoided the Scylla of rationalism toward which Russian common sense could draw it, while also avoiding the Charybdis of unrestrained mysticism, toward which it is drawn by that trait of the Russian nature which Dostoevsky defined as the tendency to transgress boundaries and to stare into abysses. These two properties have remained in the Russian character, and they explain the existence of numerous sects in the Orthodox Church which fall into two main groups according to these two properties. Adherents of the sects of the first category, guided by common sense, reject Orthodox dogmatics and liturgy as incomprehensible and contradictory for the human mind. Leo Tolstoy is the most typical and most eloquent representative of this tendency. The second group is the group of mystical sects, the khlysts being their chief representative.

There is one other branch of Orthodoxy—the Old Believers. Initially, they represented Orthodoxy in its purest form, but under the influence of their "Protestant" state they assimilated certain false qualities; nevertheless, in general, they are still close to the Orthodox ideal we have sketched in the present essay. Torn away from the dominant church by external forces, the Old Believers would nevertheless have broken away sooner or later from that part of the Russian nation which began to assimilate European civilization, to forsake the Orthodox way of life and betray the faith of the fathers. The Old Believers split away from Orthodoxy during the cultural crisis in Russian society at the end of the seventeenth century, i.e., during a period of cultural innovations in clothing and in everyday life in general on the eve of the epoch of Peter the Great. Having destroyed the Orthodox way of life, Peter's reform struck a powerful blow against Orthodoxy, depriving it, at least in cities and in the educated class, of its body—its way of life. The results of the second historical blow against Orthodoxy—the Revolution[18]—cannot yet be determined. In any case, the Revolution has accelerated that decline and degeneration of the Orthodox way of life, and thus of Orthodoxy itself, which has long been taking place because of capitalism with its cities and factories. Even though cultural (nonpolitical) history moves slowly, Orthodoxy is approaching a point of crisis, where it must degenerate utterly or change and be reborn. We say "change" because, in its everyday structure, Orthodoxy is closely connected with life, and life changes and breaks this structure, thereby breaking Orthodoxy as well. On the other hand, Orthodoxy is strongly and intimately connected even with political history—through the autocracy of the Tsar. The faith in this autocracy, a mystical relation to it, is one of the necessary elements of Orthodoxy; and therefore changes in the government of the country represent a new blow directed against Or-

---

18. That is, the Revolution of 1905.

thodoxy. A third crack in Orthodoxy is the ever-increasing disorder in the church, her violation of her own fundamental canons. What we find here is a huge contradiction between the conservatism of Orthodoxy and its *de facto* divergence from conservatism in the direction of destroying the ecclesial structure. This contradiction is now generally recognized and is becoming an important factor determining the future of Orthodoxy.

The Salt of the Earth

*The Story of the Life of Hieromonk Abba Isidore,
Starets of the Gethsemane Skete*

*Compiled and Told in Order
by His Unworthy Spiritual Son, Pavel Florensky*

Foreword Addressed to My Pious Brother-Reader

Father Isidore is no longer with us. He is no longer with us. He is gone. His fragrance was like a flower's, and we sorrow because he has faded. He shone to us like a bright little sun, and the light has gone out. He was our rock of faith—where is our support now? Everything about him amazes us: his love, meekness, and humility; his impartiality, directness, and independence; his unpretentiousness, unselfishness, and poverty; his radiance, tranquility, and spirituality; finally, his prayer. But what amazes us most about him is that he transcended the world. He was in the world, but he was also not of this world. He lived among people, but not as a man. He did not disdain anyone or anything, but he himself was above everything; and all earthly things drooped low and pitifully before his gentle smile. With his gaze he demolished all human conventions, for he lived above the world and was free with a supreme, spiritual freedom. It seemed that he didn't walk on the earth but was suspended by invisible threads from another country. This filled him with inner lightness; and when anything heavy and earthly approached him, it lost its oppressive weight. With a gentle smile, as if playing, he knew how to subvert ordinary human life into joy, and he did this with impunity. He could allow himself things that transcended the righteousness of the law, and he'd do this with such luminous clarity that these acts of his always had a *symbolic* meaning. Simple and everyday things were for him not just simple and everyday things, but projected long roots into *other* worlds, to a "new earth."

And now, reflecting on and exploring with our hearts that "which we have seen with our eyes, which we have looked upon, and our hands have handled,"[1] we delve deeper and deeper into Father Isidore's life. The *symbolic meaning* of his life becomes more and more noticeable, and the labor of writing becomes harder and harder. There are no words to describe the subtle fragrance of spirituality that always accompanied Father Isidore like a cloud, especially since there is very little about his life that can be expressed verbally and externally. For, externally, his life was simple, containing neither interesting events nor captivating words.

Forgive me, gentle reader, for my ineptitude in this work I am undertaking; and if Father Isidore does not appear before you more like an Angel from heaven than a man of earth, the fault will lie not with the revered Starets, but with the inept writer of his life. I have done my best to write truly about Father Isidore, but every time I reread my manuscript an obscure feeling comes over me that I have not grasped his true nature.

Chapter 1

In which the pious reader learns about Father Isidore's cell

In order to satisfy your curiosity, pious reader, about how Father Isidore lives, let us take a walk together to his cell. We exit the Monastery of St. Sergius of Radonezh, go through the Posad, and cross the field near the Skete ponds. Then after crossing the bridge, going past the Bogoliubivaya Kinoviya Monastery, and traversing the woods, we find ourselves between the Gethsemane and Chernigov Sketes. But before going to the Starets's home, let us not forget to pray in the underground church of the Chernigov Mother of God, the miraculous icon of these parts. The Starets loves her so much, that without doubt he will ask us if we visited her, a question he poses to every guest.

But now let us go without further ado to the Gethsemane Skete. We climb up a wooden staircase and traverse a graveyard. And over there we see Father Isidore's little house.

---

1. 1 John 1:1.

This house, in which Father Isidore lived twice[2] and in which he died, is situated in the right corner of the Skete (in relation to the main entrance), at the very wall. Previously, this house had belonged to the Athos starets Samuil (called Ioanniky as hieromonk) and then to Father Avraamy, who, before living there, had spent many years beneath the earth, in the so-called "caves" adjoining the underground church of the Chernigov Mother of God. Father Isidore's house is a tiny log structure consisting of a little cell into which four or five men could squeeze with great difficulty and sit on little benches; a "little vestibule" (Father Isidore's name for it) in which two men could sit with difficulty; and a tiny entryway. A kind of closet was attached to the "little vestibule," and Father Isidore set up his samovar there. The entryway and the closet were minuscule; the samovar took up the whole closet, and only two people at a time could pass through the entryway, and only if they were skinny. During the last two years of Father Isidore's life, a cold entryway was added to the house, but it was so small that two men could barely stand in it at the same time.

But in this toy house there are many nooks and corners. Whenever you enter this house, it's as if you keep trying to remember, but can't remember, some sweet half-forgotten dream that is dear to your heart. It's all so simple and poor, but also special, warm to the gaze, and serene. Things have their eyes; and Father Isidore's furnishings greet you with such welcoming glances when you enter and escort you with such sweet gazes when you leave. When you enter, holy icons look straight out at you. Each of them has its own story; each of them is associated with some important name, yet important not here on earth, but in the kingdom of heaven. Beneath the icons there is a stand with a mother-of-pearl Jerusalem cross, an old tattered Gospel with a worn and glossy leather cover, and an icon-lamp on a blue glass base. All the walls of the cell are covered with photographs of people associated spiritually with Father Isidore, as well as with pictures, poems, and fruit-drop wrappers. None of it was worth more than pennies, but for Father Isidore everything was fruitful. Everything there was a symbol of the heavenly, a reminder of things on high. The glorious abbot of Mt. Sinai, St. John of the Ladder, says that both worldly and spiritual songs excite joy, divine love, and tears in those who love God, whereas for those who love sensual delights, it is the other way around.

I also think that if Father Isidore had had real paintings on his walls,

---

2. He lived there before and after living at the Paraclete Skete. More about this later. (Florensky's note.)

instead of cheap pictures, his cell would have lost its meek sweetness: God loves humility and his power is manifested in poverty.

So, you enter the cell. To the right of the icons is a window, beneath which there is a little table with books, letters, and papers scattered over it. To the left of the icons stands a little bench; and then there is a little table on which lie a worn *epitrachēlion*,[3] cuffs with tattered edges, and different necessaries; and then a little shelf. Above the table there are two little windows. On the sills Father Isidore has placed what he calls his "flowers": jars with moss, tin cans with weeds pulled out by the gardener, a corked water-filled bottle to be used as a "vase" for his "flowers," a bottle with a broken willow branch. It is impossible to remember everything that was on the windowsills.

In the "little vestibule" there is a little cupboard with cups and saucers and a little table on which the tea was sometimes placed. There are also wooden hangers made of dry sticks, resembling a stag's antlers. Father Isidore would show them to every visitor.

If you take the entryway to the end, you'll come out into a tiny garden, not more than two yards wide. Lying between the Skete wall and Father Isidore's house, this garden encircles the house and is enclosed on two sides by a tall plank fence with a gate. Father Isidore calls this his "Inner Hermitage"; there he finds seclusion for prayer and spiritual reflection. Tall willows hang over the "Inner Hermitage," sometimes whitening it with their flying fluff. And looking round with childlike joy, Father Isidore exclaims: "It's snowing." Grass, nettles, onions also grow there, some in tin cans found by Father Isidore in the garbage, and some in the earth. Toads live in Father Isidore's garden, as well as many other creatures. A little table has been fashioned out of a stump, and there is another stump for sitting, as well as a seat made of stones carried here from various places by the master of the "Inner Hermitage." Everything the eye sees here has a symbolic meaning: the willow represents the Oak of Mamre, under which our ancestor Abraham received the Holy Trinity; the seat of stones represents the cliff of the Thebaid where hermits lived; the branches with a wooden cross between them which were nailed to the tree in the corner of the "Hermitage" (opposite the gate) and which resembled a stag's antlers, these branches represented, according to Father Isidore, the vision of St. Eustathius Placidas.[4] No corner in the "Inner Hermitage" is without meaning. The very air is filled with memories of our

---

3. A stole worn by priests and bishops around the neck with the two adjacent sides sewn or buttoned together, leaving enough space through which to place the head.

4. Allusion to St. Eustathius Placidas's vision of a radiant cross between a stag's antlers.

holy ancestors and of the saints; and for Father Isidore the events of Sacred and Ecclesiastical History are much closer and much more vivid than the tedious hurly-burly of the world.

If you open the gate, you'll go from the "Inner Hermitage" into the "Outer Hermitage," which is situated in front of his house. This is an unenclosed place, only slightly protected by trees and bushes. Here, beneath a leafy bower, a round table was anchored into the ground, and it is surrounded by what Father Isidore calls his "furniture"—a "couch," an "armchair," a "chair," and so on, all made of crooked tree-limbs and boards. Father Isidore made this furniture himself. It's hard to imagine anything clumsier.

In the summertime Father Isidore would sometimes treat visitors to tea in this "Outer Hermitage." Leading a visitor to the "furniture," he'd declare with a smile: "I have a couch. It's a perfect place to lie down and rest. I often rest here. It's perfect." "You should lie down and rest here, Father," he'd sometimes say to the Bishop. Perfect, indeed! Just imagine lying down on tree-branches, some of which stick you in the side! Around the "furniture," there were a few small planted beds, two with vegetables and one with strawberries. There was also a currant bush.

Chapter 2

In which it is told how the Starets would have greeted the pious reader if the latter, while visiting the Gethsemane Skete in order to venerate its treasures, had dropped in to see the Starets

After that survey of Father Isidore's domain, let us go now, patient reader, to pay him a visit. He receives all visitors affectionately regardless of whether their visit is convenient or not; and he even greets strangers as if they were dear friends or relatives. You may not believe it, pious reader, but all people are his dear friends or relatives—everyone is a father, mother, brother, or sister to him, and even more than that.

We approach the door. If the key is sticking out, that means he's home. However, he's almost always at home, and if he's not at home, there is no doubt that he will soon return. He leaves home only to go to church, to attend the liturgy; and, very rarely, he also goes to the Posad, to see the Bishop or visit the Academy, or to see other spiritual children of his. But we are happy to find that the key is sticking out of the keyhole, and that means the master is at home. We knock meekly with one finger. He doesn't open the door. He probably doesn't hear us—his hearing is bad. Or he may already have a visitor, whose confession he is hearing or with whom he is having an intimate conversation. Let us knock more loudly. That's what it was—he didn't hear the first knock, perhaps because he was immersed in prayer. We can now hear him approaching the door with his elderly step, and opening it. He never asks who's there; he receives everyone, and although this has caused him trouble in the past, he never diverges from this established rule. He comes out in loose white canvas overalls and a white canvas skullcap. Quite often when he greets visitors he wears white canvas trousers and a white canvas shirt, which is not tucked in; above the shirt he wears a paramandyas;[5] and he is usually barefoot or wears soft leather shoes, though at very rare times he wears boots. He greets us, telling us we are welcome.

We enter and take off our coats. The master shows us his artful hangers. Together with him, we cross ourselves before the icons, and then we ask for his blessing. He blesses and kisses each of us, and then he asks us to sit down. We all feel, for some reason, that this blessing is not an ordinary one, that it is *special*. But no one can say what is special about it. The special thing might be that his blessing is done with complete sincerity and conviction; and it is true that the Starets is deeply convinced that the blessing is filled with power, and is not just an empty ritual. Or the special thing might be Father Isidore's inner *love*—not trumpeting itself, yet obvious to everyone—for the one being blessed. But that is far from being the whole thing. There's something else, but what it is can't be deciphered by the rational understanding. Finally, you stop trying to understand it rationally, and say simply: "It is God's grace. Such power has always emanated from saints." This renunciation of rational explanation fills us with tranquility, and as the visit progresses, *everything* seems clear and self-evident.

Father Isidore would always say something that lifts one's spirits. If two of us come to see him, he calls us the travelers to Emmaus; and if three come, that's extraordinarily good, for God appeared to Abraham in the form of three pilgrims. Sometimes Father Isidore would remark affectionately that it was for us, and for no one else, that he had been waiting, and that, as if on purpose, a previous visitor had brought him a tasty snack, which we could enjoy; or that God himself had sent us, because he had a special task he needed us to perform, a task he often thought up on the spot, in order

---

5. A piece of square cloth worn on the back, embroidered with the instruments of the Passion, and connected by ties to a wooden cross worn over the heart. The paramandyas represents the yoke of Christ.

to make us happy. Yes! If we had not forgotten to bring him a treat, we were not bashful about giving it to him: Father Isidore receives as simply as he gives—he thanks us and is joyful. For he always has visitors, and usually he has almost nothing to offer them; but he never lets anyone leave without giving him some little gift.

Then, he begins to take us around his cell. If you're a first-time visitor, he'll tell you the stories of the people depicted in the photographs. He'll recite a religious poem. He'll show you his flowers. Then he'll ask you to sit down and read to you a verse rendition of the Psalms composed by a blind priest. Or he'll ask if you want to accompany him in singing, from one of his books, something from the burial rite of the Mother of God performed in the Gethsemane Skete. Or he'll even ask you to take the book home and to copy out the relevant passages so that you could sing them later by yourself. Or he'll tell you something from the life of St. George the Recluse. Or he'll recall the writer Nikolai Gogol (Father Isidore's brother served as a valet for the Counts Tolstoy and was present at the death of Gogol), whom he revered, chiefly, it seems for the following verses (which he attributed to Gogol and distributed widely):

> O Most Holy Mother, to Thee
> I dare my voice to raise, etc.[6]

Then he leaves the visitors and goes to set up the samovar and to prepare some refreshments, which he offers joyfully. One of us sits down on Father Isidore's bed; another in an armchair; yet another on the little bench; we pray and start on the tea. After the refreshments, Father Isidore hands out gifts, teaches us his prayer of the Savior's five wounds, tells us his most cherished thoughts (about which below), gives us handwritten sheets with prayers and verses, blesses us, and says goodbye.

Chapter 3

In which Father Isidore's refreshments are described

Whenever someone comes to visit Father Isidore, the gray-haired Abba bestirs himself and starts running around like a young attendant, exerting

---

6. It is not known whether Gogol actually wrote these verses.

himself to offer food and drink to the visitor, whoever he may be. The Abba is anxious lest the visitor leave without being offered refreshments. He sets up the samovar and brings out into the "little vestibule" everything he has to offer. And when inexperienced visitors, embarrassed by this hustle and bustle, try to stop Father Isidore, imploring him to run around less, he always cites the example of Abraham, whose hospitality made him worthy of receiving the Holy Trinity, and he continues to scurry back and forth. Nothing can deter him, and those who have visited him several times no longer try to stop him from bustling around. If you try to stop him, he'll say, as always, that not only Abraham, but that we ourselves could be visited by God in the form of a guest. And Father Isidore bestirs himself even more furiously.

And God save you, pious reader, from bashfully refusing any of the refreshments offered to you. Believe me, the Starets will be deeply pained by your refusal. He will say that no one can refuse love. In reality, these are not just refreshments put out on a table; they are love made material. All that he possesses in his poverty, he brings out to his visitors; if he remembers anything else, he'll light up with joy, leap up, and run to get it. A piece of watermelon brought by a previous visitor, an apple, some biscuits or gingerbread, a few fruit-drops—all this is shared equally among the visitors. He leaves nothing for himself, saying that he has already eaten. But if he is asked to partake of the refreshments, he will be afraid that a refusal may offend his visitors and so he will take something—solely in order to please them.

Father Isidore likes to mix things that are considered unmixable. For example, he had a jar of his famous jam—a mixture of ordinary cherry jam, figs, cranberries, raisins, kvas, and black radish, I think. He'd sometimes explain how he prepared this jam, adding with a smile: "Some people don't like it, but I think it tastes good." He'd offer this jam to only a few select visitors, the "perfect" ones in whom he has confidence, as he liked to joke. To all others he offered ordinary jam. There were reasons for this: those who were not properly trained could barely swallow a single spoonful of this ascetic jam. Father Isidore, on the other hand, would eat several spoonfuls and praise it.

Even in these small things such as Father Isidore's "furniture" and his "jam," one can see a subtle yet very instructive irony in relation to the luxurious things valued by the world—one can see his independence from the world, his transcendence of it. "You think you can astonish me, a bearer of the Spirit of God, with your furniture and with your jams, with your comforts, but I do not pay any attention to you with all your comforts, for if the Spirit is present, then even my furniture and my jam are good, but if he is absent, then all your things are worth nothing." That, I think, is what Father Isidore meant to say with his "furniture" and his "jam." If this subtle irony can be called a holy foolishness, then Father Isidore can be called a "fool for Christ's sake." This holy foolishness was, I think, innate to him, and therefore there was nothing in it that was invented, premeditated, or artificial.

Father Isidore sometimes prepared meals in the same style as his jam. He'd make a salad by throwing together lettuce, olives, and anything else he had on hand, resulting in a mixture that no one wanted to eat, though he'd keep saying with an inviting smile: "But just try it."

Here, as in many other cases, it is impossible to draw a line of demarcation between his simplicity and love, on the one hand, and his independence from all the things in the world, on the other. He subverted everything, but he did this without the slightest smugness and without showing off. His simplicity was full of irony; his irony was simplicity itself. He could subvert all conventionality and look at everything with the eye of eternity but, amazingly, he did it without offending anyone. He would attack your complacency, throw you off the heights of human self-satisfaction, and trample your conceited smugness into the mud. But, amazingly, it was impossible to get angry at his attacks: Father Isidore would look at you with such childlike innocence as if he had no idea what he had just done. He demolished all your positions, but not a trace of smugness, self-satisfaction, or pride could be seen in his clear, wide-open eyes. It was as if it was not he who had done all this. He demolished your conceited complacency, but it is impossible to explain how he did it. The best analogy might be a man charged with electricity: when he touches another person, the latter feels a shock, but he doesn't believe his eyes—for the person touching him looks like a mere man. That's how it was with Father Isidore: he'd shock us with his electricity, while standing there as before, in his loose white overalls or in his canvas trousers and shirt, smiling affectionately. And you'd think: "He's just a nice old man, nothing more!"

But let us return to Father Isidore's refreshments. One day certain distinguished personages came to visit Father Isidore in his cell, and they found him at his samovar. The Abba was cooking potatoes in it. He offered his visitors tea, but they refused, not wanting any part of it.[7] Father Isidore then overturned the samovar and emptied the water, spilling the potatoes onto

---

7. The tea would have a potato flavor.

the floor. "Don't be afraid of the water. It's warm and will dry up soon. As for the potatoes, I'll finish cooking them later," he declared to his visitors, and started setting up the samovar again, having understood why the visitors had refused.

One day the Bishop paid a visit to Father Isidore, who was digging in the garden in his undergarments. The Bishop laughed: "What a dandy you are, what a dandy." "All right, all right. Sit down, Father," Father Isidore laughed too, and brought out the refreshments.

I don't remember if it was then, or some other time, that Father Isidore was sitting with Bishop E. in the "Inner Hermitage." In front of them there was a wobbly little table with glasses of tea, some biscuits in a rusty sardine can, and one and a half pieces of old gingerbread. They became immersed in conversation, but meanwhile it had started raining, so the two of them hid under "the Oak of Mamre" and continued talking. After it had stopped raining, Father Isidore gathered up the tea things left on the table and saw that the biscuits were floating in the sardine can. A few days later, the Bishop was again drinking tea at Father Isidore's, and the Starets again brought out the can with the biscuits, proposing that the Bishop finish eating what had been left over. "But they were drenched then," the Bishop said, dubiously. "I poured out the water and dried the biscuits, and now they're as good as new," the Starets explained.

Here is another incident that has remained in our memory. One day Bishop E. was walking in the woods near the Vifaniya Hermitage, and he encountered two Vifaniya seminarians walking toward him. "What are you doing?" the Bishop asked. "Taking a stroll." "Rather than counting the trees, it would be better if you visited some people." "Who?" "Have you heard of Father Idisdore?" They started talking, and the Bishop took them to see the Starets. Father Isidore greeted them the way he always greeted everyone: with gladness and love. He offered them biscuits and kvas, and then started a conversation with them. When they left, the seminarians were radiant and ecstatic.

Yes, pious reader! You may not believe that, even now, as I am writing these lines, tears of gratitude and tenderness are filling my eyes as I recall Father Isidore's refreshments. For those chunks of watermelon, those biscuits and pieces of apple, were not just food; they were always chunks and pieces of love and tenderness.

Chapter 4

Which tells the reader about the gifts that Father Isidore would give to everyone he met

If, taken to the extreme, the doing of good to others can (not completely accurately) be called a *passion*, then we can say that Father Isidore's sole passion was the giving of gifts. No one left the Father's cell without a gift. He never came to see anyone without a gift, never went anywhere with empty hands. He'd always bring something: a *prosphoron*, oil from the Mother of God, a sheet with prayers, or an icon. Even in someone else's house, he concerned himself with refreshments. He'd visit, for example, the Bishop or someone else, and he'd take out a black radish, a frozen apple, a jar of jam, a piece of gingerbread, or something else.

When he gave gifts, he thought not of their utility, but manifested his love; and therefore he was not embarrassed if the gift was a very small one. In the summer he'd sometimes bring a cucumber from his garden, or a dozen of his own raspberries on a leaf, and he'd present them with joy.

Even when he didn't personally visit someone, he tried to offer him a sign of love—some little gift. Sometimes when you visited him, he'd give you some gift, and then he'd also give you a commission: "Here's a piece of gingerbread—bring it over to Sergii. Here's a little *prosphoron*—take it to . . . (he'd name someone else)."

Once someone came to visit him who had spent the summer away from Sergiev Posad. The Starets was delighted: "Ah, you're here. All this time I've been saving those two berries on that bush for you." Indeed, in spite of the fact that autumn had come, there were two berries still hanging on a raspberry bush. The Starets plucked them, placed them on a leaf of grass, and offered them with love. And then he remembered that he had not yet sent the black radish he had selected for Bishop E.

He went to pull it out of the ground. A visitor offered to help him, because the old Abba could barely walk, and was tugging in vain on the radish-plant leaves. But the Abba refused: "If you're giving a gift, you have to do it yourself." He kept tugging and tugging until the leaves were torn off. He stood perplexed above the plant. But then he had an idea. He ran to get a knife and a cup, and began to pour water around the plant in order to soften the soil. He then dug around the plant with the knife, pulled the black radish out, and triumphantly went to wash it in the barrel. After washing it, he wrapped it in clean paper and handed it over to be delivered to the Bishop, with the words: "Let him eat it. It's delicious." But when he received his black radish, the Bishop kissed it and hid it in a place of honor.

Father Isidore especially loved to give gifts to those who came to visit him. He'd be visibly tormented until he'd decide what gift he would give to his visitor. He'd keep looking through all his possessions, and wouldn't grow calm until he found a suitable gift. He would be that way not only with laypersons and with clergy from outside the Skete, but even with his brothers in the Skete.

"I'd bring him dinner," one novice recalled. "And every time he'd give me three pieces of candy." "That's for you, to console you. You worked hard—you brought dinner." "But the candies cost money. I was embarrassed to accept the gift."

But there were a great many such cases: Father Isidore consoled many people by giving them little gifts. In extreme cases, for lack of anything else, he'd give away things that, for him, were necessities of life.

Not long before his death, he gave away all his possessions. But we'll recount that below.

Chapter 5

Which shows the reader how lovingly Father Isidore behaved toward all people

To manifest love for people—for rich or poor, for noble or peasant, for those of high rank or low, for pure (if there are any who are pure) or sinful, for Orthodox or non-Orthodox, even for non-Christians and pagans—was, for Father Isidore, just as necessary as, and even more necessary than, breathing. He did good works right and left, without thinking about it, simply and naturally—as if not suspecting that he was doing anything special, anything exceptional or unique. He'd never let a person go without telling him something instructive, comforting, and encouraging. When he walked past, he'd always say something pleasant. If he saw a gloomy face, he'd always dissipate the sorrow. If someone needed assistance, Father Isidore would give him everything he had. If that wasn't enough, he'd ask others—carefully, humbly, meekly, even shyly. If even that wasn't enough, he'd give away everything that came his way. And since seekers of assistance always crowded around Father Isidore, he never had anything for himself. Whenever he received any money from anyone, it would always disappear by the next day. He knew it was impossible for him to refuse anyone who asked, and so whenever he acquired a three-ruble note he'd always make haste to change it into a number of coins that he could hand out to several needy persons. Otherwise, he'd give away all his money to the first person who asked. He'd send money all over Russia—to some convict languishing in prison, to some soldier stationed far away from home, and so on. He'd often give away his meager dinner, and leave himself nothing to eat. "A poor man comes to me," Father Isidore says, trying to justify himself. "And he tells me that he hasn't eaten for three days, and to prove this is true, he kisses the dirty hem of my cassock. How could I not give him my dinner?" That was his justification. But he often gave things away without waiting to be asked. And people often deceived him.

He was put him in charge of the clothing and linens for the Skete, but here too, he gave everything away. One of the brothers at the Skete recalled that "Father Isidore's whole life was based on love and dedicated to the poor. Those who were poor, those who were downtrodden justly or unjustly, would go at once to Father Isidore, and to no one else. No one left him without being comforted. He gave everything away like the widow in the Gospel story. Once, someone asked to borrow Father Isidore's boots because he had to go somewhere, but then he vanished. And Father Isidore walked around all winter in flimsy shoes and socks."

"Who took the boots?"

"Do you really think he would say?"

Knowing that he would give everything away, the authorities at the Skete stopped issuing him new clothing. One of the brothers recounted the following: "He had always possessed a childlike simplicity and an unbounded love for people. Yes, there was poverty . . . No one can deny that. The many years I lived here, I never saw him wearing a new cassock! And no one ever saw him wearing new boots. He always wore what the authorities gave him, but they never gave him any good stuff, because they knew he'd give it away." In fact, Father Isidore didn't even have a decent outer cassock, and when he had to leave the Skete, to see the Bishop or visit the Academy, he had to borrow Father Avraamy's. That cassock had a past: it was first worn by Father Galaktion in the Lavra, and then Father Avraamy bought it from him for ten rubles. He and Father Isidore were close friends.

According to Father Avraamy, "Father Isidore was drawn more to people of the world. . . . All kinds of people visited him."

All kinds of people: monks and priests, actors and teachers, students and seminarians, soldiers, merchants, peasants, workers—they all came to see him. They came asking for money. They came seeking answers to perplexing questions or seeking to be comforted because life had made them weary. They came with heavy sins, fearful of punishment. They came with great joy, desiring to give him something that he would pass on to the poor. They came because they wanted to make peace with their enemies, to improve their family lives, to heal ailments, to expel demons. They came for all sorts of reasons. He met all of them with love and tried to satisfy all of them. But he especially loved the outcasts, even those who were justifiably so. When all had turned away from a man, it was here that Father Isidore's love bloomed with its greatest intensity. Take the case of one family, for example. There were rumors about its many dark deeds: that it had deceived many people, that it was being investigated by the police. But Father Isidore treated this family with a special solicitude: he sent the family members gifts, gave them whatever he had, did whatever he could to take care of them, and asked that others do the same.

He also showed a particular tenderness toward Jews, again probably because they were outcasts. Whenever you went to see him, he'd always recount something about some "little Jew" (his phrase) who had accepted Christianity because of his love. He had godsons who were "little Jews," and he continued to assist them throughout their lives. On his cell wall there hung a photograph of one such Jew with his family (a barber, as I recall), and Father Isidore would always explain to new guests what a good man he was, as if he was afraid that someone would offend his "little Jew" and say something bad about him. One such "little Jew" was subject to conscription, but because of his simplicity of soul (at least that's how Father Isidore explained it) he ran away when he was summoned to report for duty, for which he was sent to prison. From prison he sent Father Isidore letters filled with anguish and unbearable agony; he complained that he had been reduced to the state of a pauper, begged Father Isidore to pray for him and to send money, and wrote that only the memory of Father Isidore and the icon he had given him kept him from committing suicide. Father Isidore worried about him as if he was his own son, sent him everything he could, asked all his visitors to send something to the "little Jew," and wrote to him in his barely decipherable elderly scrawl. This was one of many cases; it would be impossible to remember or record all of them. Father Isidore's life overflowed with good deeds.

In the same way, a year or two before he died, Father Isidore took a young Korean under his wing, in spite of the fact that he would be suspected of associating with a Japanese spy.[8]

---

8. This was at the time of the Russo-Japanese War.

It often happened that he'd feed someone for a prolonged period of time, sharing his own meals with him. There was one man he fed for an entire winter, but this man stole Father Isidore's alarm clock, and Father Isidore even saw him do it. Father Isidore complained to one of the brothers: "None of this is important, but he also took my hammer, and now I can't nail anything to the wall." The hammer turned up later, but when the Starets was asked, "What about the alarm clock that was stolen from you?" he'd say, smiling guiltily: "Not stolen, taken." And he'd change the conversation.

In the same way, for about three years, right up to his death, he took care of a worker who had lost his arm in a machine accident. Father Isidore called him the "one-armed man." He fed the "one-armed man" with a spoon, dressed and undressed him, gave him money, and repeatedly prevented his attempts at suicide. Whenever he received a gift from anyone, he immediately gave it to the "one-armed man." There was no one Father Isidore didn't ask for assistance. Whatever the topic of discussion, Father Isidore invariably turned the conversation to the "one-armed man" and implored that everyone come to his aid. He caused Father Isidore many worries. But, from many examples, let me describe just one. Once a student came to see Father Isidore, and he witnessed the following spectacle: the worker was excitedly telling Father Isidore that he had to shoot or hang himself, because revolutionaries had supposedly told him to do it as a sentence pronounced on him. Father Isidore turned to the student and complained about the worker. But if even the Starets's words couldn't move the worker, would he really have listened to the student? And of course he didn't listen to him. So, not being able to convince him, the Starets and the student got down on their knees and prayed that the "one-armed man" come to his senses. Father Isidore then rushed off to the Starets Varnava to seek his assistance, but Father Varnava, probably having foreknowledge of what was going on, refused to talk to the "one-armed man." And then, with the "one-armed man" in tow, the ancient Abba Isidore staggered out of the Skete to the student's room in the monastery hotel. There they treated the worker to tea and begged and implored him to give up his intention. Father Isidore tried different things: he broke a *prosphoron* and gave pieces of it to the worker; he removed from his neck his holy treasure, his mother-of-pearl cross that had been brought to him by some pilgrim from Old Jerusalem—and put it around the worker's neck; he got some money from somewhere (he never had any of his own, of course!), gave it to the worker, and told him that the Lord had sent him this money to comfort him. But the hardened heart is not wounded by love. The eighty-year-old Starets then bowed down to the ground before the worker and implored him to come to his senses. The student also bowed down to the ground, as did his young wife, who was present all this time. The worker then bowed down before the Starets. Only God knows how all this imploring and bowing would have ended if a hotel servant had not knocked on the door and asked the student to vacate the room, because it had become known that the "one-armed man" was politically suspect. The student had to gather up his belongings and leave the hotel as quickly as possible. As for Father Isidore, he stood at the Skete gates, watching the student and his wife depart and repeating the Savior's words: "Blessed are they who are persecuted for righteousness' sake."

Chapter 6

In which the Orthodox reader learns about Abba Isidore's kindness toward all of God's creatures, toward wordless animals, plants of the earth, and everything in which life breathes—a kindness that likens human beings to God the Creator

Father Isidore showed kindness toward all living beings, and even toward unintelligent creatures. He showed concern not only for those made in the image of God but also for wordless animals—for the creatures who groan in pain together with man. He cared for and fed beasts and birds; he even took care of reptiles, frogs, mice, and rats. Even when the old Abba was sick, he did not forget his younger brothers: he told others to feed his family. Even just before his death, he asked members of a family he knew about the health of their cat: "So, how's the cat? Is it better?" he asked. "Yes, it's better." "Well, thank God, thank God."

It happened sometimes that a cat would injure a bird, and the injured bird would be lying on the road. Father Isidore would bend down with difficulty and pick up the injured bird. And so, a little sparrow with an injured wing would live in the Starets's cell until it was healed.

Once he was once asked: "Father, don't the mice bother you?" He smiled: "Not at all. I give them dinner and supper, and so they sit calmly. In the past all they did was make scratching noises all over the cell. But now that I put food out for them, near their hole, they've stopped running around. No, they don't bother me at all."

"I have a guest now. I don't live alone anymore," the Starets once said to the Bishop. The Bishop looked around inquisitively. "It's a frog that has come into the Hermitage," Father Isidore explained with a joyous smile. "But they run away," the Bishop said. "Yes, she ran away, but then she came back. I sing to her and talk to her, and now she doesn't run away." Indeed, a large frog was sitting on one of the stones of the "Thebaid" (about which the attentive reader already knows). Lowering his gray beard above the wordless creature and looking directly into her eyes with his clear eyes, with his elderly voice he sang her the Psalms of the meek King David.

Another Abba, St. Macarius the Great, used to say that just as the sun, in illuminating dirt and impurity, is not thereby made dirty but remains pure, so God's grace enters every soul and remains untainted. Likewise, from Abba Isidore of Gethsemane grace emanated on all beings that approached him, on human beings as well as on animals, but nonetheless the Abba remained above the world: with the help of the Mother of God, "he was created above the world's confusion."

The Starets had a special love for plants, for grasses, for flowers, for everything growing in the earth. He sees a weed that had been plucked out, and he picks it up and plants it in his "Inner Hermitage" or in his room—in a little box or in a sardine can that he found somewhere on the road. He acted that way because he pitied the wordless and gentle children of earth. For the same reason he stuck nettles all over the "Hermitage." And for the same reason he picked up branches that had fallen off and put them in water.

The Starets did not allow others to harm God's creatures wantonly. One of the brothers recounted that "once, after one of the services a few of us gathered at Father Isidore's. Right under the window, some sort of leafy fungus was growing; and without asking, we cut it. Father Isidore came out and asked, 'Who did that?' One of the brothers said, 'Mikhail cut it, but I brought him here.' 'Then, pray toward the Church of the Resurrection.' The brother got down on his knees and prayed. Father Isidore then called him over and gave him three pieces of candy to comfort him for having spoken crossly to him. Father Isidore had nurtured this fungus; he had watered it."

I could tell you many other things, pious reader, about the Starets's kindness toward all creatures. But what I've recounted is sufficient to attest that he was truly a lamenter for the world and an abba (i.e., father) not only to people but to everything that breathes and lives on the earth.

Chapter 7

Which shows how meek, gentle, and peace-loving Abba Isidore was, and which also tells how he forgave every offense against him

Father Isidore was free and independent. But he was full of meekness, gentleness, and forgiveness. He never judged anyone and was never angry at anyone; he was patient with everyone and there was no end to his forgiveness. If he noticed that he had made someone angry, he immediately asked for forgiveness, even if he hadn't done anything. If anyone offended him by word, and the offender's heart could not be softened despite all of Father Isidore's efforts, he would go away and wait for an opportune occasion to try again.

And he constantly urged others to do the same, serving as a model of meekness for them. If judgmental words were said in his presence, he would meekly, yet firmly and powerfully, put an end to them—and he did this in such a way that all words would cease. If he saw that some conflict had arisen between two men, or if, simply, their mutual love had cooled, he would urge them to make peace and ask each other's forgiveness; he'd particularly urge the one with whom he was speaking at the moment even though he might even be completely right in the matter. Father Isidore would ask, implore, and, finally, *demand*; he would do so gently and meekly, yet insistently and decisively, in such a way that no one would dare disobey him.

What took place between this spiritual father and his spiritual children was known only to them, and to their Father in heaven. And Father Isidore never revealed any of it either by word or even by a single movement of his head. It would all sink forever in the spiritual depths of the Starets, like a pebble in a deep lake. After the matter had ended, he'd not only expunge it from his soul and memory, but even seemed to expel it from being itself. In other words, it did *not exist*, and there was nothing to talk about. But it is worth recounting, pious reader, several incidents of this kind from Father Isidore's life.

At one point, he housed, fed, and supported a seminarian who had been expelled. But the seminarian turned out to be ungrateful; inspired by man's ancient enemy, the devil, he was possessed by an evil thought: he planned to kill Father Isidore and to steal his meager property. In Father Isidore's absence, he began to rummage through everything, looking for money. But then the Starets showed up. The seminarian went after him with a knife, demanding: "Give me your money!" But Father Isidore didn't have any money. Whenever he had any, he'd give it to the first person who asked.

While the seminarian, wielding his knife, was demanding the nonexistent money, a number of brothers ran in to protect the Starets.

The Abbot reproached the Starets:

"Why do you bring them (i.e., the indigent) into your home?"

The Starets apologized:

"But, Father, you can't ask impossible things from me, an old man! This is my only comfort!"

And so the Abbot couldn't do anything. Father Isidore continued to bring into his home men who sometimes did him harm. But he concealed this carefully, and we would learn of it only accidentally.

What happened next? The seminarian was tried, but Father Isidore saved the villain from punishment. During Father Isidore's testimony at the trial, he was asked whether the seminarian had intended to kill him. He answered: "No, he didn't intend to kill me." The judges were astonished, of course: "Didn't he go after you with a knife and shout that he was going to kill you?"

"Yes, he shouted... People shout all kinds of things, but do they necessarily want to kill you?"

The judges informed the seminarian that he was being released because of Father Isidore's testimony.

Here is another incident: Father Isidore was once insulted in the kitchen. He came into the kitchen to ask for something, but the cellarer's assistant rudely refused to give him what he was asking for. Just think, pious reader, would someone like Father Isidore ask for something extra? But even if he did ask for something extra, who would dare judge him? But the refusal here was so rude that it was clearly an insult. Whether it was for this sin or for some other reason, the offender became very sick soon after the offense and lay on his deathbed. As soon as Father Isidore learned about this, he went to see the offender to ask for his forgiveness: "I may have offended you by asking you to give me what I may not have needed." Soon after this, the cellarer's assistant recovered.

Father Isidore not only forgave transgressions against himself, but even covered with his love his brother's sin by trying to hide it from others. For example, a certain novice, or it may have been a layperson wearing a novice's clothing, frequently came to see him. Father Isidore always offered him tea and went out of his way to help him. But this "novice" behaved poorly toward Father Isidore: he'd go to visit the Starets's spiritual children and ask for things in the Starets's name. It's not known whether Father Isidore suspected this, but one day the truth came out: The "novice" went to see one of Father Isidore's spiritual sons and asked for envelopes, stamps, and letter-writing paper in the Starets's name. The spiritual son said that he was going to visit Father Isidore that same day and would bring him all these things himself. He went to Father Isidore's and handed him a package: "Here's what you asked for." But Father Isidore denied it: "No, I didn't ask for this." "But the novice told me you wanted these items." Father Isidore reflected for a moment and suddenly realized that his name had been used under false pretenses, but he made every effort to cover up his brother's sin. Dismayed by this unexpected discovery and clearly ashamed for his brother, he decided to stop insisting that he had not asked for the postal items. "It's good you brought this—it will be very useful," he said, taking the package and changing the subject. And so he did not expose the sinner, did not condemn him.

Not only did Father Isidore personally forgive transgressions, but he also urged others to do the same. To establish peace was a necessity for him. Here is an example of this, and from this example the reader will also learn about Father Isidore's relationship with the celebrated Starets Varnava, who later became his spiritual son. A certain deacon, a student of the Theological Academy, recounts that he visited Father Isidore shortly before the latter's death. The Starets was reading the Life of Father Varnava and therefore spoke about this book, approving it; but he also noted that the story told on page 17 was inaccurate. This is how Father Isidore retold the story:

One day, a soldier acquaintance of his paid a visit to Father Varnava, who at that time was still the novice Vasily. Father Varnava received him cordially and presented him with a book of holy Gospels that he himself had received as a gift from his Starets, Daniil. When he learned about this incident, Father Daniil summoned the novice and asked him about this book of Gospels; and when Father Varnava told him the whole truth, Father Daniil became furious and told him never to appear before his eyes again. This is where Father Isidore came to the rescue. Sorrowing greatly, Father Varnava went to see his friend and teacher Father Isidore (who was teaching him to decipher the stresses in the sacred texts) and described his grief to him, seeing no way to repair what had happened. But Father Isidore found a way: "Don't worry. I have the same sort of Gospel book. Take it and give it to the soldier, who's still in the hotel; and take yours back from him. And then we'll go together to the Starets to ask for his forgiveness." And that's what they did. Father Isidore went down on his knees before Starets Daniil and implored him to forgive his friend, while the guilty novice wept. The Starets's heart was softened by this loving request, and he was reconciled with Father Varnava.

Chapter 8

In which the pure-hearted reader will see great humility in the Holy Spirit combined with great independence

I will tell you, attentive reader, that great modesty and profound humility dwelt in the heart of our Father Isidore. He rarely spoke about his works of God, and when he did so, it was always for the purpose of edification. For the most part he concealed them. He never thrust himself forward, never spoke about himself in such a way as to elevate himself above others. The good works he did he concealed not only from others, but even from himself: he did them and then seemed to forget about them. Truly, in the words of our Lord and Savior Jesus Christ, his right hand did not know what his left hand was doing. Therefore, he did not have a high opinion of himself, but always regarded himself as nothing and believed sincerely that he was the worst of men. Sometimes great joy would erupt in the heart of a visitor when he contemplated Father Isidore's incarnate heavenly beauty, and he would exclaim: "Father, how good you are!" But the perplexed Abba would dispute this: "What do you mean, good? I'm bad—the worst of men."

The Abba was free of pride. He could ask anyone for anything, even get down on his knees before anyone and kiss the hand of anyone, if spiritual healing demanded it. He humbled himself simply, without exertion or affectation, as if the humbling of oneself were an ordinary matter. But great spiritual humility was combined in him with great independence. The Starets did not feel superior to any man, no matter how insignificant, contemptible, and sinful this man may have been. But there was also no man before whom the Starets would have been untrue to himself, no matter how important and influential this man may have been. The Abba spoke his mind to everyone, and especially to men of authority. Let me also tell you, pious reader, that the Abba feared no one, groveled before no one, forgot his human dignity for no one, always felt independent and free, and was subordinate only to God.

Once, when he was still just a beardless cell-attendant of the Deputy Abbot of the Lavra, Antonii, he intruded into a conversation between Antonii and the Metropolitan of Moscow, Filaret. The great Filaret and the wise Antonii were sitting at their tea and reflecting in unison on the necessity of an ecumenical council and on union with the Catholics. But the question arose, who would take the lead at the council? It could be foreseen that neither the Orthodox nor the Catholics would concede in this matter, and so the council would not come to pass. At this point, Father Isidore entered, carrying a tray of tea things. "The Mother of God will take the lead," he said. "The chairman's place should remain vacant: it will be reserved for the Mother of God."

His entire life, Father Isidore nurtured the idea of the necessity of the unification of the churches, and their schism was for him a *personal* sorrow and a *personal* insult. "All of us are of one Mother born/And Her suffering is not to be borne"—he'd sorrowfully recite these verses from memory and do it repeatedly. It was obvious that the thought of the schism afflicted him greatly. Sometimes he'd add: "It's all because of a single letter—we're Cafolics and they're Catholics.[9] It's necessary to pray to the Mother of God. The union cannot be accomplished by human powers, but it will be accomplished through Her." Father Isidore associated the union of the Eastern and Western churches with the final destiny of the world; and sometimes, pointing to the anti-Christian movement in Russia and abroad, he expressed his most hidden and cherished thought: "The time of the Antichrist is at hand. There will soon be such persecution of Christians that we will have to hide."

When Father Isidore spoke these words, you had to believe they would come to pass. His cloudless face would grow dark; his clear smile would vanish for a moment; his eyes would gaze seriously, piercing the future. There would be a sense of terror: *something* was coming, advancing toward us. . . . But this moment would pass; and the prophetic seriousness would hide, fade, vanish. But this single moment would affect us for a long time.

The thought of the unity of the churches, in conjunction with these terrible forebodings, was one of his most cherished thoughts. Once he even wrote letters about these things to Tsar Alexander III, Gladstone, and Bismarck. The letters were written in pencil, barely grammatical, and in Russian, of course. To Gladstone and Bismarck he also sent, in addition to the letters, some of our liturgical books and Gogol's prayer to the Mother of God. It isn't known if Gladstone and Bismarck ever received these things, but we do know that the letter to the Tsar reached the Court, which sent a reprimand to the Skete. Afterwards, Father Isidore would repeatedly tell the story of this exploit of his, and laugh at how unexpectedly it had turned out. But he continued to be fearless and independent.

He himself used to recount other incidents of his life that clearly revealed how independent he was.

When Leonid was Deputy Abbot of the Trinity Lavra of St. Sergius, fear possessed the monks. Leonid had been a military man and he introduced

---

9. The Orthodox Church is called "One, Holy, Catholic (*kafolicheskaya* in Russian), and Apostolic."

a military discipline into the monastery. One time, he commanded that the last hermits saving themselves in the caves (where now stands the Church of the Chernigov Mother of God) be dragged out from under the earth and be made to have their meals together with everyone else. "Time to put an end to this kind of fasting!" he said.

Everyone trembled before this pastor, who commanded the monastery like a regiment. As the pious reader will no doubt foresee, the Deputy Abbot soon had his eye on the ever-fearless Father Isidore. Father Isidore, being summoned, entered the Deputy Abbot's apartment. Father Leonid expected Father Isidore to come straight up to him to kiss his hand, but Father Isidore first began to pray before the icons. Father Leonid was enraged, and he found an excuse to vent his fury. Since childhood Father Isidore's right arm had been somewhat damaged, making it impossible for him to bring it all the way up to his left shoulder. So, Father Leonid shouted at him: "Fool! You don't even know how to cross yourself!" Father Isidore, calm as always, looked directly into the Deputy Abbot's eyes, and said simply and without any trace of defiance: "I am not afraid of you." Father Leonid went into a frenzy and spewed out a stream of abuse. But Father Isidore declared once more: "I am not afraid of you." They say that the Deputy Abbot practically had to grab him physically and push him out of the apartment. But this incident seemed to have had a sobering effect on Father Leonid, and afterwards he became more restrained. Father Isidore would recount this whole incident with a smile, acting out both roles.

A similar incident occurred when he was living in the Paraclete Skete. Father Isidore wanted to have a partition put up in his cell, creating a storeroom for his extra stuff. But the authorities became suspicious of him, who was already a starets: "What for? For what purpose?" A desire to slander him was what lay behind these questions. Then he declared: "I am putting it up in order to keep women there!" For that answer he was expelled from the Paraclete.

In view of Father Isidore's straightforwardness, boldness, and independence, all high personages who visited the Skete were carefully shielded from him. Following in the footsteps of Bishop Filaret, the founder of the Skete, the Metropolitan of Moscow, Sergii, once lived there. With staff in hand, he sometimes strolled through the Skete without any ceremony. Every effort was made to keep Father Isidore from talking to the Metropolitan, but one day he couldn't be shielded. Our Abba ran into the Metropolitan and said to him: "Look, Father: they write in the newspapers that there's famine in India, that the Indians are starving. We, on the other hand, have more than enough of everything. You should send them money" (i.e., from the Lavra).

To prevent the repetition of such a conversation, the Metropolitan's attendant issued the following order: "If Father Isidore shows up, don't let him near."

Not long before his death, Father Isidore went against everyone once again. This is what happened: Between the Iversky Women's Monastery on the Vyksa, which had been founded by Starets Varnava, and the Skete where Father Varnava lived, a dispute arose about who should have the founder's body when he died. Varnava himself asked that he be buried in the monastery he had founded, but the Skete wanted the Starets's body for itself. The Iversky nuns petitioned the court, which polled the Skete brothers to find out who was for the surrender of the body and who was against it. Only two of the elders were "for"; Father Isidore was one of them.

Even near death Father Isidore remained true to himself. There was an elder brother who was responsible for the material needs of the brothers and who was known for his hard-heartedness. In spite of the fact that he was dying, Father Isidore went to see this brother and presented him with an icon of the Mother of God called "The Softening of Cruel Hearts." This gift combined everything: tenderness toward the brothers, a desire to act on the hard-hearted man by kindness, a prayer to the Mother of God for her help, and a strong yet subtle hint to the sinful brother.

As always, the meek Father Isidore was not afraid of judging. But he judged with such love that those being judged rarely got angry at him.

Chapter 9

In which the writer tries to give the reader an idea of Father Isidore's ascetic labors

I will now tell you, my very patient reader, what I know about the *ascetic labors* of the Great Starets. But you should know that Father Isidore concealed his ascetic labors in great silence—as if in the secret inner hermitage of his soul. In ancient times, a certain brother came to a skete to see Abba Arsenius of Egypt, and when he looked through the door, he saw that Starets Arsenius seemed to be on fire, and this vision terrified him. In the same way, we can get an idea of Father Isidore's ascetic labors only by stealing a look through the gate of his inner hermitage. The things I will relate are things of which I have only a fragmentary and haphazard knowledge.

Father Isidore never interrupted his fasting; and in his constant fasting it pleased him to abstain from speech. He was always abstinent in food and drink, of course, because he never had much food and drink. He never had much of anything, and if anything was brought to him, he'd give away to others not only what was brought to him, but sometimes even his own meals. Moreover, even the little he had he ate not in such a way as to enjoy the natural and legitimate sweetness of the food, but in such a way as to worsen the taste of the food. He used to say: "Food shouldn't be too tasty." I've already described the jam and the salads he made. The story of his raspberry jam is particularly remarkable. This is how Father Efrem, hieromonk of the Savvinsko-Zvenigorod Monastery, Father Isidore's spiritual son and friend, recounts it:

> It does not surprise me that, when the Skete Fathers are asked about Father Isidore, they always find it hard to describe clearly the ascetic side of the Starets's life. In a strange way, the following incident may give some idea of his ascetic life.
>
> When I was living in the St. Sergius Lavra, I remember that once, during the Dormition Fast, Father Isidore paid a visit to the Lavra from the Paraclete Skete. He came by to see me. I prepared some tea and started to serve him; with the tea I served a superb raspberry jam. As the Starets was partaking of the tea and jam, he remarked: "This jam is excellent; they say it's good for colds." I said: "Yes, raspberries are considered to be a warming and invigorating agent." I then proposed that he take the whole jar of it back with him to the Skete. He looked at me and at the jar with a slightly inquisitive glance and said: "The jar is really big (it contained 5–6 pounds of jam), but if you can spare it, I'll take it—and save it for the winter." I carefully wrapped the jar in sheets of newspaper and tied it around with a napkin, and Father Isidore carried it home in a bundle with other provisions.
>
> The day after this visit the weather was warm and summery, and the Lavra hieromonk Feodor (who, too, was devoted to the Starets) and I decided to ride to the Paraclete Skete and visit Father Isidore. We arrived and knocked on the door of his cell, while saying a prayer (as was our custom). The door opened, and Father Isidore met us with an angelically radiant smile and with the greeting:
>
> "Dear guests! Welcome! So, you miss me already! Well, let's go to the stumps.[10] I'll take the samovar there, and we'll have some tea."

---

10. Next to the cell there was a little garden with a round table. It was encircled by chairs that Father Isidore had made out of tree-stumps and branches. (Florensky's note.)

By chance, on a shelf in the vestibule, I spotted the jar of jam I had given him yesterday, but more than half of it was already gone, and slices of fresh cucumber were mixed into what remained. I couldn't restrain myself from shouting:

"Father, it's a sin and a shame to ruin good jam by putting cucumber slices in it!"

The Starets answered good-naturedly:

"Don't get upset! Things shouldn't be too good: they'll sweeten you up too much. It's better if they're half and half."

"But what did you do with the jam? Did you put it in other jars?"

"Yes, I distributed it. Yesterday, after I returned from visiting you, I put some in a teacup and took it to the blind old monk, Father Ammony, and I also gave a little to Ignasha the canonarch, and a tiny bit to Vaniusha the bell-ringer. All of them are friends of yours, I think."

"I never heard of them."

"I told them that Serenya (a diminutive for my name in the world, Sergii) has sent you this jam, so you should mention his name in your prayers. And so all things will be well."

"But Father, you wanted to save the jam for the winter."

"You keep harping on this . . . You should go to the stumps and have your tea. I have nothing else to offer you—no one was expecting you today."

That gives an idea of how Father Isidore fasted. But he put a higher value on prayer; he lived by it, breathed it, was nourished by it. As the Starets Avraamy attests, Father Isidore ceaselessly repeated the prayer of Jesus in his mind.

In a corner of his inner hermitage, kneeling on a large stone, he'd often pray long hours, competing with Seraphim, the wonder-worker of Sarov. Every vigil and every liturgy he'd spend kneeling on the cold floor in the lower tier of the Church of St. Filaret the Charitable. He'd ceaselessly remember the Lord Jesus Christ and often, with deep heart-piercing love, he'd repeat the prayer of his five wounds (with which the reader will become familiar below if, with God's blessing, this writer finishes writing the Life of Father Isidore).

As for Father Isidore's most important labor, his labor of prayer, I do not even know what to say. Breathing is a necessity for human beings; yet, pious reader, if you were asked about the breathing of your father in the flesh, could you say much about it? Not much, for breathing is something completely natural for human beings. Likewise, prayer was something completely natural for Father Isidore. We did not notice how he breathed into himself the grace of God, just as you do not notice how your father in the flesh breathes air into his lungs. It would be another thing if your father in the flesh rarely breathed air into his lungs and if our father in the spirit rarely breathed grace into himself—not more than once or twice a day. But such was not the Starets's life of prayer. Everyone felt that Father Isidore didn't cease praying when he was conversing or when he was going about his household chores, but no one dared to ask him about this. Truth be told, such questions seemed idle and superfluous.

Chapter 10

Which tells the reader about the spiritual freedom of the grace-filled Starets Isidore and also about how he would disregard fasts

Father Isidore's profound humility was combined in him with an extreme disregard for what people thought. In the same way, his asceticism was combined with complete spiritual freedom. Truly, he was aware that "the Son of Man is the Lord also of the sabbath" and that "the sabbath was made for man, and not man for the sabbath." He was not subject to the law, but was free. He lived according to the rules of the church, but at every moment of his life he knew the difference between the spirit and the letter of these rules. And if it was necessary, he would freely and powerfully violate the letter in order to preserve the spirit. That is why people said about him things like "I didn't see anything exceptional in his life. His life wasn't particularly strict: he didn't despise material things. He'd bathe in the bathhouse. He'd have a little wine from time to time."

But there would also be outright violations of the church rules. Once, on a fast day, Father Avraamy visited a certain family. The Starets was offered an omelet.

"I can't. I'm afraid," Father Avraamy refused.

But Father Isidore just ate an omelet that was offered him.

In order not to offend his hosts, Father Isidore disregarded the fast. He used to say: "It's better to disregard the fast than to offend people by refusing."

On another occasion the two fathers visited the same family. Again, it was a fast day. They were offered butter. Father Isidore spread it on his bread and ate it, whereas Father Avraamy refused it.

"Why aren't you eating?" Father Isidore asked.
"It's Friday."
"I order you to eat."
"I'm not your spiritual son," Father Avraamy objected.

Once, in the first week of the Great Fast,[11] Father Isidore informed the Bishop of the following:

"Father, forgive me, for I have sinned: I ate forbidden food during the first week of the Great Fast."
"What happened?" the Bishop asked.
"Some milk was left over, and since it was a pity to pour it out, I drank it."

So, Father Isidore ate forbidden food twice during the first week of the Great Fast, and this happened just a few years before his death, when he was very elderly. But what is the explanation for these incidents? Perhaps, he was training himself for the ultimate humility? Or, perhaps, he was teaching humility to his interlocutor?

Also, Father Isidore did not refuse wine. He'd say: "It would be much worse to offend a person by refusing." When he was offered some at a meal, he'd drink a glass and sometimes a glass and a half. When he was very elderly, he'd drink up to three, but never more.

Also, he did not seem to follow the usual prayer rule. The Bishop asked him once:

"What rule do you follow, Father?"
"I don't have any particular rule."
"What do you mean, you don't have any? Didn't you serve with strict rule-followers?"
"I just don't have any. When I asked the Starets on Athos (Father Isidore once lived on Old Athos) about the rule, he said: 'Why do you need a rule? I myself don't have one. Here's a rule for you—constantly keep saying: Lord, have mercy. A long prayer, you'll forget, but this you won't forget—it's just three words.'"

"It's such a simple rule," Father Isidore concluded with a smile. "But I can't even manage to do something so simple."

---

11. In the Catholic Church, this corresponds to Lent.

However, it is necessary to understand the meaning of what he said. Father Isidore did not reject the rule, of course; and of course his prayers consisted of much more than just "Lord, have mercy." But his answer manifested both his great humility and his great freedom of spirit; and that is what he taught others.

Sometimes he'd leave the Skete without asking permission. One of the fathers recounted the following: "We had a recluse, Father Alexander. Father Isidore was close to Father Alexander: they confessed their sins to each other. Father Isidore did not take sins that seriously. I'd sometimes encounter him outside the Skete and ask: 'Father, did you ask permission?' 'Just say nothing about this.' We asked to go see Bishop E., but the Abbot didn't give us permission. He said: 'He'll laugh at you. I'll tell him myself.' Afterwards, Father Isidore said: 'The Abbot has his own politics.' And he'd continue going to the Bishop."

Father Isidore's freedom of spirit is also clearly attested, pious reader, by something that was a fairly frequent occurrence: during confession, wearing his *epitrachēlion* around his neck and a single cuff, he'd go to tend to his samovar, leaving alone the person whose confession he was hearing and instructing him to read his sins off from a list glued to a piece of cardboard.

Soaring above the world, Father Isidore could enter it with impunity. He did not despise or disdain the world, and he was not afraid of it. It was that he always possessed the power to overcome the world and to let it, purified, into his consciousness. The temptation of the world did not tempt him, and the seductive splendor of the world did not seduce his pure heart.

Father Efrem recounted the following incident: He once entered his cell and saw that there was a novel by Paul de Kock[12] on his table. Father Efrem conjectured that one of the monks had put the book there as a joke. But at that moment Father Isidore arrived and, to Father Efrem's extreme amazement, he said that he had put the book there.

"But do you know what kind of book this is? Where did you get it?" asked the astonished Father Efrem. Father Isidore said that one of the brothers had brought him the book, probably as a joke.

"You're a learned man," he said to Father Efrem. "And so I'm giving the book to you."

"But it's indecent."

"That's all right. Read it. Discard the bad things, but gather the good things into your heart."

---

12. Charles Paul de Kock (1793–1871), French writer, author of risqué novels.

That was an example of Father Isidore's freedom of spirit. He did everything lightly, without strain, as if playing. And in every unconstrained movement of his soul, you felt power—a mighty power much greater than all the exertions of ordinary men.

That was how he was in the presence of people. But what he did when he was alone with God—no one knows and can understand except his Divine Interlocutor.

Chapter 11

Which informs the reader about what would happen during confession with Father Isidore

No matter what day or hour you came to see Father Isidore, he'd never refuse to hear your confession. Furthermore, when he was asked, he—burdened with years and with sickness—would never refuse to go to your home, in Posad, to hear your confession even though it was about two miles from the Skete to Posad.

"People with all sorts of sins constantly swarmed around Father Isidore," one Starets recalled. "Some lived outside the law. All sorts of men came to see him—some with swords. The time of the strikes[13] was especially dangerous for him. They'd come to see him and say: 'We cut down so many men with our swords, it didn't depend on us—the authorities told us to do it.' His courage was amazing—he could handle anything. Once I saw men with swords coming out of his cell—these were the kind of men he was acquainted with."

"You said, Father, that someone had cut down men with his sword?"

"A soldier."

Even a few days before his death, barely able to sit up on his deathbed, Father Isidore kept hearing confessions.

The desire of the repentant man to cleanse himself—that was what Father Isidore's spiritual gaze was directed at during confession. He gave few if any admonitions during confession. His spiritual simplicity softened even the old, hardened sores in people's souls. He'd recount: "A man would come to see me. He'd be carrying a sin around for twenty years, but he'd tell it to me."

---

13. Allusion to the Revolution of 1905. The "men with swords" were soldiers who were ordered to kill protestors.

Even during an ordinary meeting with Father Isidore, his gaze would warm and calm a disturbed soul, as if piercing it with a meek solar ray. When Father Isidore would look at a sinful brother whose soul was unclean, the brother would avert his eyes because it was impossible for him to bear the radiance of Father Isidore's gaze. Once, someone who had never seen Father Isidore before, a man with a heavily burdened conscience, fell on his knees before the Abba and asked for his prayers. One of the Skete brothers recalled meeting the Starets in the garden: "He took my hand and gazed into my eyes as if he could see through me. I was raising and lowering my head, and he said: 'Peace be with you, Misha.'"

Father Isidore would usually hand a list of sins to the person confessing and tell him to read it out loud and to make a mental note of the ones that applied to him. Sometimes, during such a reading, Father Isidore would even leave his cell wearing his tattered *epitrachēlion* and his single ancient cuff, to prepare refreshments for the person confessing.

He never got angry. If the sin was bad, he wouldn't become enraged, but would commiserate with the sinner. Whatever was confessed, he remained calm and equable, and said lovingly: "You should pray more." In particular, he'd advise the sinner to seek the Mother of God's intercession. But he'd always tell the sinner about the efficacy of the prayer of the Savior's five wounds and explain how to say it.

Father Isidore's confession, though outwardly simple, was utterly special because it was filled with intimations of eternity. Ordinarily, at confession you'd see a man before you. But here, it was just the opposite: the person confessing saw before him not a man, not even a witness of the Lord, but Eternity Itself. Eternal truth itself looked at you and saw you, but it did so without looking and without seeing. It was as if you were confessing before the Universe. No complaint, no reproach, not even a single movement was visible on Father Isidore's face. He didn't even ask any particular questions. In other words, everyone coming to him for confession knew that he had entered the kingdom of *freedom*.

So far we have talked about the confession of laypersons and, in general, of persons not from the Skete.

Father Isidore was not the designated confessor for everyone in the Skete, although, earlier, in the course of eight years, he used to confess the hieromonks. However, it would often happen that, in the hope of reforming one brother or another, the Father Confessor officially designated by the Skete would treat this brother too severely or even chase him away: "I don't want to see you again."

The sinner would be on the verge of despairing or of becoming embittered; and then, with sorrow in his soul, he would come to Father Isidore. The Starets would receive everyone; and his mere gaze would soften the despairing and embittered soul. But the official Father Confessor would be filled with anger at Father Isidore, who had acted in defiance of his intentions; and he even complained to the Abbot, asserting that Father Isidore's approach could not reform the brothers. But despite all prohibitions, Father Isidore could not refuse to see the brothers who came to him to repent; and seeing their despair, he acted with love, not with severity. He did not impose penances but, on the contrary, tried to comfort, to encourage, to calm, to instill peace in the soul. For example, if one of the brothers drank, Father Isidore would receive him and chase out the cruel despair and hopelessness.

But he could also act differently. Sometimes, brothers came to Father Isidore not because the Father Confessor had chased them away, but because they wanted to avoid the expected penance. Father Isidore received these brothers too, but he did impose penance. "This is for a double sin," he'd say. "For avoiding the Father Confessor and for the sin you came to confess."

One brother had eaten some sausage. He had been offered some at the Lavra and didn't have the strength to refuse. This brother was afraid to go to the Father Confessor, so he went to Father Isidore and told him what had happened.

"So, you filled up on sausage?" asked Father Isidore.

"What do you mean, 'filled up'? I just had three slices."

"All right—three hundred reverences to the ground."

"But, Father, it was only three slices."

"No, otherwise I won't forgive you. Go then to the Father Confessor. Three hundred reverences to the ground."

"I only ate a little. They offered it to me."

"It's for a double sin. For the sausage and for wanting to avoid the Father Confessor."

But in Father Isidore's severity there was much softness. He knew that the Father Confessor would impose more than three hundred reverences. The brother had no choice but to agree to the penance imposed by Father Isidore.

Chapter 12

Which contains "The Conversation about the Rock," where a certain professor describes his visit to Father Isidore and what ensued

One day a certain professor invited me (the writer of Father Isidore's life, which you are holding in your hands, dear reader) to pay him a visit and began telling me about his visit to Father Isidore and how the Starets heard his confession. The memory of this confession profoundly agitated the professor's soul. For a long time he could not find the appropriate words, but kept returning to the beginning of his story. He finally succeeded in stopping the tears that had been unceasingly filling his eyes at the thought of Father Isidore and in collecting his thoughts to some extent. Then, still not satisfied with his words, he told me to write down the following account, which he called:

"The Conversation about the Rock"
I have had it up to here with the intelligentsia,[14] and the last thing I want is to make it seem that it was nothing more than a member of the intelligentsia becoming "infatuated" with Father Isidore. That is not what happened at all. The fact of the matter is that I (a professor, a member of the intelligentsia, a sick man—write whatever you like) slammed into this Starets with my forehead, and that nothing intermediary remained between me and him, between me and Christ. I went to the Starets, driven crazy by church questions, by politics, by the bishops, by Merezhkovsky, by the Theological Academy and its professors. But all the rationalism and spite I came with melted away in Father Isidore's cell. But then it returned, and I was sick again. Down to the smallest details, his clothing, his eyes—there persists in me the memory of having slammed into something hard. The cell, the flowers with no fragrance. The pure air. You breathe freely. I am unable to describe the cell—I usually can't remember details. But there was something awfully luminous, pure, and light in the cell—something utterly amazing.

---

14. The caste of professional intellectuals, who at this time were attempting to find a rapprochement between the Russian Orthodox Church and secular society. Specifically, this refers to the "Religious-Philosophical Meetings" organized among others by the prominent writer Dmitry Merezhkovsky and including bishops and professors of the Moscow Theological Academy. The author of "The Conversation about the Rock" felt that this effort was marred by the intelligentsia's rationalism, negating the authentic religiosity represented by Father Isidore and other monks and ascetics.

I have now collected my thoughts to some extent and will describe my visit in a more systematic way.

I entered the cell, knowing what a cell is. I was about fifty years old. I had seen both monks and priests. Sent by the Bishop to his confessor, I came with a sense of formal humility. It wasn't that I was comforted the way I would have been comforted by any priest whom I would have considered my father and judge as far as my confession and my conduct were concerned. No, it was different. With a friend I entered the small cell in the corner of the monastery. I was startled by the brightness, cleanliness, and simplicity of the cell; and I thought that everything would be as it always had been, that a cordial, proper monk would receive me cordially and properly, that I would confess properly, and that everything would be as it should be. But it was all different. It suddenly seemed to me that this simple cell contained *infinite power*. I didn't know why that was so, and my doubt whispered to me: "It's your nerves—you're being overdramatic and imagining something that's not there."

The old man, *clearly* understanding who and what I was (I realize this now), greeted me as if he was a stupid, ignorant monk; and in a conversation that lasted several minutes and in which I tried to prove and explain something to him, I saw *clearly* that I couldn't explain anything to him or tell him anything. I saw that if I started explaining, he'd briefly and clearly answer that I was smarter than he was in theology and philosophy, that I knew everything better than he did, from philosophy to catechism, and that it was unfathomable why I would have come to him, a Starets, to seek and ask about something. I felt then that I had come to seek *something else*, and I started to weep. To my weeping the Starets responded with a prayer and by saying "blessed are those who weep, for they shall be comforted." And I understood what he meant to tell me with this prayer and with the words about those who weep: "That is how I respond to you, and that is how you should respond to yourself, if you've only come to me for a catechetical or homiletic response."

Once again I became ashamed. I felt then—simply and clearly—that, by God's grace, I was exactly where I had to be; and I asked the Starets to hear my confession and that of my friend who had come with me. It was then that I experienced what I can only call an "impression of the church."

The Starets, dressed as he was in untucked shirt, canvas trousers, and soft slippers, got up calmly and said:

"All right."

He took out his *epitrachēlion* and put it on. He then energetically buttoned his old brocade cuff to his shirtsleeve and blessed God. Then, turning toward my friend and me, he told us to read Psalm 50,[15] the Creed, and a number of prayers. I could barely read the Psalm and the prayers, even though I knew them in three languages. Making mistake after mistake, I felt, when I was corrected, that some *power* was supporting and guiding me.

When we had finished reading the prayers, he handed me a little book from which I was to read the confession of sins according to the rule. Here, he looked at me and at my friend standing next to me, and his look told me that he, with the power vested in him, did not need my chatter and quibbles, but that I, together with my brother standing next to me, should read what is written, repenting and confessing what I hear and see.

I was ashamed that I was emphasizing individual words of the confessional prayer. I imagined the Starets was telling me:

"Why is that needed? Why do I need your brilliant logic and comprehension?"

After he had read the prayer of absolution, I could say only one thing:

"I hear in my soul, I do not know why: 'Christ is risen from the dead.'"

He completed the hymn:

"Trampling down death by death, and upon those in the tombs bestowing life!"

Then I wept again, and he told me again that I would be comforted. And when I was leaving, he kissed my hand.

I know only one thing: that I saw the Rock and upon it the church and that in the future I would be able to resolve all the questions besetting me by recalling that vision.

And apart from this magnificence I can say nothing. For me this has always remained a great shock. The church revealed herself for a moment and then hid—the church in canvas trousers and gold cuffs and an *epitrachēlion* on the Rock. There was never anything like this . . . For Father Isidore was not what people call a "celebrated" or popular confessor. I've known and seen confessors and elders who have been referred to as "peasants" and I've known those who have been referred to as "intellectuals." But the fact is that I, an aristocrat, saw him neither as a peasant nor as an intellectual. The fact is that none of my definitions were of any use to me. I repeat: He is neither the one nor the other; he is more. He is not Varnava (whom I've never seen, but about whom I've heard that he conducts this business in a kind of peasant way). Nor is he one of the refined confessors

---

15. In the Septuagint numbering.

who are so abundant in Moscow. He is something in between; that is to say, he is something great that is not reducible to my definitions.

I am acquainted with a certain bishop. He, too, is full of grace. But his grace has to be taken by force: he does not bestow it unless he is made to. By contrast, dealings with Father Isidore were characterized by an extraordinary lightness and ease. Let me clarify what I mean.

The so-called peasant-priests are extraordinarily "easy." I know perfectly well how easy it is to confess before all kinds of village priests—be they ignorant peasants or black-hundredists.[16] But with them you always feel that there remains something in you which they cannot understand and which you do not dare demand they understand.

But here it was different. Here, there was a direct and immediate lightness and ease. This absence of a double curtain is extremely rare. And this is how I summarize my impression as a whole:

I, an educated intellectual, am familiar with all the conventionalities with which one can approach a confessor's soul. But I was completely flummoxed: none of these conventionalities were of any use; there was nothing of this sort in Father's Isidore's soul.

That was how he concluded his narrative.

Chapter 13

Which will tell the reader what Father Isidore taught in his conversations

Abba Isidore did not like to lecture. He did not like scholarly argumentation, and he'd tell others to stay away from it:

"Don't be overly curious about these things," he'd say. "It's dangerous for a monk to be overly curious."

He spoke very harshly concerning the *Dogmatics* of Makary, Metropolitan of Moscow; and he said about its author that "Makary himself had drowned because of this," i.e., because of his effort to squeeze living faith in the vise of reason.

Father Isidore was very wary when discussing faith.

---

16. Members of a reactionary movement supporting autocracy and nationalistic Orthodoxy.

"I was a little taken aback by their (i.e., Isidore's and Varnava's) prejudices," a certain Starets recalls.

"What prejudices?"

"Those typical of the common people. They don't know anything, Isidore and Varnava. They don't comply with Makary's catechism. From Father Varnava I even hear attacks against Metropolitan Makary. They don't know how to distinguish between dogma and morality. Dogmatic theology is one thing and moral theology is another thing. And then there's accusatory theology..."

Saying this, the Starets was right in his own way. It's true that Father Isidore did not concern himself with theologies, for he had a *spiritual life* in God and a *spiritual* knowledge of God, and in this life in God it was not possible to draw lines of demarcation separating the various subjects of scholastic teaching. Father Isidore's soul disdained any order established by separation into books, chapters, sections, and subsections, for *another* order reigned in his soul—an order given not by teachers and professors, but by the Holy Spirit. And one often wanted to ask about Father Isidore: "How does he know the Holy Scripture without having received any formal instruction?"

I repeat, gentle reader, that Father Isidore's power consisted not in wise words but in the spiritual *power* that accompanied his words, even the most ordinary ones. But if you are still curious to know what he conversed about, I will present here a few examples; however, in reading them, you must keep firmly in mind that, if his words are separated from the one who spoke them, they will lose their Isidorian essence and wither like little blue flowers of flax torn from the stem.

Father Efrem recounted the following: "I recall that when the letters of Metropolitan Filaret to Archimandrite Antonii, the Deputy Abbot of the Lavra, were published, I read in one of them the Metropolitan's note: 'Isidore answered well.' At the first opportunity, I went to see Father Isidore and asked him what it meant that he had 'answered well.' The Starets told me the following:

> Three of us came to the Metropolitan to be ordained: I as a hieromonk and the two others as hierodeacons. The Metropolitan first questioned the younger monks. He asked the youngest: "By what do you hope to be saved?"
>
> "By humility," he answered.
>
> "Do you have a lot of it?" the Metropolitan asked. And then he asked the other monk:
>
> "By what do *you* hope to be saved?"

"By your holy prayers," he answered.

The Metropolitan became enraged.

"Where did you learn such hypocrisy?" And then he asked me:

"And you, by what do you hoped to be saved?"

"By the passion on the cross and death of our Savior the Lord Jesus Christ."

The Metropolitan crossed himself and said:

"Memorize that answer and remember it always."

Father Efrem also wrote the following about Father Isidore: "He had a profound knowledge of the dogmatic truths of the holy Orthodox faith, and when he was asked questions about these truths, his answers were always wholly correct, based on Holy Scripture and the Holy Fathers."

The Mother of God, the church, and the Savior's passion and death were the subjects about which Father Isidore spoke most frequently. However, these were not separate questions for him, but were interwoven into one.

He would frequently compare the "birth" of the proto-mother Eve from Adam's rib to the "birth" of the Mother-Church from Christ's rib. Father Isidore equated Adam's miraculous sleep with the Lord's mysterious sleep of death, and the removal of Adam's rib with the piercing of the Lord's side by the lance. For Father Isidore the miraculous flowing of blood and water out of Christ's wound represented the birth of the church; and in some mysterious fashion he associated this birth of the church with the wound made by the sword in the heart of the Mother of God. He associated the suffering of the Mother of God with the grace of the church. "Christ gave birth to the church," he'd sometimes say, "and we all became one."

The peak of Father Isidore's theologizing was his Prayer of Jesus, which implicitly included the foregoing ideas. The reader will become acquainted with this prayer in the following chapter.

The Starets venerated and loved God's saints, and he had a profound, vital, heartfelt connection with them. In his soul he always lived among the saints; they were his family, and even closer than a family. He felt special veneration for St. Seraphim the Wonder-worker of Sarov, the monk George the Recluse, Tikhon of Zadonsk, and a few others. In his conversations he'd often refer to these bearers of the life of grace; he didn't like to speak in his *own* name.

Often with profound tenderness he'd repeat after St. Seraphim:

"My joy, my joy! Acquire the spirit of peace and thousands of souls will be saved around you."

When the conversation would turn to idle words, and to angry words in particular, he'd point out the power of words, often reciting the verses of George the Recluse:

Words are the sparks of the soul.
Hasten to eternity, my spirit.

More frequently, usually when saying goodbye, he'd say:

Soul exhorts soul:
Beware of anger and of idle words
And you will be a Christian theologian.

Father Isidore also loved to recite (and he did so in a very animated way) a rendition in verse of one of the Psalms, which he had read once in some magazine and had liked enormously. He'd become very excited, and read with great expression and power. Sometimes he'd hand a visitor a very thick book—a verse rendition of the Psalms composed by some blind priest; and drawing attention to this last circumstance ("Just think: he was blind!"), he'd ask the visitor to read the rather heavy verses out loud. Sometimes he'd read Derzhavin's ode "God." But more often he'd talk very warmly of Gogol and recite the verse prayer to the Most Holy Theotokos attributed to him:

O Most Holy Mother, to thee
I dare my voice to raise, etc.

For some reason he loved this poem. He'd also recite a verse prayer about Christ's cross:

Glorious is the power of Christ's cross.
It shines everywhere, etc.

But most often Father Isidore compelled visitors to sing from the Burial Rite of the Mother of God performed in the Gethsemane Skete on August 17, when her Dormition and Assumption are celebrated:

Blessed Empress, illuminate me with the light of Your Son.
The angelic host was amazed when it saw You given over to death,

Your soul placed in God's hands, and ascending with God,
Most Immaculate One, with divine and heavenly glory. And so on.

That was what the gray-haired Father Isidore sang to the Virgin Mary. When he'd finish reciting the verses, he'd ask his visitors to copy them and sing them as often as possible at home. He'd always say that purity, peace, and meekness come from the Mother of God and that she, who suffered much, would come to help those who call to her.

He'd invariably ask his visitors whether they had already seen the Mother of God (in the Chernigov underground church), and if they said no, he'd ask them to go to her to pray.

Whenever a pair of friends would come to see Father Isidore, he'd always express his joy and approval of their friendship. He'd repeat insistently that people should live in peace. He'd conclude by reciting the verses "A brother strengthens a brother/The way a fortress strengthens a city," as if he foresaw the possibility of the two falling apart.

Whenever anyone complained to the Abba about sickness or some misfortune, he'd say almost with envy (if it is permissible to use this inappropriate word): "You see how much God loves you—he remembers you."

Once, one of the brothers was sick. Father Isidore ran into him and asked:

"How are you, Misha?"

"I'm not well, Father."

"Don't you know that if God visits you with some sickness or misfortune, that means that he loves you? The Lord visits us with sicknesses now, but that will be counted in our favor in the next world."[17]

Chapter 14

Which is the most edifying chapter since it acquaints the reader with Father Isidore's grace-bestowing Prayer of Jesus, which provides great spiritual comfort to all those who say it with understanding

All who came to Father Isidore were taught by him to say his Prayer of Jesus, which he had composed himself or which perhaps had been revealed to him

---

17. This chapter has been slightly abbreviated.

from above. The Abba himself said this prayer ceaselessly. He regarded this prayer (which will be given below) as extremely important in the struggle against evil thoughts and as full of the power of grace. There is reason to think that it was revealed to him in a vision, but he never elaborated on the origin of the prayer, although he insistently counseled everyone to say it.

This prayer—the prayer of the Savior's five wounds and of the sword that pierced the soul of His Most Pure Mother—was most effective in calming the agitations of the soul, moderating anger and rage, and expelling foul thoughts and erotic reveries. That was what the Starets affirmed, and as proof he said he knew of a case where this prayer was successful in expelling the demons from a certain woman.

The Starets would recite this prayer facing his icons. He'd take his time reciting the first part, as if waiting for something; meanwhile, he would be looking at the holy crucifix. While saying the second part, he would be looking at the icon of the Most Pure Virgin. He would recite this part rapidly, with animation and joyful hope. After reciting this short prayer, the Starets would be transfigured even in outward appearance. It was as if light radiated from his eyes, and he beamed with a festive joy like that described in the Song of Songs and in the narrative of the Marriage of the Lamb in the Revelation of St. John. Before anywhere else, the grace-bestowing effect of the prayer would first be visible in Father Isidore himself.

He knew that. That was why he repeatedly counseled others to treat themselves with this medicine.

"Cross yourself *with understanding*—this way. And the temptation will pass," he'd tell visitors who complained of temptation, depression, or frustration. And he'd cross himself, reciting his Prayer of Jesus. "If you feel afflicted, say this prayer" (and he would recite it). "Turn to the Mother of God. She is pure and loves purity—and she will help you."

It was with words like these that Father Isidore exhorted others to recite his prayer of the Savior's five wounds and of the sword that pierced the heart of His Most Pure Mother, the Virgin Mary. But as long as Father Isidore was alive, this prayer was not well received for some reason either by the Skete brothers or by laypersons. Amazingly, hardly anyone even remembered it, even though clearly it was not difficult or long. Some even thought it was indecent that the Starets was teaching everyone, even educated people, to recite such a "peasant" prayer, one not taken from a book.

"He composed the prayer himself," one of the brothers recounted. "Wherever he'd go, he'd push his prayer and his notebooks (i.e., his prayer sheets) on people. I'm amazed he was so bold."

That's how it was when the spirit-bearing Starets was still alive. But as soon as he departed this world, many people realized that they didn't know the prayer of the five wounds and copied it out for themselves in order to use it in their prayers, while others memorized it. Many people attest to the great grace-bestowing power of Father Isidore's prayer, especially against evil thoughts and foul images. Speaking from his personal experience, one of the brothers said that "the prayer of the Savior's five wounds is so powerful that demons cannot withstand it."

And now, pious reader, I present to you this last earthly gift of our Abba, the whitened Starets Isidore. Recite it for the healing of your soul and body and teach it to your dear ones, in memory of the Starets, and through his prayers may the Lord shed his grace on you.

The Prayer of the Savior's Five Wounds, Which the Starets Isidore taught his spiritual children to recite

Where does it hurt?

Placing your hand on your brow, say:

"**Lord**, whose head was crowned by a wreath of thorns, unto blood and brain, for the sake of my sins."

Lowering your hand to your right foot, say:

"**Jesus**, whose right foot was pierced by an iron nail, for the sake of my sins."

Placing your hand on your left foot, say:

"**Christ**, whose left foot was pierced by an iron nail, for the sake of my sins."

Raising your hand to your right shoulder, say:

"**Son**, whose right arm was pierced by an iron nail, for the sake of my sins."

Moving your hand to your left shoulder, say:

"**Of God**, whose left arm was pierced by an iron nail, for the sake of my sins. And whose side was pierced by a lance, and blood and water flowed out it, for the redemption and salvation of our souls. Through the Mother of God, give me understanding."

Facing an icon of the Mother of God, say:

"The sword pierced your soul too, so that from many hearts will be opened a source of repentantly grateful and heartfelt tears of all humankind."[18]

---

18. The initial words from each line of the prayer form the first phrase of the traditional

Chapter 15

Written to inform the humble and wise reader that Father Isidore had the gifts of prescience and miracle-working

Is there any need to remind you, pious reader, that in and of themselves, the gifts of prescience and miracle-working (or any other gift) do not yet mean that the Spirit of God dwells in those who possess these gifts? As a good Christian, you know, of course, that the kingdom of God consists in righteousness and peace and joy in the Holy Spirit, not in miracles or prescience or healing; and the fathers of the church have proclaimed this in their wise writings. But you also know that, when he seeks the kingdom of God, the lover of God also acquires—together with the Spirit—his gifts. The Savior said: "But seek ye first the kingdom of God . . . and all these things shall be added unto you."[19]

That truly describes Father Isidore. He never chased after the things at which people marvel, but, like a certain wise merchant, he sought above all the precious pearl of his soul. God was enthroned in his soul, and with God came the spiritual joy and superabundant life promised by the Savior to his disciples. And this living fluid, pouring abundantly out of Father Isidore's transparent heart, as if it were an overfull crystal vessel, worked miracles and gave unfathomable powers to the Starets.

Those who visited Father Isidore did not doubt that he saw and knew things hidden from ordinary men. But these obvious gifts were as nothing compared to the personal presence of the Abba, for who looks at the adornments of the king's palace when the king himself is present? Also, he spoke unwillingly about his spiritual gifts, for he regarded them as a natural consequence of life in God. So, when people would speak to him about his prescience, he'd answer calmly:

"God is with us. He is close to us. He sees with our eyes."

Many who visited him reported that Father Isidore would often start the conversation by talking about the business that had brought them to him, although they hadn't yet mentioned it, and this occurred not just once or

---

Prayer of Jesus: "Lord Jesus Christ, Son of God, have mercy upon me, a sinner." The last sentence of the prayer is based on Simeon's words to the Mother of God in the temple (Luke 2:35).

19. Matthew 6:33.

twice but multiple times, and it was reported not just by one or two visitors, but by many of them. You'd visit him, and he'd begin by offering advice concerning the matter you came to ask him about. Such occurrences seemed so commonplace to his disciples that they did not bother to record them; and now they have virtually disappeared from the common memory. But by chance several such incidents were recorded, and I will recount them in order to edify those who never had the opportunity to meet the Starets.

One of Father Isidore's acquaintances had to travel somewhere far away from Sergiev Posad. On the return trip an unexpected encounter caused him vague agitation. He had unexpectedly encountered the wife of one of his acquaintances, and she told him that her husband had been experiencing a moral crisis and had fallen into despair. The necessary thing would have been to leave the train at the next station and go see his acquaintance, but for some reason this thought never entered his head, or perhaps a demon hid it from him with his tail, as the saying goes. He arrived in Sergiev Posad just in time for the divine liturgy, during which he suddenly realized that he had to go back immediately in order to make up for his omission. And since the train to that city didn't leave until late at night, he had time to visit Father Isidore to receive his blessing.

A snowstorm was brewing when he got to Father Isidore's house. Before he could enter, the Starets met him at the door and, even before blessing him, pointed to the snowflakes whirling in the air and said: "Look, look, good deeds are swirling like flies! You have to go right away: the trains might stop running!" He confirmed that it was urgent to go that very night, blessed the man who needed help, and even wrote him a letter in his trembling elderly scrawl.

Here is another incident: One day one of Father Isidore's spiritual sons, Father G., came to see him. He confessed to Father Isidore and then offered him two rubles. Father Isidore took the money. Father G. thought: "Why did he take the money? He knows I'm poor." Father Isidore said nothing in response to this thought. During the ensuing conversation, a pauper came to see Father Isidore; the Starets had told this pauper to come in the evening to receive some money, though he did not have any money when he had invited him. Father Isidore gave the two rubles to this beggar, and said: "This kind man here, who is visiting me, has given you this money." Afterwards, as Father G. was leaving, Father Isidore took him aside and said: "Don't be upset because I took the two rubles from you: prayers through them—through laypersons—reach God more easily than from you and me." Father G. interpreted this incident as an indisputable case of prescience.

If Father Isidore was paid a visit by someone who had sin in his soul, or was quarreling with his friend, or whose love had cooled, the Starets would always begin the conversation by mentioning this sin, or with two or three questions he'd compel the visitor to confess and repent. This had become such a common event that, when anyone remained obstinate in his sin, he'd make every effort to avoid Father Isidore.

Life in the *other* world became Father Isidore's *customary* life. In his dreams he'd often see the Mother of God and St. Seraphim and other saints and hear their grace-filled exhortations. For example, here is the story of how Bishop E. first met Father Isidore. Bishop E. recalls:

> Prior to 1904 I had never met Father Isidore. I had, however, heard much about him when I was still a student at the Moscow Theological Academy. We first met in May 1904. It was a marvelous day; I had gone out into the Academy garden. A bent old man with a crutch and wearing a skullcap hobbled toward me. He came up to me and said:
> "Father, you're the Bishop, aren't you?"
> "Yes, I am. What is it you need?"
> "I'm Father Isidore."
> "I'm very glad to meet you."
> "I have a reason for seeing you. Last night the Mother of God came to me and said: 'Why is it you have not yet asked for the blessing of the new Bishop?' So, here I am."

With his great sensitivity, Father Isidore also understood the signs from inanimate creation. For example, he'd often tell the story of how, when he was standing in church one day in his hometown, he saw a ball of fire engulf the iconostasis. He saw in this ball of fire a divine sign that told him he should become a monk. Smiling slightly, he'd invariably add: "Some may say this was a natural event. But I am of a different opinion."

And that's how it was. Skeptics (may the pious reader not be tempted by them!) would give a "scientific" explanation and say that this was "ball lightning." And what if it was? Can't God speak to us through ball lightning? He holds all of creation in his hands and speaks to us through it; but our hearts have grown coarse and we do not understand God's words. But with his pure heart Father Isidore listened to creation; he heard God's word in creation and therefore the whole world was filled for him with miraculous signs and secret messages. For him, a spirit-bearing person, ball lightning too was a miracle, whereas an earthly soul will not regard even the end of the world as a divine sign. A sinner, desiring to live without God, will be punished by losing the sight of his heart's eyes: he does not see or know God and does not understand the signs of his wrath, and therefore nothing impels him to take stock of himself and repent; he lives as if asleep, but does not understand that and thinks his dreams are waking reality.

The Starets did not live that way: he was always wakeful and vigilant in spirit. He listened to God's creation, and God's creation listened to him. Invisible threads united him with the hidden heart of creation. The world was a sign for Father Isidore and Father Isidore was a sign for the world. Truly, what occurred around the Starets did not occur around others.

He himself recounted the following incident. On the day of the Dormition of the Mother of God, a day when women are allowed to enter the Skete, a woman came to see him and complained of constant headaches. "You should cross yourself with understanding," the Starets said and taught her his prayer of the Savior's five wounds. She started to make the sign of the cross with understanding, but before she could raise her hand to her brow, she trembled all over and fell to the ground in convulsions, and black foam started coming out of her mouth. Father Isidore had this woman carried from the Skete to the Chernigov Mother of God, into the underground church. There, her sickness was healed.

Chapter 16

About Father Isidore's cross and about how little he was understood by those around him

Father Isidore's entire life was a heavy cross, but he bore it patiently. This cross-bearing, more than anything else, convinces us that Father Isidore had his own special transcendent world from which he drew his powers and his strength. Life in God seems possible to us only if certain *conditions* are realized: it seems to us that we can maintain our equilibrium only if we enjoy social esteem and if we possess material resources and similar goods, which Abba Isaac the Syrian, one of the holy fathers, likens to putrid corruption. In contrast, Father Isidore's faith was a living, self-actuating power that never deserted him. His life was wholly unlike ours.

He had once been a manor serf in a noble's house, but he never remembered his former masters with hatred or even with bitterness. Moreover, as long as his former mistress, the princess, was alive, he would pay her an annual visit with a *prosphoron* and a string of round-rolls.

He had been persecuted everywhere, but he recounted his travails so calmly and with such a happy smile that he could have been talking about somebody else. He had to leave Old Athos for lack of money. In the Paraclete Hermitage he'd gather round him children from the neighboring villages, give them tea to drink, teach them prayers, and hand each of them a few kopecks from his meager resources. The authorities didn't like this and they began to spread rumors that he drank and brought women into his cell. Finally, they manufactured some truly ugly story, expelled him from the Hermitage, and sent him to the Gethsemane Skete.

The persecutions in his life were endless. But what was he persecuted for? For hearing the confessions of brothers who were on the verge of despair because of the father confessor's severity; for receiving strangers; for giving bread to the poor; for leaving the Skete without permission in order to comfort someone in the Posad; for being candid with the authorities.

The younger brothers loved him fervently, but the elder ones, with a few exceptions, disliked him just as fervently. They could not stand his independence and candor, in spite of his great humility. He was despised for his lack of ostentation in fasting, but his worst fault—in the eyes of the brothers who considered themselves learned—was his simplicity and "lack of education." Some even considered him a fool or a crazy person and called him a "queer bird" (and that was one of their gentler expressions).

Father Isidore was a monk for sixty years, but he never received any honors, not even a "thigh shield."[20] The eighty-year-old Starets lived alone in his little house and had to do everything with his own hands, for he didn't have an attendant. He had let himself go to such an extent that, during his sickness, his face with covered with a layer of dirt, and Bishop E., who visited him, had to take lice out of his gray hairs. He got a helper only six days before his death.

Poverty, sickness, contempt, insults, persecution—these were the thorns strewn on the path of Father Isidore's life. But in these thorns he preserved a tranquility, joy, and fullness of life that others do not possess and do not acquire even in the most favorable conditions.

What was the most notable thing about Father Isidore? Surely, it was the fact that in every situation he remained a Christian. Christianity was

---

20. The "thigh shield" (*nabedrennik*) is a vestment awarded to priests for long and dedicated service to the church.

his constant element, unconnected with the world and with its natural and social conditions. For him Christianity was not an exotic element, but the very essence of life—not a decoration, but the very fabric of life. Not understood during his life, Father Isidore remains, it seems, not understood after his death. Those who had been around him have not yet realized what a treasure they have lost. But the Starets's light shines the more brightly in this night without understanding.

Chapter 17

Which recalls the meager information that exists about Father Isidore's life, the place of his birth, his subsequent life, and the spiritual influences upon him

You now know, pious reader, what Father Isidore was like; and you probably also want to know how he became what he was. To satisfy your curiosity, I will present what little I know of his biography.

He was born in the village of Lyskovo in the Makar'evsky Region of the Nizhny Novgorod District, and he was baptized as Ioann. His parents were manor serfs of the Princes Gruzinsky; their given names were Andrey and Paraskeva and their surname was Kozin. Ioann gave his surname either as Gruzinsky or as Kozin, but usually as Gruzinsky. The exact year of Ioann's birth is unknown. According to the Starets Avraamy, Ioann was born in the year of the death of St. Seraphim of Sarov. But not long before his death, Ioann repeatedly recounted a memorable conversation he had had with his mother on the day of St. Seraphim's death. "A marvelous fragrance permeated the air," he recalled. "I asked my mother where it came from, and she told me that St. Seraphim had just died." Two or three days later, news came of St. Seraphim's death. According to the first piece of information, Ioann would have been born in 1833 (the year of Seraphim's death); whereas, according to the second piece of information, it must be assumed that in 1833 Ioann was old enough so that later he could remember something that had happened that year. Ioann himself affirmed that he was born in 1814.

In any event, a beam of light entered Ioann's life from St. Seraphim's radiance. When she was carrying Ioann in her womb, his mother walked to Sarov to see St. Seraphim. The Saint summoned her out of an enormous crowd, bowed down to the ground before her, and foretold that she would give birth to a great monk and that his name would be Isidore. In later years, in the Skete, Father Isidore became a close friend of one of Seraphim's disciples.

We know very little about Ioann's childhood, adolescence, and youth—only what he himself told us. Of particular interest is his participation in the domestic theater of the Princes Gruzinsky. He played Filka and other comic roles; his love of verse and art must date back to that time. But despite his attraction to such worldly entertainments, the youth did not forget his soul. Even then he yearned for the ascetic life of a monk.

"When at night my father and mother would be busy with household chores," he recounted not long before his death, "I'd turn to the wall and gaze at a picture of the monks Zosimas and Sabbatius, and see green meadows and monasteries."

Then Ioann saw a sign that transformed those youthful thoughts into a firm decision. He was praying in the Church of the Protection of the Mother of God in his hometown. Lightning in the form of a full moon (as the Starets himself described it later), shining brightly, passed along the iconostasis, accompanied by an explosion of thunder. No one was hurt, but the iconostasis was blackened. This sign (the old-timers there remember it) had a powerful effect on Ioann. "The lightning struck and warmed him," is how one of the brothers expressed it. "My thought went to Athos," is what the Starets himself said. However, Ioann was not able to put that thought into action then, and instead he entered the Gethsemane Skete, founded by Metropolitan Filaret. There he was reunited with the Deputy Abbot Antonii, who too was a native of the village of Lyskovo and was an illegitimate son of Prince Gruzinsky. By the way, it should be mentioned that, judging by the fact that he had adopted the surname Gruzinsky as well as by the slenderness of his body and by his somewhat eastern nose and face, it wouldn't be outrageous to suppose that Ioann too was not entirely of common peasant stock. It is not impossible that he too was descended from princes.

Deputy Abbot Antonii invited Ioann to be his cell-attendant. Ioann was then a beardless youth. In addition to being Antonii's servant, he also wrote out prayers for the remembrance of the living and the dead. He also read in church and sang in the choir in his light bass voice. At that time he became acquainted with Father Avraamy, who later replaced him as Antonii's attendant. At the Deputy Abbot's he frequently saw Filaret, Metropolitan of Moscow, and many other notables of that period.

At first, Antonii and Ioann were close friends, a friendship that was perhaps reinforced by the fact that they were relatives. But later their friendship cooled. The Deputy Abbot became close to Metropolitan Filaret and his mind became full of ambition. Ioann did not refrain from telling the Deputy Abbot the truth and no doubt by his very presence reminded him of the past—of the time when Antonii, as a serf, was a medic attending to Prince Gruzinsky. The Deputy Abbot grew weary of Ioann and would say: "He is too heavy for me."

The period when Father Isidore began his life as a monk was a very special one in the history of Gethsemane Skete. The memory of St. Seraphim of Sarov was still alive. A whole host of true monks shone their light out into the world from the depths of the woods where the Skete now stands; a myriad of great men would come from the world to warm their souls with the light of these monks, to acquire strength and boldness from them. There was no brick enclosure then; the monks lived apart and each of them bore his own particular ascesis. Some of the monks descended into the recesses of the earth: there, they built an entire monastery with a church and even dug a well. When the underground bell would ring, underground monks bearing candles would come out of their coffin-like cells, in which one could barely lie down, and through narrow damp underground passageways they would gather for the night prayer. They would read the Psalms and sing the Alleluia hymn, and then they would disperse to their cells. It was very stuffy in the underground church, so wooden pipes had been built to bring fresh air in from outside. Sometimes, at night, Father Antonii would listen to the singing of the monks coming out of those pipes. At times, Metropolitan Filaret lived in the Skete.

In 1869, Brother Ioann was tonsured into the mantle together with Father German, who is now the abbot of the Zosima Hermitage, just beyond the Paraclete. Both Ioann (in monasticism called Isidore) and German were received from the Holy Gospel by the Starets hieroschemamonk Alexander, who a little later also received Varnava (d. 1906) as his spiritual son.

It is worth noting that this trinity of spiritual Elders—Isidore, German, and Varnava—is connected by ties of spiritual brotherhood. Father Isidore, as born spiritually from Father Alexander before the other two, was venerated by them as the eldest and therefore after Father Alexander's death he took Alexander's place as the spiritual father of his orphaned younger brothers.

The Paraclete Hermitage did not yet exist at that time. When it was built as a refuge for lovers of the strictest solitude, Father Isidore made his home there. He was placed on an accelerated path to becoming a hieromonk. In 1863 he was ordained as a hierodeacon and in 1865 as a hieromonk. He never rose higher; he was offered the schema[21] when he was very old, but he refused it—because of his humility.

---

21. To be ordained a schemamonk is the highest honor an Orthodox monk can achieve.

There was a time when Father Isidore was preparing to go to America to preach together with Bishop Ioann. The Deputy Abbot had a new fur coat made for Father Isidore for the long journey, but for some reason Father Isidore didn't go and the fur coat went to America by itself without its owner. About five years after entering the Paraclete Hermitage, Father Isidore fulfilled a long-time desire of his—to spend time on Old Athos. He spent one year in this ancient nursery of monasticism. That year the Athos elders planned to erect a cross on top of glorious Mount Athos, and Father Isidore participated actively in this holy endeavor.

But for lack of resources to pay for a cell, Father Isidore soon had to leave this monastic kingdom and return to his native land. He again settled in the Paraclete, but he did not stay there long, for he was persecuted, slandered, and finally expelled. He moved back to the Gethsemane Skete, where he lived uninterruptedly until his blessed death.

Of the events of this period, the most important one was the appointment of Father Isidore as the confessor for all the hieromonks. This happened after the death of Father Varnava in 1906.

Chapter 18

Which tells about Father Isidore's blessed death

That is how Father Isidore's serene life transpired. His death, too, was incomparably serene. It even seemed that he did not die, but gradually went to sleep; his breathing grew fainter and fainter until it disappeared: he took a last breath and his life flew away with that breath.

Until the last moment he did not lose his usual gaiety and clear consciousness, remaining alert even on his deathbed. Even his memory of persons, of names, of spiritual verses, or of the particular circumstances of people's lives did not wane. His sickness—the hemorrhoids, diarrhea, and hemorrhaging—was agonizing, but he never complained. When he was asked about his health, he'd reply, invariably smiling: "It's fine, thank God. It's fine, everything's fine." His body had shriveled up completely; his arms had withered, becoming like lashes covered with skin. The sickness had produced a severe deterioration in his body. His face, formerly rather plump, had wasted away; his cheeks had become sunken, his nose was thin and pointy. Toward the end Father Isidore didn't even have the strength to smile. But his eyes—the clear eyes of the radiant Starets—shined like bright stars with an amazing effulgence. While his enfeebled body still lay in this world, his eyes seemed to shine already from the other world. Anyone who had the honor of seeing them knows what a blessed death is.

The Starets had been sick for a long time, but starting in Holy Week of 1907 his sickness had become more noticeable, and with the feast of the Dormition the hemorrhaging had become so severe that he had to stop attending divine services, except to receive the Holy Gifts.

With the beginning of the Philippian Fast he took to his bed without rising, and it was clear that his sickness would end only in death. The Abba ate almost nothing, causing him to grow even weaker. In the last week of his life he accepted nothing but a little cold water—from a teaspoon.

During his remaining days, he taught his visitors even more zealously and insistently, repeating his favorite thoughts. Most frequently he repeated the prayer of the Savior's five wounds. Constantly remembering the poor, he'd say: "One who has must give to one who has not." He'd also say: "A righteous man will punish a sinner with mercy" and "one who is merciful makes a loan to God, and God will repay everything." He implored the authorities to help the sick and the poor—in the monastery as well as in the world. He spoke of mercy: "Mercy will be praised at the judgment."

He continued to be interested in church affairs. He kept talking about union with the Old Catholics; he said it didn't matter who was first and reaffirmed that the Mother of God will sit at the head of the council. He said goodbye to the brothers and to his spiritual children. He gave each of them a commission: to help the individuals he had been taking care of. He asked them not to forget the poor; he divided his meager property among them and blessed them. He asked one of them to change a ruble into small coins and to distribute them among the poor.

It was obvious that this leave-taking with the world greatly fatigued him, whose body already lay half-dead, but he did not want to stop his final activity. When Bishop E., his spiritual son, came to see Father Isidore three days before his death, he asked him if he was afraid of death. Father Isidore answered with a smile: "No, not at all. What is there to be afraid of? Thank God—I am not afraid, not at all. Thank God." And he continued dividing his meager property in the most painstaking manner, making sure to give away even the smallest items. He asked the Bishop to choose whatever he wanted, and he gave him his staff and his half-mantle.

Although he could no longer move, he offered to hear the Bishop's confession. Despite the Bishop's protests, he did hear his confession. Then he said "I am going away" and he gave the Bishop his confession book, which was torn and smudged from long use. Even on his deathbed he remembered to render this last service to his spiritual son.

He then remembered something else and told the attendant: "I have six potatoes over there. Distribute them to the poor." He asked him to do the same with the jam that was left over, and he even made sure that a piece of bread would be given away.

The Starets told Father Izrail: "I would prefer to be laid out in my *epitrachēlion*, but it's too fine. Ask the brother in charge of clothing for a worse one to lay me out in, and give this one to his Eminence (i.e., Bishop Evdokim)."

The *epitrachēlion* that Father Isidore did not want to waste was extremely ancient, tattered, and threadbare. He had heard confessions in it his entire life; he had never parted with it; but before his death he parted with it. That was a supreme sacrifice of love, for we cannot imagine what that *epitrachēlion* meant for Father Isidore.

Two days before his death, on February 2, at about four in the morning, Father Isidore asked to receive communion. After the early liturgy, at about six in the morning, the Holy Gifts were brought to him and he received communion.

The attendant said to him:

"Father, you are dying!"

"Enough, enough," Father Isidore contradicted him affectionately. "Just think what you are saying! No one is dead for God. All are alive. 'He who believes in Me will not die . . .' I am not dying. God is not the God of the dead, but the God of the living."

The next day, at about two, two students of the Theological Academy came to see him and brought him ten rubles. Father Isidore asked Brother Ivan, his cell-attendant, to give him a little box; he put the money into it and ordered that it be distributed to the poor.

After resting a little, he said to the attendant: "Go, brother, and get the father confessor."

The father confessor came at seven in the evening. He looked at the sick man and said:

"You're in bad shape, bounteous father."

"I am very bad, and so I want to receive communion. If I live through the night, come to me on my Angel day."[22] (He remembered that February 4 was his Angel day.)

The father confessor left at about eight. Brother Ivan started to read from

---

22. His name-day, the feast day of the saint after whom he was named.

the Lives of the Holy Fathers and Father Isidore's Gospel book. Ivan noticed that Father Isidore was moving his fingers, and he said:

"Let me cut your fingernails!"

"Tomorrow," Father Isidore said.

The attendant began to read from the Holy Gospel again, but the Starets said to him:

"Brother Ivan, give me my cross."

When Ivan handed him the cross, Father Isidore crossed himself with it and blessed Ivan, and then he gave it back to him. Ivan read a little more from the Holy Gospel and then he saw that Father Isidore was getting worse. He then asked for the Starets's forgiveness and for his prayers, and he started reading from the Holy Gospel again. Father Isidore interrupted him:

"Brother Ivan, put out the light."

But the attendant did not fulfill this request, but instead asked:

"Why, Father?"

Father Isidore's breathing became more rapid, and he said again:

"Put out the light."

Brother Ivan blew out one of the icon-lamps, and then he went out into the little vestibule, because earlier Father Isidore had said to him:

"Don't look at me when I'm dying. When the great Anthony was dying, he sent his disciple to get water, and then he died. When St. Seraphim was dying, he shut the door to his cell, and then he died. That is the way it has been with all the servants of God: no one saw them die. You too must go away: read or go to sleep."

When he was still healthy, Father Isidore would tell his disciples that it was even a sin to watch a man die, and here he would refer to the testimony of St. Paul of Thebes and of many other saints. The Starets's demand that the light be put out was not a caprice. No, he had a firm and immutable conviction that when a person is dying, he must concentrate totally and free himself entirely of all worldly things so that he could remain alone with God.

What the dying man did in his last minutes, what he felt and thought in the stillness and inner tranquility, undisturbed even by the habitual sight of the humble cell and the meager light from the icon-lamp—these are things we can never know, and even if we could know them, our minds would be powerless to fathom them. The Abba's soul had access to things that are beyond our understanding. But what is remarkable, my brother-reader, is that, in spite of his great humility, Father Isidore, at the moment of death when he was face to face with God, compared himself to the Spirit-bearing ascetic saints, and he did so using expressions that made this comparison seem the most natural of things. In another man this would have been overweening pride and intolerable impudence. But on Father Isidore's lips such audacity was so natural that it was almost unnoticeable. This near-death testimony that he gave about himself is of great value for us, for who could appreciate this spirit-bearer and understand him better than he himself?

And so, Brother Ivan put out the light and left the cell. Father Isidore was breathing rapidly. Brother Ivan lay down on the floor in the little vestibule and, listening to the breathing of the dying man, he dozed. It was half past nine. Awakening from his slumber, he leaped to his feet and began to listen. It was quiet in the cell. He went up to Father Isidore. The Starets's mouth was open. Brother Ivan felt the body; it was still warm. He understood that the Starets's soul had gone to God. It was then eleven in the evening. Brother Ivan ran to awaken the hieromonk Father Izrail. He came and performed the *panikhida*.[23]

So, at eleven at night on February 3, 1908, on the eve of his Angel day, the great Starets of the Gethsemane Skete died. He was, most likely, about eighty-four years old.

Chapter 20

Which tells the curious reader about Father Isidore's grace-filled burial, about his countenance after his blessed passing from life in this world, and about his grave

The next day the news of Father Isidore's death spread throughout Sergiev Posad, and then reached Moscow. On February 5 at eight in the morning, the Starets's large spiritual family gathered in the Church of Filaret the Charitable in the Skete to take its last farewell of him. Bishop E. was there, as were a number of Moscow hierarchs, Skete brothers, and students of the Theological Academy and other laypersons. Even some women had made it into the church, even though they were not permitted to enter the Skete. The gathering was solemn, yet also sorrowful, for all present had the painful sense that the world had lost a help that would never again be seen. A few wept bitterly. The Bishop officiated at the service.

When it was over, the Bishop summoned to the coffin those who had been closest to Father Isidore. They formed a tight ring around the coffin, and the Bishop gently lifted the black cloth from Father Isidore's face.

---

23. The Orthodox last rites.

The Salt of the Earth

The Starets lay there as if alive—with a shrunken face but without the slightest trace of corruption. It was as if the hand of death had not touched him. A light smile shone on his closed lips; his chest seemed to be breathing. A profound peace and stillness wafted from this coffin—one felt not the coldness of the grave, but the fragrant coolness of a clear evening. The Starets in his coffin was like the sun setting over ripe white grain-fields. One saw not the majestic silence of a corpse and not the solemn detachment of a dead person, but blissful repose in God: Father Isidore was here—he was asleep, not at all terrifying, not at all frightening, but serene and tranquil, meeker than meek. When he had been alive, his gaze had always brought comfort into the world. But Father Isidore had never been like this. With his hood drawn over his brow and with his head inclined slightly to the left, he lay radiant and bright (not with the waxen pallor of death): he was so inexpressibly fine that you wanted to ask his blessing and your tears flowed spontaneously—not from sorrow and anguish now, but from pure tenderness and rapture before this beauty that has defeated death. This was the first coffin we had ever seen that did not fill us with terror. Within it lay "spiritual beauty incarnate" (to quote St. Gregory of Nyssa)—the beauty of the sabbath.

When the service had ended and all those present had said farewell to the Starets, Bishop E. stood over this unpainted pine coffin, this treasure bequeathed to the Gethsemane Skete, and spoke the funeral oration. He briefly related everything the reader already knows about Father Isidore, and then he defined the significance of the Starets in the history of monasticism, declaring that Father Isidore was the last flower of the ancient Thebaid, the last representative of monasticism. This, roughly, is what the Bishop said: "At the present time, we do not have a monasticism; we need to create it. Father Isidore was a harbinger of this future monasticism, which had its beginning in the distant Thebaid. Amen."

The oil was poured. Rapidly, the coffin was nailed shut. The sobs of a few elders—comrades in monasticism of the Starets—resounded. And Father Isidore was carried to his final resting place, past his little wooden house, where a *panikhida* was served. It was cold and snowing. For a while the sky became ominous and the wind blew furiously. But despite the cold wind, nobody wanted to leave this yellow mound, newly formed near the chapel in the brothers' graveyard. The winter passed. The spring, too, passed—a spring without Father Isidore. Toward the summer his grave was tidied: sod was placed around it; flowers were planted; a white wooden cross was erected with a black inscription and a ruby-colored lamp with an everlasting flame.

The front of the cross bore the inscription: "Beneath this cross is buried the body of God's servant Hieromonk Father Isidore. Tonsured into the Skete in 1852, died on February 4, 1908. He was . . . years old." (The number of years was erased intentionally, because it turned out to be erroneous.)

Inexpensive icons hang there: of St. Seraphim, of St. Feodor, the Chenstokhov Mother of God, a copper crucifix, and others—all of them donated by unknown venerators of the grace-filled Starets.

The back of the cross bore the inscription: "Lord, receive my spirit with peace." On the cross hangs a tin lantern, painted green. Within it a lamp burns everlastingly, just as everlastingly as Father Isidore burned before the Lord Jesus Christ.

Chapter 21

The last one, a chapter the reader can skip if he does not have time, since it doesn't contain any new information about Father Isidore

A certain brother once asked St. Niphon of Constantia: "At the present time there is a multitude of saints all over the world. Will it be that way too at the end of this age?" Niphont answered:

> My son, until the end of this age there will be no lack of Prophets of the Lord God, just as there will be no lack of servants of satan. However, in the last times, God's true laborers will successfully conceal themselves from people and will not perform signs and miracles among them, as at the present time, but will follow a path of active doing combined with humility; and in the kingdom of heaven they will turn out to be greater than the fathers celebrated for their signs, because no one will perform miracles then before the eyes of men, miracles that would ignite the hearts of men and inspire them zealously to accomplish spiritual exploits. Those occupying the thrones of priesthood throughout the world will lack all skill and will be ignorant of the art of virtue. The monastic leaders will be no different, for they will be seduced by sensualism and ambition, and will be a temptation for men, rather than a model. Thus, virtue will be despised more and more; cupidity will reign, and woe to the monks who grow rich with gold, for they will not see the face of the Living God. . . . And so, my son, as I said before, many will be afflicted with ignorance and fall into the abyss.

That was the prophecy pronounced by the Constantia Bishop. Remembering Father Isidore, one is struck by the accuracy of the ancient prophecy:

"in the last times, the saints will successfully conceal themselves from people." This prophecy becomes even more striking when we reflect on Father Isidore's affirmation that the last times are at hand and that a persecution is coming that once again will force Christians to hide in the bowels of the earth.

For, with his divinely wise simplicity, Father Isidore was able to conceal himself not only from the world, but even from his brothers and fellow monks. There was nothing remarkable about Father Isidore, but the remarkable thing was that there was nothing remarkable.

He was truly a bearer of the Spirit of God. That is why the thing that was remarkable about Father Isidore remains inexpressible with our words and ungraspable by our minds. An integral unity in himself, Father Isidore becomes entirely contradictory when we try to express him with our words, when we say: "He was this or he was that." Yes, he fasted. But he also disregarded fasts. Yes, he was humble. But he was also independent. Yes, he was detached from the world. But he also loved all creatures like no one else. Yes, he lived in God. But he also read newspapers and recited poetry. Yes, he was meek. But he was also strict. In other words, he was a total contradiction for the rationalizing mind. But for the purified mind he was an integral unity like no one else. Spiritual unity is seen as a contradiction by the rationalizing mind. He was both in the world and not of this world. He despised nothing, and yet he always remained in heavenly places.

He was spiritual, spirit-bearing; looking at him, one could understand the nature of Christian spirituality and the meaning of the Christian "not of this world." It was not by chance that the respected and experienced Varnava, Starets of the Gethsemane Skete, was Isidore's spiritual son and even called him the "second Seraphim," and that the Starets Avraamy, who lived an ascetic life in the "caves" and has resided in the Skete for fifty-five years, says about Father Isidore that "he manifested a meekness of doves." "At the present time I never met anyone like this Starets"—that is what many of the brothers say.

Having praised the Lord our God for the wondrous sign given to us in Father Isidore, I lay down my pen with brotherly gratitude to you, pious reader, my faithful companion on this path we followed through the spiritual meadow, breathing a pure air filled with sublime fragrances. May a serene peace descend into your soul, pious reader, similar to that which ceaselessly and abundantly filled Father Isidore's soul, and may the unfading light of joy shine within you. Amen.[24]

---

24. This final paragraph has been abbreviated.

Appendix[25]

Prayer to the Mother of God
(Attributed to Nikolai Gogol)

> O Most Holy Mother, to Thee
> I dare my voice to raise,
> Tears streaming down my face.
> Hear me in this sorrowful hour,
> Accept my ardent prayers,
>
> Deliver my spirit from woes and evils,
> Pour loving tenderness into my heart,
> Direct me to the path of salvation.
> Give me strength to overcome my willfulness
> And to endure all things for God.
> Be my protective veil in my bitter life:
> Do not let me die in sorrow.
> Thou art the refuge of all who are unfortunate,
> The intercessor for us all!
> O protect me when I hear the voice
> Of God's dread judgment,
> When eternity brings an end to time,
> The trumpet's voice raises the dead,
> And the book of conscience exposes
> The entire burden of my sins.
> Thou art the fortress of the faithful!
> To Thee my whole soul prays:
> Save me, Thou who art my consolation.
> Have mercy on me!

---

25. Florensky's appendix contains four prayers that Father Isidore used to recite and distribute: (1) the prayer to the Mother of God attributed to Gogol; (2) the prayer beginning "Blessed Empress," sung in the Gethsemane Skete on the Feast of the Dormition; (3) a prayer devoted to Christ's cross; and (4) a monastic prayer to the Lord Christ, imploring him to overcome all temptations. Only the prayer attributed to Gogol is reproduced here.

Index

Afanas'ev, A. N., 155, 155n12
Aksakow, A. N., 22, 15n20
Alexander III, 185
Alfonso VI of León and Castile, 54
Alphabetical Patericon (1491), 63–64, 65
Amvrosy of Optina, ixn9
Anarchy, 73–79
Andersen, Hans Christian: "Man without a Shadow," 15; *Norwegian Fairy-Tales*, 14
Andronik, Igumen, vin1; "Pavel Florensky, Student of the Moscow Theological Academy," ix, ixn8
Anthony of Padua, death of, 217
Anthropodicy, xii, 120
Antimins, 16, 16n23
Arago, François, 31
Arsenius of Egypt, 187
Athanasius, 65

Bald Mountain, 16, 16n22
Balzac, Honoré de, theory of the daguerreotype, 15
Baptism, xi, 40, 52, 62, 65, 100, 101, 137n18
Basil the Great, 121, 121n4
Bely, Andrey, vin2, viii, 69n47
Bismarck, Otto von, 185
Black-Hundredists, 199, 199n16
Borgia, Francis, 57

Borromeo, Charles, 57
Bourneville, Désiré Magloire, 16, 16n21
Boxel, Hugo, 2
Brentano, Clemens, 57
Bugaev, N. F., vi, vin2, viii; theory of discontinuity, vin2
Burial Rite of the Mother of God, 202–3
Byzantine Orthodoxy, 142–43

Calmet, Augustin, *Dissertation sur les Apparitions des esprits et sur les Vampires ou les Revenans de Hongrie, de Moravie etc.*, 17–18, 19–20
Cantor, Georg, 133
Catherine of Siena, 57
Catholicism, 142, 148, 160, 161
Chernigov-Gethsemane Icon of the Mother of God, 165, 203
Church, the, apostolic, comparison of to the Christian church of Florensky's day, 139–41
Clement of Alexandria, 83
Consciousness, and the opposition between that which is appropriate and that which is inappropriate (Russian *dolzhnoe* and *nedolzhnoe*), 5–7, 5n6
Crookes, William, 22

Da Vinci, Leonardo, 13
Deification, 120, 121–22

Derzhavin, Gavrila, "God," 202
Descartes, René, 82
Dogma, 120
Dogmatics, xii, 119–38 *passim*; vs. dogmatism, xii, 125–33; need for as a truly living religious worldview, 126, 128, 133–35; sequence of phases in, 138 (table); worshiping God "in Spirit and in truth," 120–24
Dostoevsky, Fyodor, 82, 158, 160, 162; *The Brothers Karamazov*, ixn9, 27, 56n30, 67, 123; *Diary of a Writer*, 22; on "responsiveness," 65; theory of demons, 22

Eckermann, Johann Peter, 9
Elchaninov, Alexander, 25n1
Emiliani, Jerome, 57
Emmerich, Anne Catherine, 57–58
Empyrean, the: distinguishing of from the empirical, 39–46, 54–56; and mathematics, 46–49; and moral acts, 42–46; and mystical perception, 50–52; and science, 41–42. *See also* Sacraments: perceptions during the reception of
Encyclical of the Eastern Patriarchs (May 6, 1848), 148
Ephrem the Syrian, 90
Erdan, A., *La France mystique: Tableau des excentricités religieuses de ce temps*, 31n10
Eucharist/Holy Communion, 56, 62–65, 101, 141, 147, 149; and transubstantiation, 39–40
Eucharistic sense (*flair eucharistique*), 56–58
Eustathius Placidas, vision of, 167, 167n4
Evil, 75; love of, 75

Fall, the, 36
Father Isidore. *See* Isidore, Father
Father Serapion. *See* Serapion, Father
Feofan of Tambov and Shatsk, 52
Filaret, Archbishop (Gumilevsky), *Orthodox Dogmatic Theology*, 127n11

Filaret, Metropolitan (Drozdov), 115, 184, 186, 200–201, 212, 213; *An Extensive Christian Catechesis of the Orthodox Catholic Eastern Church*, 127n11
Florensky, Pavel: birth of, vi; "Data towards a Description of the Life of Archimandrite Serapion Mashkin," 97n18; *Detiam moim*, vii–viii, viiin5; "Dogmatism and Dogmatics," xii; education of, vi–vii, viii; "The Empyrean and the Empirical," x; fascination of with the interplay of religious and scientific themes, ix; "The Goal and Meaning of Progress," x; involvement of in the Symbolist movement, viii; Kandidat thesis of, vi; Letter I in *Khristianin*, 98–102; Letter II in *Khristianin*, 102–11; "Letters and Notes of Archimandrite Serapion Mashkin," 97n16; master's dissertation of, vii; mentoring of by Father Isidore, ix, xiii; "Orthodoxy," xii; *The Pillar and Ground of the Truth*, xi, 98n1; "The Prize of the High Calling," x–xi, 97n16; as publisher and editor of Father Serapion's works, 97; "Questions of Religious Self-Knowledge," xi; sacraments as a central theme of his theology, xi; "The Salt of the Earth," ix, xiii; life and study in Sergiev Posad, vi, viin3, xiii; spiritual crisis and mystical experiences of, vii–viii; standard edition of his works, xiii; "Superstition and Miracle," ix; university teaching career of, vii, viii
Florensov, Antonii, viii, ix, 184, 200, 212–13
Fonvizin, Denis, *The Minor*, 82, 82n4

George the Recluse, 170, 201, 202
Georgievski, Evlogy, 159
Gethsemane Skete (monastic community), xiii, 212, 213
Gladstone, William, 185
Goethe, Johann Wolfgang von, 9–10, 13; *Faust*, 9, 33

Index

Gogol, Nikolai, 202; Prayer to the Mother of God, 170, 170n6, 222
Gregory of Nyssa, 219
Gruzinsky, Ioann. *See* Isidore, Father
Guyot, M., "My Verses of Yesterday," 124

Harnack, A. von, *The Essence of Christianity*, 140
Hegel, Georg Wilhelm Friedrich, 82
Hierodeacon, 91n14
Hieromonk, xiii, 91n13
Hoffmann, E. T. A., 15, 21; *The Devil's Elixirs*, 22; *Life and Opinions of Tomcat Murr*, 13–14; "The Sandman," 22; *The Serapion Brethren*, 21–22
Hugo, Victor, *Toilers of the Sea*, 45
Hume, David, 82

Imbert-Gourbeyre, Antoine: on *flair eucharistique*, 56, 57; *La Stigmatisation*, 56n31
Isaac the Syrian, 68, 209
Isidore, Father (Ioann Gruzinsky), 164–65; ascetic labors of, 187–90; biography of, 211–14; cell of, 165–68; and "The Conversation about the Rock," 196–99; cross of, 209–11; death of, 214–18; gifts given by to everyone he met, 174–75; gifts of prescience and miracle-working of, 206–9; greeting of visitors by, 168–70; hearing of confessions by, 193–95, 214; humility and independence of, 184–87; kindness of toward all of God's creatures, 179–80; love of for all people, 175–79; meekness, gentleness, and forgiveness of, 181–83; mentoring of Florensky by, ix, xiii; postmortem countenance, burial, and grave of, 218–20; Prayer of the Savior's Five Wounds, 170, 201, 203–5, 205 (text), 205–6n18, 209, 215; prayers that he used to recite and distribute, 222n25; refreshments of, 170–73; spiritual freedom of, 190–93; the symbolic meaning of his life, 165; teaching of in his conversations, 199–203

Isidore of Pelusium, 80
Ivanov, Vyacheslav: "*Mi fur serpi amiche*," 120; "Tantalus," 121

Jahenny, Marie-Julie, 57
James, William: conception of reality, 35n16; Florensky's satirization of, 35–36
Jesus: activity and empirical existence of, 38; as both human and divine, 37; as the bread of life, 33–34; death and resurrection of, 32; divinity of, 35; incarnation of, 36–37; redemptive mission of, 38–39
John Moschus, *The Spiritual Meadow*, 62, 63, 64–65
John of the Ladder, 166
John the Chozebite, 62
Justin Martyr, 137n18

Kant, Immanuel, 82; *Critiques*, 92
Kepler, Johannes, 9
Khomiakov, Aleksei, 82; "Some Remarks by an Orthodox Christian concerning the Western Communions, on the Occasion of a Brochure by Mr. Laurentie," 149
Khristianin, letters to the editor of: from Alexander Sokolov, 117–18; from "A monk," 116; from Priest D. G. T., 111–15
Kliuchevsky, V. O., *Course of Russian History*, Seventeenth Lecture, 145–46
Kock, Charles Paul de, 192, 192n12
Kozin, Andrey, 211
Kozin, Ioann. *See* Isidore, Father
Kozin, Paraskeva, 211

Lato, Luisa, 57
Legends, 69–70; uniformity of the plot of, 70
Leman, Alfred, *Illustrated History of Superstitions and Witchcraft*, 4, 4n4, 14
Lermontov, Mikhail, 10
Leskov, Nikolai, 158; "At the Edge of the World," 161

Levitsky, I., "Ephesus or Jerusalem?," 57n33
Littré, Émile, *Dictionaire de la langue française*, 3–4
Lopatin, L. M., vi
Lucian, *Life of Demonax*, 83
Lucia of Parnia, 57
Lutheranism, 159, 160

Macarius of Alexandria (the Younger), 63
Macarius of Egypt (the Great), 180
Makary, Metropolitan (M. Bulgakov), 85, 200; *Orthodox Dogmatic Theology*, 127nn11–12, 128, 199
Maksimov, S., *The Unclean Power*, 11n14
Malevansky (Bishop Sylvester), *An Essay on Orthodox Dogmatic Theology*, 126–27n11
Marie de la Croix, 57
Mashkin, Vladimir Mikhailovich. *See* Serapion, Father
Maupassant, Guy de, 21
Merezhkovsky, Dmitry, 82, 196, 196n14
Mihailovich, Aleksei, 150
Minsky, N. M., *The Religion of the Future (Philosophical Conversations)*, 135, 135n16
Miracles, 8–9, 12, 14, 62–65
Monoideism, 80
Moscow Theological Academy, vin3, xiii
Motovilov, Nikolay, ixn9, 99n2
Myers, F. W. H., *The Subliminal Consciousness*, 57, 57n3
Mysticism/Mystics, 83–84
Myths, 69

Nekrasov, Nikolay, "A Moral Man," 44–45
Nesterov, Mikhail, 94, 94n15
Nevsky, Alexander, 150
Nietzsche, Friedrich, 158; *The Gay Science*, 125
Nikitin, Ivan, 89n11
Nikolaevich, Konstantin, 95
Nilus, S., *The Great in the Small*, 99n2

Niphon of Constantia, 220
Novoselov, M. A., *Forgotten Path of Experiential God-Knowledge*, 52

Occultism, 8, 11–12, 14, 23–24
Old Believers, 139–40, 162; veneration of relics by, 16
Olga of Kiev, 146
Origen, xi, 81, 91, 95
Orthodox Church, as "One, Holy, Catholic, and Apostolic," 27n2, 139n1, 185n9
Orthodoxy, 142. *See also* Byzantine Orthodoxy; Russian Orthodoxy
Ovsianiko-Kulikovsky, Dmitry, 67n45; on works of art as an induction, 67
Owen, Robert Dale, 15, 22

Paganism, Slavic, 143–44
Pascal, Blaise, 31; *Pensées*, 12, 31n11, 157
Paul of Thebes, 217
Peter the Great, 162
Petrov, Grigory Spiridonovich, 111, 111n8, 114
Philosophy, 28, 80–83, 85
Pobedonostsev, K. P., *Moskovsky Sbornik*, 158
Prayer of Jesus, 206n18
Prayer of the Savior's Five Wounds (Father Isidore), 170, 201, 203–5, 205 (text), 205–6n18, 209, 215
Prayer to the Mother of God (attributed to Nikolai Gogol), 170, 170n6, 222
Progress, principles related to, 71–79; hierarchical order vs. anarchic order, 73–74; obligatoriness, 71–72; theocracy vs. anarchy, 73–79; unity, 71–73
Protestantism, 142, 148, 161
Pushkin, Alexander, 7

Reichart, Kiriak, 161
Rozanov, V. V., 82; *In the Proximity of Church Walls*, 132
Rufinus of Aquileia, comp., *The Lives of the Desert Fathers*, 63
Russian national character, 145–46
Russian Orthodoxy, 150, 157–63; and

the church, 148–51; and everyday life, 151–54; and nature, 154–57; origin of, 142–46
Russian Revolution (1905), 162, 193, 193n13
Russo-Japanese War (1904–1905), 177n8

Sabbatius of Solovski, 212
Sacraments, 99–102, 120; and the difference between the empirical and the empyrean, 39–40; differentiation of from ceremonies and rituals, 50; letters to the editor of *Khristianin* on, 111–18; and mystical perception, 50, 51–52; perceptions during the reception of, 56–70; view of as ceremonies that signify, 100. *See also* Baptism; Eucharist/Holy Communion
Sagée, Emilie, double appearances of, 15
Schelling, Friedrich Wilhelm Joseph von, 28; use of the word "tautegorically" by, 69n47
Schemamonk, 213, 213n21
Seraphim of Sarov, ixn9, 98, 114, 201, 211; death of, 211, 217
Serapion, Father (Vladimir Mikhailovich Mashkin), x–xi, 80, 82, 84–97 *passim*; on attacks of evil, 87–88; candor of, 92–93; on Christian philosophy, 85; chronology of his life, 81–82n3; gravesite of, 89; humility of, 91; immersion of in prayer, 85–87; interest of in nature and the natural sciences, 93–94; last will and testament of, 89; observance of the "hours" by, 85–86; political radicalism of, 91; poverty of, 88–89, 91; sincerity of, 84–85; struggle of with pride, 90–91
Sergius of Radonezh, xiii, 64
Skovoroda, Gregory, 82
Sokolov, Alexander, 117–18
Sologub, Fyodor, "Shadows," 15
Solovyov, Vladimir, xi, 12, 80, 81, 82, 86, 91, 93–94, 95; "Nemesis," 7; theocracy as a key concept in his writings, x; *Three Conversations*, 24

Spinoza, Baruch: *Ethics*, 97; on superstition, 2–3
Spiritism, three categories of responses to, 22
"Stoglav" (The Book of One Hundred Chapters), 144, 144n6, 152
Superstition, 1; definitions of, 2–4, 5; and doubles, 15; Florensky's definition of, 11, 13, 21; and relics, 16–17; and the resurrection of a corpse, 17–18; and shadows, 15; two sides of (inner and outward), 5; and vampires, 18–20. *See also* Occultism
Suvorov, Alexander, 15
Swammerdam, Jan, 9, 9n10
Symbolist movement, viii, 56, 56n29
Symbols, 55–56

Tasso, Torquato, *Jerusalem Delivered*, 20, 20n30
Teinturier, E., 16, 16n21
Theocracy, x, 73–79
Theodicy, xii, 120
Tikhon of Zadonsk, 201
Tolstoy, Leo, 67, 82, 100, 111, 114, 129, 162
Trinity Lavra of St. Sergius, vin3, xiii; Uspensky (Dormition) Cathedral of, 122, 122n6
Troitsky, Sergey Semyonovich, 119n1
Trubetskoy, S. N., vi, 82; *The Doctrine of the Logos*, 10–11

Valiac, Maréchal, 20–21
Varangians, 146
Vasnetsov, Viktor, 94, 94n15
Veniaminov, Innokenty, 148
Vladimir the Great, and Christianity, 146–47
Volzhsky, A. S., "The Life of F. M. Dostoevsky and Its Religious Meaning," 160, 160n17
Vvedensy, Aleksey, 96

Worldviews: catholic Christianity as the absolute worldview, 27; naturalistic worldview, 35, 53, 56; religious worldview, 8, 10, 25–27, 55; scientific worldview, 8, 10, 11, 12; spiritual worldview, 35; superstitious worldview (*see* Occultism); symbolic worldview, 56; worldview of the Jews, 10

Worshiping God "in spirit and in truth," 120–24; as veneration of God the Holy Being, 120, 122; as worship "to the known God," 122–23

Zöllner, Johann Karl Friedrich, 22

Zosimas of Palestine, 212

www.ingramcontent.com/pod-product-compliance
Lightning Source LLC
Chambersburg PA
CBHW032004220426
43664CB00005B/132